SOCIAL CHAUCER

Social Chaucer

Paul Strohm

Harvard University Press
Cambridge, Massachusetts
London, England
1989

Printed in the United States of America
10 9 8 7 6 5 4 3 2 1

Publication of this book has been aided by a grant
from the Andrew W. Mellon Foundation.

This book is printed on acid-free paper, and its binding materials
have been chosen for strength and durability.

Library of Congress Cataloging-in-Publication Data

Strohm, Paul, 1938–
Social Chaucer / Paul Strohm.
p. cm.
Bibliography: p.
Includes index.
ISBN 0-674-81198-4 (alk. paper)
1. Chaucer, Geoffrey, d. 1400—Political and social views.
2. Chaucer, Geoffrey, d. 1400—Contemporary England. 3. England—Social conditions—Medieval period, 1066–1485. 4. Literature and society—England—History. 5. Social structure in literature.
I. Title.
PR1913.S59S77 1989 89-30655
821'.1—dc19 CIP

Acknowledgments

THIS STUDY began some years ago, prompted by several fortunate convergences: my reading in Arnold Hauser, staunch advocate of social meaning in an era of aestheticism, with his assertion of the relation between new styles and emergent social groups; my encounter with M. D. Chenu's description of vertical and horizontal social formations; a conversation with sociologist Irving Zeitlin, who—upon learning that I had written my dissertation on the implied audience of a mystery cycle—asked if I knew anything about its real one.

Since then, my belief in the collaborative nature of inquiry has been confirmed and reconfirmed. Anthony Shipps of the Indiana University Library has been constantly and graciously responsive to my requests for assistance. Daniel Rubey gave important advice on several preliminary articles that, though they find no place in this study, opened the way to it. Discussions with Margaretta Fulton of Harvard University Press provided early and continuing guidance. Barbara Hanawalt read my first two chapters when I most needed a historian's advice. Clifford Flanigan, Mary Ellen Brown, Tamara Goeglein, Samuel Rosenberg, David Anderson, and Richard F. Green offered timely suggestions. I wish particularly to mention the professional generosity of David Wallace, who read and commented on the entire manuscript, with the acumen and vital insight so amply revealed in his own scholarship.

Finally, I dedicate this book to my colleague Alfred David, whose life and career have exemplified for me the delight in learning and the high personal principle that sum up the best in our profession. Alfred and his wife Linda have been my valued advisers and steadfast friends.

Contents

Preface

PREVIOUS studies have sought to situate Chaucer in history by describing his position (or seeming lack of position) on salient events of the day. Scrutiny has been given to his stance on the peasants' rising, the debate over peace with France, and other discrete events. Yet, in my judgment, the structure of late medieval social relations provides an interpretative context for events in his life and themes in his poetry at least as rich as that offered by particular moments in political history.

I will approach the complex and shifting structure of social relations in Chaucer's lifetime through a variety of contemporary texts, including statutes, poll taxes, and political treatises as well as fictional narratives. Some of these texts look so much like raw data that they have been treated as if they were repositories of unmediated fact. I will, however, treat all these texts as attempts at self-understanding, as imaginary constructions of social reality in their own right. Rather than viewing Chaucer's poetry in relation to a separate body of information, I will place his imaginary depictions of social relations in a larger field of such depictions. My object is to gain social knowledge from the texts in this study, but knowledge of the particular sort that texts afford.

This language of textuality may suggest certain reservations on my part about the accessibility of social information in texts, but I am in fact thoroughly persuaded that the worldly affiliations and practical business of texts lie open to careful investigation. To be sure, several social paradigms are reproduced again and again in writings by Chaucer and others, in ways that would seem to suggest that certain ideas have a timeless and self-enclosed "literary" life of their own. But, for all the persistence of such paradigms, they are rarely reproduced without modification, and in noting their modification we can trace the influence of absent historical and social causes.[1]

The most persistent and prestigious social model of the high middle ages was, for example, that of the hierarchy, with its insistence on a divinely sanctioned and eternal order of vertically arrayed estates. Yet many fourteenth-century texts stretch and modify this received model in order to include new and previously unrecognized social groupings. Registered in this modification are many new developments: the decline of the knightly class and its separation from the aristocracy, the elevation of esquires to gentle status, the recognition of a still broader grouping of gentlepersons, and the entry of citizens and burgesses to new civil importance, to name a few.

Similarly indicative of new developments is the rapid fourteenth-century elaboration of an alternative social paradigm, which opposed to the hierarchy of high medieval tradition a depiction of social relations as horizontally arrayed, communal, secular, and bound in finite time. Behind this alternative paradigm may be felt the pressure of new forms of social relation based less on domination and subordination and more on ties of common interest and experience. Indeed, historians have shown us that the later fourteenth century was precisely the time when the last vestiges of vassalage (sanctified by oath and secured by land tenure) were being replaced by new forms of indentured service (defined by contract and remunerated by cash payment). Other, less formal, kinds of retaining brought people together in retinues, factions, and sworn and unsworn associations for the accomplishment of temporary goals. These developments required modification of a system in which loyalties were defined vertically in terms of ties to a social superior, in favor of horizontal agreements between persons in similar social situations. Part of this shift occurs within the textual realm; within the realm, that is, of imaginative productions through which people become aware of conflict and fight it out.[2]

Chaucer's own poetry embraces a lively contention between vertical and horizontal forms of social depiction. This contention is in turn involved in that social transformation of the late middle ages usually described as the transition from feudalism to capitalism, with the vertical or hierarchical view of social relations complexly linked with the feudal system of land tenure and the horizontal or communal view with guilds, confraternities, and other nonagrarian formations. Enormous explanatory power resides in the potential link between rival forms of social depiction and rival systems of production, though such connections must be regarded as an informing hypothesis rather than as a matter settled once and for all. Arguing against confident connections are the unsettled state of our own debate on the transition from feudalism to capitalism[3] and the unevenness with which the transition occurred.[4]

Partly because of this unevenness, fourteenth-century social groups are often mixed in character. The entrepreneurial nobleman and the knightly tradesman are regularly encountered, and one would be hard pressed to decide whether Chaucer and his fellow king's knights and esquires belonged to a "retinue" developed to grapple with the administrative problems of late feudalism or to a "bureaucracy" developed to deal with record keeping and exchange under emergent capitalism. As R. J. Holton has wisely cautioned, this is a period "uneasily poised between feudalism and capitalism, where quasi-modern elements appear in traditional guise, and traditionalism seems to bring forth dynamic consequences of an unintended kind."[5] In this mixed situation, members of a single social group might draw on elements of hierarchical or antihierarchical ideology, depending on the matter at hand. Aristocrats, and even kings courting the city of London, eagerly joined confraternities and guilds. No one could be more hierarchical than a devout fourteenth-century merchant at prayer. Needed in this situation is not broader and broader generalization, but rather more particularity—about the composition and situation of the group employing a certain form of social depiction, and the uses the depiction might be asked to serve.

All people in the late fourteenth century appear to have been exposed to the claims and counterclaims of hierarchical and antihierarchical ideas about their social experience. Chaucer and his associates were, however, exposed with the greatest intensity of all. For they found themselves in a highly ambiguous social location that can only be understood by a mixed appeal both to vertical and to horizontal forms of understanding: they were gentle in rank, but insecurely so; linked to the nobility, but less by sworn and eternal ties than by temporary contracts; members of a feudal retinue that actually combined elements of a political party and a precocious bureaucracy.

Just as Chaucer's life was intersected by contrary social experiences and competing systems of social explanation, so does his poetry provide an intersection for different, ideologically charged ideas about social relations. I do not use the term "intersection" to suggest that different currents pass through it on their way to somewhere else, but rather in its sense as *carrefour*—a crowded and public place of commingling, where systems converge in stimulating disarray.[6] My later chapters deal with some of the occasions on which Chaucer introduces varied social concerns directly into his poetry, as when he considers the oaths and bonds that cement, or fail to cement, social relations. I go on to suggest that some apparently neutral categories—including such formal matters as temporality in narrative—are themselves the bearers of recognized social meaning, that "aesthetic" contentions may actually be placed, in Chaucer's remarkable hands, in the service of "social" understanding.

My interest in the historicity of Chaucer's texts enhances my interest in his authorial activity. Recent criticism has, to be sure, discouraged excessive deference to the sovereign author and has sharpened our sense of the various ways in which meaning enters a text independent of the agency or will of a particular author. I hope that this book will reflect my own awareness of such matters as the role of an audience in the shaping and reception of meaning, the senses in which a text exists as a system apart from the intentions that accompanied its inscription, the reliance of any author on socially created genres and forms. Nevertheless, I reject the conception of the author as a hapless scribe or "reproducer" of ideology, subject to a material insertion over which he or she has no control.[7] I view Chaucer not only as producing but as responding to the social implications of his material. Supported by personal exposure to multiple centers of textual and social authority, he enters not just into reproduction but into analysis, negotiation, and reconstrual of the materials he takes in hand.[8]

I hasten to assure the reader that I will not parade Chaucer as an impresario of fully developed social solutions. Much of our attraction to his texts involves their provisional and unfinished qualities, their willingness to entertain alternatives without pressing for premature resolution, their frankly exploratory approach to the utopian and the transcendent. Chaucer's very success in opening his text to materials of varied ideological implication is what persuades me to disagree with those critics who minimize the possibility of escape from a single hegemonic or dominant ideology.[9] Emphasizing the power of a unitary ideology to efface alternative formations, such theories require a shift of critical attention from matters overtly treated to those that are omitted, erased, or repressed.[10] Chaucer certainly defines the boundaries of his texts in part by acts of exclusion. No nobleperson tells a tale on the way to Canterbury, and no peasant either. Yet I continue to be impressed more by what his text includes than by how much it omits: by the amount of conflictual matter to which it gives space and by its deep implication in urgent social contests of the time. Rather than viewing Chaucer's poetry as hegemonic and exclusionary, I associate myself with those critics who assert the possibility of unresolved contention, of a struggle between hegemony and counter-hegemony, of texts as places crowded with many voices representing many centers of social authority.[11]

SOCIAL CHAUCER

1 ⊠ Chaucer and the Structure of Social Relations

THOSE fourteenth-century knights and esquires in royal service, whose ranks included Geoffrey Chaucer and his closest associates, enjoyed a social position of marked precariousness and promise. Available to them were greatly expanded opportunities to enter the upper ranks of the social hierarchy, not on the traditional bases of military service and land tenure, but through the skilled and specialized services they were able to provide. Operating outside formal social definitions, associated at times with the landed gentry and at times with the civil servants and lawyers, they comprised a distinctive grouping, with their own priorities, aspirations, and loyalties.

Seeking accommodation within the "descending" hierarchy of tradition, these new careerists would decisively alter its form. For they were penetrating it in ad hoc and unpredictable ways that challenged previously orderly conceptions of social degree. Their emergence, and consolidation of their newly achieved positions, could not have occurred without alteration of the ties and covenants between lords and those who served them. Old relations of vassalage based on land tenure were extensively redefined, opening the way to more flexible forms of service and more varied remuneration: sacral, sworn bonds were replaced by voluntary agreements; permanent loyalties gave way to more temporary arrangements; vertical ties of domination and subordination—while by no means wholly superseded—were everywhere set in competition with lateral ties among people in similar social situations.

These changes are largely undocumented, in the sense that they were only belatedly and haphazardly incorporated into written social description. Legal codes, sermons, and other traditionally sanctioned sources are conservative, static, and tantalizingly vague in relation to the very social groups and forms of relation we would most wish discussed. Fortunately, however, various documents of a limited and occasional nature do offer fleeting insight into the changes that were occurring. Propelled by pragmatic objectives into new areas of social description, such documents as sumptuary statutes, poll-tax ordinances, parliamentary summonses, indentures for service, and statutes governing the composition of retinues offer valuable insight into new forms of social relation in Chaucer's day. An appreciation of these new forms should, in turn, help us to a more particular sense of Chaucer's social location, and the elements of which he sought to construct his own social self-understanding.

Social Description

Thirteenth- and fourteenth-century social description tends to be conservative in its deference to principles of social hierarchy.[1] This deference is apparent both in its disproportionate attention to the landowning lords and their ecclesiastical counterparts (as opposed to more recently emergent groups of the "middle strata" [2]) and in its emphasis on relations of orderly subordination among social levels (as opposed to a more organic emphasis on interdependency).

A typical conspectus of society in the thirteenth and fourteenth centuries occurs in the legal compilation attributed to Henry de Bracton, which emphasizes a hierarchical ordering of estates with persons of eminence chosen to rule and others arrayed under them ("sub eis").[3] Bracton provides for emperors, kings, and princes; dukes; counts or barons; magnates or vavasours; and knights; following is a generalized body of freemen and villains ("liberi et villani"). Within the spiritual ranks hierarchy also prevails, with the pope supervising the affairs of archbishops, bishops, and an undifferentiated mass of other prelates ("alii prelati inferiores").

Although Bracton here accepts the influential model of the "three estates" of society, consisting of knights (or kings), priests, and peasants, he employs it in a form that poses no threat to hierarchical principles. His presentation of the three estates downplays notions of interdependence, emphasizing instead the separate levels at which the the estates exercise their functions.[4] Hierarchy is maintained by a detailed attention to the secular and religious aristocracies, on the one hand, and a more sketchy but dutiful attention to the peasantry on the other, without acknowledgment of "middle" or other intervening categories that could blur this strict separation of social levels. Hierarchy is further underscored by emphasis on social difference among persons ("differentia personarum") and on the orderly submission of inferiors ("inferiores") to their superiors within the social order.

Bracton's particular rendering of the social hierarchy is hardly descriptive of a thirteenth- or fourteenth-century English state of affairs. It is conceived within its own textual tradition of classical and Italian jurisprudence, and many of its terms and concepts have no direct English counterparts.[5] Its very casualness about matters of description suggests that its purpose is less descriptive than ideological, in its support for particular forms of social practice.[6] Bracton's conception of society is of course highly traditional, in its nostalgic and oversimplified "allusion" to the twelfth and thirteenth centuries, when the system of aristocratic land tenure it presupposes was most securely in place. At the same time, its ideological work is accomplished in part through "illusion": its omission of classes outside the model of the three estates, its relative neglect of social interdependence, its suggestion that the system it describes exists beyond time and change.[7]

Bracton's description is typical of ideologically conditioned texts in presenting its system as self-evident, as the only possible form of social organization. Taking such texts at face value, we have sometimes tended to regard "feudalism" as a more orderly system than it ever was. But alternative, nonhierarchical or even antihierarchical, traditions of social description were available as well, existing throughout the middle ages but coming into special prominence in the fourteenth century. If the hierarchical descriptions sought to portray land tenure as the ordained and inevitable basis of secular authority, texts in this counter-tradition found value in the social activities of other, sometimes unlanded, social groupings. If hierarchical descriptions sought support in the vertical and transcendent Pseudo-Dionysian cosmology, these alternative texts reasserted more horizontal and organic metaphors, deriving ultimately from classical ideas of the body politic and the "corporate" state.

These alternative tendencies may be found in various late fourteenth-century documents, including the sermons of Bishop Thomas Brinton. With respect to the addition of new orders, Brinton consistently follows the fourteenth-century habit of recognizing a fourth social category, between the lords on the one hand and the peasants on the other. In a sermon of 1375, he divides society into four kinds of men ("genera hominum") according to vocation: prelates and ecclesiastics, kings and princes, merchants ("mercatores"), and workers ("operarii et laboratores").[8] Brinton's choice of merchants already represents a noteworthy modification of the three-estates model, though somewhat sketchy in comparison with such contemporary formulations as Philippe de Mézières' postulation of a hypothetical fourth estate consisting of "nobles non chevaliers et de bourgeoisie," nonknightly gentlepersons and the bourgeoisie.[9]

Fortunately, Brinton has a good deal more to say about this estate elsewhere in his sermons. In elaborating the role of this fourth estate, he relies upon an alternative metaphorical and textual tradition that placed particular emphasis on the functional interdependence of the estates of society. The idea of interdependence, or what Bracton calls *connexio,* had always been implicit in the three-estates theory, but was invoked only rarely, usually in perfunctory justification of the special privileges of those in positions of civil and spiritual responsibility. More congenial to the concept of functional interdependence were those social descriptions employing the metaphor of the social body or body politic. This metaphor had already been elaborated in the twelfth century by John of Salisbury, himself in a tradition stretching back to Plutarch.[10] But as a social theory it came to maturity in the fourteenth century, and Brinton is very much of his own time in devoting part of a sermon on the mystical body of the Church to a body politic consisting of separate but united members. Its head (or, diplomatically, heads) is kings, princes, and prelates ("reges, principes, et prelati"); the eyes are judges and true counselors ("iudices sapientes et veraces consiliarii"); the ears are the clergy ("religiosi"); the tongue is doctors ("doctores boni"); the right hand consists of strenuous knights ("milites ad defendendum parati"); the left hand of merchants and devoted craftsmen ("mercatores et fideles mechanici"); the heart, explicitly designated as the middle position ("quasi in medio positi"), comprises citizens and burgesses ("ciues et burgenses"); the feet, which support the whole, are peasants and workers ("agricole et laborantes").[11]

We should immediately notice the considerable weight given by Brinton to the middle groups within society—especially in his characterization of knights as its right arm, merchants and faithful craftsmen as its left arm, and citizens and burgesses as its heart. This expansion is accomplished by two strategies distinctive to the later fourteenth century: a demotion of the knights and a promotion of certain categories of tradesmen.

As recently as the thirteenth century, with their ranks winnowed and their prestige both reflected and enhanced by increased costs, the knights had been firmly associated with the baronial aristocracy, not only in theory but in practice.[12] In the course of the fourteenth century, however, a decisive separation occurred—a separation that, although continuing to affirm the gentility of the knights, denied their aristocratic status.[13] This is most vividly reflected in the composition of fourteenth-century Parliament, to which the lords (including barons and sometimes bannerets) received hereditary summons, while the knights were regarded as eligible for election, along with "les autres," as representatives of the shires of the realm.[14]

The middle groups are further expanded in the other direction, by the inclusion of "fideles mechanici" (faithful craftsmen) along with merchants as society's left hand. Presumably, the craftsmen in question are the artificers and other members of craft guilds, humbler in station than those mercantile and victualing guildsmen who dominated aldermanic rolls and the common council as well as the mayoralty throughout the latter decades of the century, but here compared with them in social standing. A further indication of the influence of the middle groups is the multiplication of the terms by which they are described. No longer identified only in terms of vocation (merchant, craftsman), they are identified in terms that emphasize their civic importance (citizen, burgess) and placed at the very heart of the realm.[15]

His task of social elaboration greatly facilitated by the organic metaphor of the body politic, Brinton has expanded most formal accounts of the middle grouping of society, as well as our understanding of the different ranks and vocational identities of people within this grouping. Nevertheless, much remains unsaid about these middle strata and about groups of particular interest to students of Chaucer. Strenuous or militarily active knights are singled out, but nothing is said of knights whose rank is earned in civil or ambassadorial service. Esquires, including those in service, are omitted altogether. For a recognition of these groups and their place and role in society, we must turn to other descriptive documents, no less ideologically conditioned than those of Bracton or Brinton, but conceived for practical purposes that encouraged more detailed social description.[16]

One document committed by its very purpose to an exhaustive enumeration of the estates of society is the Statute on Diet and Apparel (1363), a short-lived ordinance originating in a petition of commons which complained that persons of diverse conditions of prosperity are adopting apparel inappropriate to their social rank ("diverses gentz de diverses Condicions usent diverse Apparaill nient appertenant a lour Estat").[17] The statute relegates to the bottom the mass of people in whom it has least interest (including carters, plowmen, shepherds, and other *garceons* attending to matters of husbandry) and begins with the ranks most interesting to the parliamentary representatives. Addressed first of all is the "servant problem," with limitation of both victuals and attire of those in the service of either lords or craftsmen. Next to be limited to apparel made of cloth worth no more than 40 shillings are the smaller craftsmen and journeymen. Then comes the category of esquires and all other gentlepersons with land or income worth less than £100 annually ("Esquiers & toutes maneres de Gentils gentz . . . qe n'ont terre ou rente a la value de Cent livres par an"), and also those esquires worth £200 annually or above ("Esquiers eantz terre ou rente a la value de Deux Centz livres par an")—the former limited to cloth worth four and a half marks and certain lesser furs. Next to be considered is a group for which no gentility is claimed but whose members enjoyed a condition of life that entitled them to certain perquisites of gentility. This is the group of "Marchantz, Citeins & Burgeis, Artificers, [&] gentz de Mestere," whose worth is computed not in the possession of land or rent but in goods and chattels. Those who "clearly" possess "biens & chateux" to the value of £500 are entitled to attire themselves in the manner of esquires and gentlepersons with lands and rents worth £100 annually; those with property valued over £1000 are entitled to dress in the manner of esquires and gentlepersons with lands and rents worth £200 annually. Next are the "Chivalers" who, like the esquires, are divided into two groups. Those with land or rent yielding up to £200 annually may adopt apparel similar to the upper class of esquires (but with an additional mark's worth of clothing) and knights worth £1000 are granted additional privileges, including jeweled headdresses for their ladies.

This enumeration devotes special attention to those groups that Philippe de Mézières would have considered "nobles non chevaliers." Esquires, for example, are mentioned separately and are treated as *gentils gentz*. The ascent of the esquires to *gentil* status in the course of the first half of the fourteenth century has been well documented by Denholm-Young and by Saul; lumped in the thirteenth century with franklins, sergeants, *valetti,* and other freeholders, the mid-fourteenth-century *esquier (armiger, scutifer)* had achieved a status of nonaristocratic gentility very close to that of the fourteenth-century knight.[18] Recognition of such realignments was nevertheless slow. Denholm-Young suggests 1370 as the date by which heralds had accepted esquires as an armigerous class, and by his standard this mention—as well as an even more notable mention of *gentils gentz* who are neither knights nor esquires—remains early.[19]

This document is also very current in its provision that those merchants, citizens, burgesses, manufacturers, and guildsmen with sufficient income (or conditions) are entitled to attire themselves in the manner of esquires and gentlepersons. "Conditions" are of course not everything. According to modern conceptions, merchants must be considered to belong to a different social class than esquires and gentlepersons, with the former possessing goods and chattels and the latter lands and rents. So too in fourteenth-century terms they belong to a different estate or rank, which for the merchants and others remains nongentle whatever their financial condition. This distinction is recognized in the fact that a merchant must, quite simply, be worth more in order to enjoy comparable privileges: £500 to be entitled to the attire of a gentleperson worth £100, and £1000 to be entitled to the attire of a gentleperson worth £200. Such a concession may be seen as somewhat grudging and, finally, concerned as much to preserve as to modify the distinction between gentle and nongentle in fourteenth-century society. Yet some penetration of the social hierarchy is acknowledged in the case of the esquires and gentlepersons, and that of the more prosperous merchants and manufacturers as well.

This practice of introducing finer and finer distinctions in order to clarify the relations of groups within the middle strata is carried on in numerous documents of the mid- and late fourteenth century.[20] But significant clarification of Chaucer's own position is contained in another document committed by its very nature to an unusually pragmatic treatment of the estates and occupational groups of society. The Poll Tax of 1379—coming at a time when desperately needed war subsidy was facilitated by a parliamentary compromise in which the king agreed to an inquiry into royal finances in return for economic support[21]—was both large and ambitiously graduated according to the ability to pay. This sense of the 1379 tax as a new departure is, in fact, richly reflected in documents of the time; the Anonimalle chronicler, for example, declared it a subsidy more marvelous than any previously seen or heard ("une subside si mervaillous qe tiel ne fuist unqes veu ne oie").[22]

As set forth in that chronicle and in the rolls of Parliament, the 1379 tax includes a very finely calibrated estimation of the estates and occupational groups by their condition or ability to pay. The rolls of Parliament divide the "diverses persones du Roialme" into four groupings.[23] The first includes dukes (assessed at 10 marks), counts (£4), barons, bannerets, and prosperous knights (40*s.*), bachelors and esquires with sufficient means to become knights (20*s.*), esquires of lesser estate (6*s.* 8*p.*), and esquires in service (3*s.* 4*d.*). The second grouping deals with legal occupations, including sergeants and apprentices at law (20*s.*) and attorneys (6*s.* 8*d.*). The third group consists essentially of substantial urban citizens, including the mayor of London (£4), aldermen of London and mayors of lesser cities (40*s.*), grand merchants of the realm (20*s.*), other merchants (13*s.* 4*p.*), a range of lesser merchants and artificers (6*s.* 8*d.*–2*s.* 6*d.*), and sergeants and franklins (6*s.* 8*d.*–40*d.*). The fourth group is more miscellaneous, including pardoners and summoners (3*s.* 4*d.*–12*d.*), hostelers below the estate of merchant (40*d.*–12*d.*), and on down to the impoverished or "verrois mendinantz."

As in many other documents of the period, society is seen in a dual perspective. Hierarchy and separation of estates are maintained, especially in the composition of the first category, which consists entirely of gentle ranks ranging from the Duke of Lancaster himself through esquires without lands, rent, or chattels. This separation is qualified, however, by a second standard of condition or economic status, according to which comparisons are made across the different groups. The mayor of London, for example, is assessed at the same rate as a count; other mayors, like barons; apprentices at law and substantial merchants, like knights. The framers of the tax seem aware of the comparative nature of their scale; we read that the mayor of London shall pay "come un Conte," the aldermen and other mayors "chescun come un Baron," and the substantial merchants "come Bachilers." The contemporary sense of the essential difference between the gentle and nongentle estates would hardly have been overridden by such comparisons. Nevertheless, likening of the conditions of the various estates could only lessen the sense of their fundamental difference.

As much as it shares with other documents of its period, the 1379 tax contains one innovation that is vitally important for an understanding of the position of the lesser gentry toward the end of the century. The 1363 statute treated the gentle estate both as a rank and—to invoke a modern sense of the term—as a single social class. Max Weber defines a social class as a number of people who hold in common certain possibilities in life determined "by economic interests in the possession of goods and opportunities for income."[24] This condition is satisfied by the expectation of the 1363 statute that all members of the gentry—whether lords, knights, esquires, or *gentils gentz*—shall enjoy a condition of life based on possession of lands or rents. The 1363 document made certain modest concessions involving marks of status to merchants and other citizens, but always treated them as members of a different social class, securing its status by possession of goods or chattels. With the Poll Tax of 1379, however, an essential change occurs, in which the gentle estate is no longer considered a single social class but is seen to embrace two distinct social classes. The gentle estate, in other words, comes to be seen in Weber's terminology as a "status group," based on the enjoyment of its members of a common "social estimation of *honor*,"[25] which contains two social classes, or groups with different social opportunities based on different sources of income. And it is specifically in the treatment of the rank of esquires that this change occurs. The 1363 statute recognized two orders of esquires but treated each (together with all other *gentils*) as enjoying a social position based on possession of lands or rents. The Poll Tax continues to recognize two orders of esquires—an upper tier with means sufficient for knighthood ("chescun Esquier qi par l'Estatut devroit estre Chivaler") and a lower tier of lesser means ("chescun Esquier de meindre estat"). But it goes on to define a *third* order of esquires, those who do not possess lands or rents or chattels but who are in service or who "have been armed" ("chescun Esquier nient possessiõnez des terres, rent, ne chateux, q'est en service ou ad este armez"). Those esquires who have been armed presumably confirmed (or, in some cases, earned) their rank in military service within the retinues of English commanders in the French, Castilian, and Scottish wars. In 1379, during a lull in the intensity of the wars with France after the great victories of Edward III and the Black Prince, the accomplishment of the rank of esquire by armed exertion is assumed already to have occurred. Another category of esquires continues its activities, however, and this is the novel category of esquires "en service."

This increasingly complicated category of esquires suggests the unusual flux within the middle strata during the second half of the fourteenth century. The lower ranks of the old elite, whose position was based on land tenure, found themselves jostled by persons who had gained gentility through household or military service, or by nongentle persons whose condition was based on the exchange of goods and chattels. The increasing specificity of documents like the 1363 statute and the 1379 poll tax brought some order to the situation by showing with greater precision the interrelations of the groups, but also highlighted contradictions within the system and ways in which the system was being challenged. The authors of these documents continue, for example, to assert the difference between the gentle and the nongentle estates, yet they also assert the equivalent claims of gentle esquires and nongentle merchants to social honor (the 1363 statute); the equal importance of knights and merchants to the well-being of the realm (Brinton); the interchangeability of belted knights and prosperous but nongentle residents of the countryside for purposes of parliamentary representation; the equivalent economic power of barons and aldermen, knights and merchants (1379 poll tax). Thus, even as the specification of new social groups contained the promise of stabilizing the vertical hierarchy by bringing it into closer alignment with real social circumstances, so too did it have the contrary effect of revealing the more conjectural and horizontal relations in which many people actually found themselves.

Chaucer's Social Position

At large within the turbulent and ill-defined middle ranks of society was Chaucer himself. Born the son of a wine merchant (who was, we sometimes forget, in royal service as deputy to the king's chief butler[26]), Chaucer was by 1368 an esquire of the king's household.[27] Earning this title in service to Edward III, he retained it after his technical move outside the household to assume a customs appointment in 1374, at which time he was styled "armiger regis"—an esquire, if not of the household, at least of the king. Later, in the 1380s and 1390s, he was to be known simply as "esquier" or "armiger," possessing the title more or less independently of the service in which he had received it. As an esquire, he was situated at a particularly volatile and ambiguous point in the social structure of his day.

Insightful commentators have taken note of his royal service on the one hand and his urban involvements on the other, and have attributed to him an amalgam of aristocratic (or court-derived) and bourgeois (or city-derived) values. A strong early formulation along these lines is that of G. K. Chesterton, who found that "Chaucer was chivalric, in the sense that he belonged, if only by adoption, to the world of chivalry and armorial blazonry . . . Chaucer was none the less *bourgeois* . . . in the sense that he himself was born and bred of burgesses . . . His figure bestrides the gap between these two last systems."[28] This analysis must now be sharpened by the added recognition that Chaucer's social grouping was not simply an uneasy amalgam of aristocratic and mercantile elements, but was *itself* a distinct segment of society with its own circumstances and commitments. Chesterton was right to see Chaucer's situation as being in some ways contradictory. Yet this contradiction must be understood not as an oscillation between two external social formations, but as lodged within his experience of his own situation. The social documents we have just considered can help us to understand the particular senses in which Chaucer's contradictory experiences of his role were inherent in the role itself.

Various sources—including Brinton's "body politic," the details of parliamentary summons, and the 1363 statute—have noticed a fourth estate or middle grouping embracing knights, esquires, other gentlepersons, merchants, citizens and burgesses, and some other prosperous guildsmen. This large grouping may be subdivided in several different ways. Although treated alike in such respects as eligibility for parliamentary summons, for example, its members are seen as belonging to two very unlike status groupings, in Weber's sense of their common "social estimation of honor." For this one broad grouping is divided between *gentils* (knights, esquires, and other *gentils gentz*) and non-*gentils* (the rest).

As a preliminary observation, then, we may say that every knight and esquire of the late fourteenth century, including Chaucer himself, was subject to two conflicting social evaluations: each shared with the great lords of the kingdom a common assessment of gentility, even as each shared with his fellow merchants, citizens, and burgesses of the middle strata the fact of nonaristocratic status or social rank.

Given the traversal of this group of knights and esquires by conflicting vertical and horizontal allegiances, Chaucer was nevertheless situated at a more than ordinarily ambiguous place in this group. For one thing, even as the rank of esquire had only recently gained access to gentility, so had royal service of the sort performed by Chaucer only recently been established as a point of entry to the rank of esquire. Persons had certainly gained gentle, and even aristocratic, status through royal service in the reigns of Edward I and Edward II,[29] but those services performed by esquires would not have conferred gentility because *esquier/armiger*—still roughly synonymous with *valettus*—had not yet gained decisive recognition as a gentle rank. Only in the second half of the fourteenth century did English esquires like Chaucer come to enjoy an estimation of gentility, at the expense of *valetti*, franklins, and other categories.[30] Then, during the Lancastrian years immediately following Chaucer's death, an increasing bureaucratization of the civil service led to a diminution of the very occupational possibilities that had led to Chaucer's elevation.[31] Chaucer was, in short, in royal service precisely when service at his level was most likely to lead to advantageous marriages, annuities and grants of offices, and gentle status—all of which Chaucer gained in the course of his service to Edward III and continued to enjoy through the reign of his grandson Richard.[32]

Other evidence suggests that, while Chaucer's economic position was typical for a king's esquire, he was not among the most prosperous members of that rank.[33] The 1363 statute, for example, distinguished between esquires with lands or rents worth less than £100 annually and those worth more than £200. In most of the years of his adult life, Chaucer's income placed him within the former category. Even in periods of general prosperity—as when he was married and benefiting from Philippa's annuities as well as his own, and later when he was serving as clerk of works—his income seldom exceeded £50. Only in two exceptional years does his income appear to have exceeded £100: in 1376 when he received a forfeit of £71 and in 1377 when he received £104 in connection with the wardship of Edmund Staplegate.[34] His modest income may even have something to do with his inclusion in the second tier of a 1369 listing of esquires of the royal household that includes sixty-three "esquiers de greindre estat" and eighty-eight "esquiers de meindre degree."[35]

Chaucer was further separated from at least some of his fellow esquires by an issue of what we would now call "social class." Even though the 1363 statute divided esquires into two strata according to income level, it still viewed all as members of a single status group (in their common estimation of social honor) and of a single class (in their similar opportunities for income in the possession of lands or rents). The 1379 poll tax treated all esquires as members of a single status group, but opened the possibility that the one status group might embody two distinct classes. In addition to the class of landowning esquires, it introduced a new class to which Chaucer obviously belonged—a class consisting of those without lands, rents, or possessions, in service or previously armed. Note that this class embraces two separate career tracks: those in service and those who have borne arms. Chaucer halfway satisfies this second stipulation, if we take "bearing arms" in the literal sense of having been armed for military duty rather than of being entitled to display a coat of arms.[36] He testified in the Scrope-Grosvenor hearing that he had been "armeez par xxvi ans" (or since his 1359–1360 military service in France).[37] Many esquires went abroad in such service, and many persons undoubtedly gained the rank of esquire through enlistment in a military retinue. Military service does not, however, appear to have been the avenue of Chaucer's promotion to esquire; the campaign in question occurred during his teenage years, and his place in the retinue was probably at the lesser rank of *valettus*.[38] His promotion to esquire appears to have been attained by the first of the two routes open to the nonlanded: it was first earned through household service to the king and was maintained by household and civil service thereafter. He was, in short, an esquire "en service," gaining through this service a status that Sylvia Thrupp has characterized as derivative gentility, a gentility "derived solely from the function exercised in the lord's behalf."[39]

Chaucer and some of his peers were thus exposed to some of the deepest contradictions that affected the middle strata of his society. The social situations of many superficially similar groups were much more sharply defined. On the one hand, those knights and esquires who possessed hereditary lands and rents had every reason to imagine themselves securely situated within a hierarchy whose most conspicuous representatives were the great aristocrats of the kingdom. On the other hand, even the greatest merchants such as Brembre and Philipot and Walworth—despite their wealth and knightly rank—possessed an unequivocal status as guildsmen of a particularly imposing sort. But Chaucer's stratum of gentlepersons "en service" eludes confident characterization. Though inserted in a social hierarchy between knights and other *gentils gentz*, they lack the traditional support of lands and rents. Though aligned by their work with the growing body of clerks, scribes, lawyers, and literate tradespeople, they are separated from that body by their gentility. Further complicating the situation is the nature of Chaucer's social ties—both to those he served and to those among whom he served.

The Transformation of Social Relations

M. D. Chenu describes a process of "desacralization" that undermined the sworn relation of vassalage and led to the replacement of "vertical and paternalistic fidelity" by "horizontal and fraternal agreement."[40] His interest is in the twelfth and thirteenth centuries and in the Continent. The transformation he describes, however, is no less evident in England—though in England its effects are manifested most strikingly in the fourteenth century. Until the last decades of the thirteenth century in England, the relation of the lord to those who followed him was still normally characterized by clear subordination, sanctified by oath, and secured by land tenure. Increasingly common in the fourteenth century—and then prevalent during its second half—was a new form of relation based on independent calculation, defined by written or oral contract, and secured by salary in the form of cash annuity. Lords were no less lords under the new system. Indeed, the social gulf between lords and members of the gentry retained for service under the new system might well have been greater than that between lord and knightly tenant under the old. But the singularity of the relation of the gentleperson in service to the lord he served was inevitably diminished under the new system. Emphasis on the voluntary and contractual nature of the new association worked against the exclusivity of the vertical ties that bound a person in service to his lord, and encouraged a new perception of horizontal ties of affinity to those sharing one's own class, rank, and social objectives.

The essence of the feudal relation of the high middle ages had been the sacralized relation of lord and vassal. As described in the classical formulation of F. L. Ganshof, this sacralization was accomplished by the act of homage embodied in the *immixio manum* in which the vassal placed his hands between those of his lord; the *vol* or declaration of will, in which the vassal swore to be faithful, in truth and without ulterior design ("fidel serai . . . per rectam fidem, sine ingan").[41] Normally the entry into vassalage was also accompanied by the free grant of a benefice *(beneficium)* or fief *(feodum)*—though in the early centuries of the practice the grant of land tenure was treated as if it were ancillary to the relation, and only in the twelfth century did a vassal begin to perform homage "for" a fief ("pro hoc beneficio").[42] The relation of lord and vassal carried within it a clear implication of vertical hierarchy. This aspect was conveyed in particular by the *immixio manum,* described by Ganshof as symbolizing the surrender of the person of the vassal to the discretion of his lord.[43]

The forms and relations of feudality may legitimately be viewed as at once symbolic and practical in their origin and long continuation. Georges Duby has reminded us of their symbolic status as "avant tout un état d'esprit, ce complexe psychologique formé dans le petit monde des guerriers peu à peu devenus des nobles."[44] Ganshof, on the other hand, has pointed out that feudality always had its "réel" element, predicated on the bestowal of the fief and the enjoyment by both lord and vassal of economic advantages from the relationship.[45] The subsequent history of feudality in the thirteenth and early fourteenth centuries shows both to be correct. Duby is sustained by the fact that the institutions of vassalage survived for well over a century after the increased circulation of money had made possible the development of relationships based on exchange of money rather than land tenure. Ganshof is sustained by the fact that the latter-day forms of the feudal relationship were still materially based, with money rather than land tenure as the vassal's reward. The latter-day forms of feudalism were based on the lord's concession of a *fief-rente* (as Lyon calls it) [46] or *feodum de bursa* (a term used by Ganshof), [47] in which rent in the form of regular cash payment replaced the occupancy of a particular landed fief. The fief-rent was a legitimate substitute for the landed *feodum* or *beneficium* in the nexus of feudal relations, so long as homage and fealty were performed for it—so long, that is, as it provided a basis for a sacral rather than contractual tie. Without homage and fealty, an agreement for service in return for payment became something other than fief-rent, and the relation it signaled was no longer properly feudal. Such desacralized and nonfeudal relations were to become common in the fourteenth century, and we will have occasion to inspect them more closely. The remarkable thing about feudal relations based on fief-rent is not, however, that they ended, but that they lasted for so long. Lyon has traced the practice as far back as the eleventh century and locates its apogee in the thirteenth and fourteenth centuries, in the latter stages of which it overlapped the development of other, nonfeudal forms of retaining. [48] The stubborn persistence of feudalism based on fief-rent shows the remarkable durability of this institution as a "état d'esprit," even after a rising money economy had altered its material basis.

Although the polite fiction of the fief-rent saved feudal appearances for centuries after the availability of cash annuities had permitted less personal and stable forms of retaining, the alternative practice of retaining by indenture for cash payment was making steady headway. Originating in the thirteenth century, this practice had overshadowed feudalism based on fief-rent by the mid-fourteenth century and completely routed it by the century's end. K. B. McFarlane, who first described this practice under the somewhat unfortunate term "bastard feudalism," located its essence in the replacement of enfeoffment by other forms of payment for service. [49] In further distinction from the contemporaneous institution of fief-rent, however, we should also note that retaining by indenture was no longer considered a sacralized or sworn relationship, but rather was wholly contractual and secular in nature. Although a few modest survivals of feudal language may be found in indentures, homage and fealty were not performed.

The forms of feudal vassalage on the one hand and indentured service on the other exist concurrently in John of Gaunt's register of

1379–1383. A number of entries record the completion of traditional or feudal homage for lands and instruct Gaunt's feodary (or agent) in steps to be taken. The entry for William Wallerant, for example, states that he has made his homage to the duke for certain lands and tenements he holds (in the feodary's county of Wiltshire) and that the feodary is now to take sufficient surety that William will do good and loyal services and customs for the lands and tenements, and pay any relief due, and that William should no longer be distrained for his homage and any sums taken from him should be returned.[50]

Gaunt's letter to his feodary was written for business purposes alone, and the economic basis of the relation is clearly revealed. Homage has been performed *for* ("pur") certain lands and tenements. Services and customs (the commutation of which could lead to added revenue for the lord) are to be offered in return, and a surety ("seurtee") is to be taken in order to assure their observance. The possibility of a relief or one-time payment for occupancy of lands is mentioned. Distraint was evidently invoked prior to homage, though provision is made for return of any chattels seized. We need not be surprised that the economic basis of vassalage is so evident; as demonstrated by Bean and others, English feudalism of the later middle ages was principally a fiscal system.[51] Nevertheless, because we are dealing with a situation of land tenure in which lands are *held of* ("tient de") the lord, homage is invoked and (since a report of a completed act of homage is now being transmitted to the feodary) has evidently been performed in person. To this limited extent, at any rate, some aspects of the old sacralized relation of lord and vassal have been retained.

The register for 1379–1383 contains twelve such records of homage for lands, but thirty-two indentures for service. A representative indenture for service is that of the esquire Thomas de Braddeley, who on 23 June 1380 was retained and attached ("retenuz et demurez") to John of Gaunt in the following manner: he is bound to serve the duke in times of both peace and war for the term of his life, and must exert himself as the duke pleases, fittingly arrayed for war. He will receive from the duke the sum of 20 marks annually, in peace or war, from the receipts of the lordship of Higham Ferrers. In peacetime he will receive sustenance and wages of court, wherever he is sent, like those of other esquires of his estate and condition, and in times of war he will have maintenance or wages of court like other esquires of his condition.[52]

No oath binds the lord and the retainer. The agreement by which Thomas is retained to serve ("servir") the duke is contractual rather than sacramental in nature. Obviously the reward Thomas is to receive for his service is a cash annuity rather than land tenure; the fact that he is to be paid from the receipts of a particular estate is probably more a matter of administrative convenience than a sentimental throwback to an earlier form of tenure. These observations are not intended to suggest that the relationship represented here is provisional or fly-by-night in nature. As Saul has pointed out, a less permanent contract than an annual retaining fee for life sufficed in cases where military service for a single campaign or other kinds of short-term service were all that was needed.[53] Here retention is for life and covers both peace and war. Military service might be involved. The duke went north ready to campaign in Scotland in August 1380, and Scottish hostilities and continental interests kept him militarily occupied throughout the decade. This indenture, like most, concludes with concrete specifications dealing with horses, equipment, prisoners, booty, and other trappings of war. Nevertheless, peacetime duties are obviously contemplated. Thomas is expected to be eligible for peacetime service in various venues (and presumably at various tasks), and his rights both to sustenance and wages are assured.[54]

Even from the small sample of indentures for service preserved in the register, we can see John of Gaunt building a retinue that will increase his influence, and provide assistance in the management of his affairs in times of peace as well as war. Evidence suggests that other lords were doing the same, though not on so grand a scale. Twentieth-century appraisals of this practice of retaining by indenture have varied. Noting that such retinues, for all their presumption of lifetime service, were relatively unstable, with movement in and out of service and even conspicuous cases of service to more than one lord at once, McFarlane first saw them as marking the "degeneration of liege homage."[55] Later he softened his view, coming to see the practice as an endeavor to preserve loyalty and good faith in new and increasingly complicated circumstances.[56] Finally, though, the question of whether we depict retaining by indenture as a degeneration or as a refinement of feudal practice is beside the point. Either way, it is a comprehensible response to the lessened importance of land tenure and the growing need for new forms of service and new ways of compensation. As McFarlane would point out in his lectures on lords and retainers, "it was precisely because the tenurial bond had become weak that a contractural one was needed."[57]

Granting that retaining by indenture sought in some ways to perpetuate older values (such as continuity of service to a single lord), the fact remains that it represents a new system of social organization. As a contract rather than a sworn oath, the indenture permits a degree of voluntarism not possible (or at least emphatically discouraged) within the system of vassalage. Elements of hierarchy persist: the lord is still the lord and the indentured retainer serves him. But the agreement to serve and to compensate service is made subsequent to a rational calculation of each party that his profit will be served. No sanctified agreement or earthly replication of the heavenly hierarchy, the indenture is entered into as a transaction between two persons, each seeking to advance his own interests.

The feudal relation of lord and vassal thrived because it met the needs of both parties: the lord's need for military assistance and income from his property and the tenant's need for land and military protection. The indentured relation of lord and retainer thrived by meeting new needs: that of the lord for service and influence and that of the retainer for an assured income and legal and political protection. As a successful adaptation to changed conditions, the indenture system spread rapidly; already cited is Saul's remarkable finding that in the fourteenth century between half and two-thirds of all Gloucestershire gentry were retained by local magnates.[58] Gloucestershire may be a partial exception; Michael J. Bennett, for example, finds a much higher proportion of Cheshire and Lancashire gentry in independent possession of manors during the same period.[59] Local variations notwithstanding, the indenture system was plainly the basic way in which fourteenth-century English knights and esquires were recruited into larger political structures (or, as they were often called in French texts of the day, *affinites*) for the enjoyment and exercise of influence.

Statutory solutions sought, by a strict definition of the limits of permissible retaining, to balance the desire of kings to dominate nobles, that of nobles to have retinues, and that of the commons to be protected from wanton thuggery.[60] Particularly notable in this regard is the comprehensive 1390 Statute on Livery and Maintenance. Not only proscribing the unlimited distribution of "liveries of company," it defines the limits of permissible retaining. In the process, the statute provides an enormously valuable review of the possible forms of relation between lords and retainers in the second half of the fourteenth century. Because of problems with the troublemaking retinues of lords and others,

> We have ordained and strictly forbidden . . . that any prelate or other man of the holy church or bachelor or esquire or other of lesser estate give any manner of such livery called livery of company, and that any

> duke, count, baron, or banneret give such livery of company to a knight or esquire, unless he is retained with him for the term of his life for peace and war by indenture without fraud or conspiracy, or unless he is a familiar servant dwelling in his household, or to any valet called yeoman or archer or to any other of lesser estate than esquire, unless he is similarly a familiar dwelling in his household.[61]

Forbidden is any retaining by prelates or by nonnoble gentry below the rank of banneret; also forbidden is retaining by lords except when it is of long duration or of persons intimately connected with their households. Retaining may be practiced by members of the hereditary aristocracy with the rank of duke, count, baron, or banneret and may involve three categories of retainers: (1) persons of the rank of knight or esquire, who are retained for life in peace or war by indenture, (2) familiar servants dwelling in the household, and (3) family servants below the rank of esquire dwelling in the household.

The first category, already familiar to us from the case of Thomas de Braddeley, is of knights and esquires who are formally retained. Not necessarily resident in the lord's household, these retainers are nevertheless presumably liable, like Thomas, to be summoned for duties on behalf of the lord. (Not specifically addressed here, but excluded from the lord's retinue by the terms of the statute, are knights and esquires who contract for shorter terms of purely military service. As in the case of Gaunt's indentures, the arrangement contemplated here is plainly to be more enduring.[62])

The second category, which is of particular interest because of the insight it offers into the situation of those "en service," consists of gentle servants, of the rank of knight or esquire, dwelling in the household. The gentility of this category is plainly indicated by its separation from the succeeding category of familiars of lesser estate than esquire.[63] The fact that we are considering knights and esquires must cause us to look once again at the phrase with which their status is characterized: "mesnal et familier." *Mesnal,* in this context, must be divorced entirely from the taint of our *menial.* Old French *mesnial* means "pertaining to a household" *(menage),* and a *mesnial* person is simply "a person connected with a household." To be connected with a royal or noble household, in the capacity of service to a lord, was in no way regarded as incompatible with gentility in the fourteenth century.[64] Included in this category of *mesnals gentils* are no doubt those knights and esquires serving in legal, managerial, and fiscal posts that predated the extensive use of indenture. Compensation for such services, not covered by an indenture agreement, was conveyed through letter patent, providing for annual annuities in return for good service. The esteem in which their service was held was not less than that of the indentured retainers, but simply expressed in a different way; knights and esquires in either capacity are, according to the statutes of Richard II and of Henry IV, equally entitled to wear the "honurable liveree" of the king.

The multiple options outlined and implied in the 1390 statute suggest that lords had broad latitude in retinue building. These magnates could create a bond by indenture payable by chancery annuity, simply by compensated household service, or (in the proscribed practice) simply by passing out a hat or robe or other sign of affiliation—perhaps even with the recipient footing the bill. No wonder John of Gaunt and the other lords defended so vigorously in 1384 and 1388 their right to distribute *signi* or other ornaments to their dependents.[65] Although we have already seen that Gaunt's retinue was formed along more stable lines than the infamous "liveried companies," he and his fellow magnates must have valued the flexibility conferred by this range of options. Yet the lords were not the only beneficiaries of a system that also opened up a multiplicity of possibilities for those retained. Those who (like the third category of esquires in the 1379 poll tax) lacked significant lands, rents, or chattels and were required to make their way "en service." were presented with opportunities to secure or earn their gentility as indentured retainers, as nonindentured members of household *(mesnals gentils)*, or in less sanctioned ways. McFarlane was correct in his conclusion that, under this system, "a man was allowed greater freedom of choice at every stage in the pursuit of his own interests."[66]

Whatever appearance of continuity was preserved by these new forms of association, one should not insist too emphatically on their similarity to earlier feudal ties between lord and tenant. Christine Carpenter, I think, overstates the case when she observes that "The written contract [of bastard feudalism] itself no more implied a commercial attitude than did the spoken pledge of the less literate feudal age."[67] Lacking a secure basis for reward through land tenure, lacking the spiritual authority of the sworn oath, dependent on more subjective and less predictable perceptions of personal advantage, and frankly temporary in nature, these new associations of lords and followers could not have rivaled in intensity those feudal bonds formed in simpler, agrarian times.

The new associations were, after all, explicitly designed to introduce more flexible conceptions of duration and remuneration into the relations of lords and those who served them. Given such motives, we can hardly doubt that one consequence would have been a withdrawal of some measure of the singular fidelity the feudal oath had sought from the retainer. Noticeable in social relations among the later fourteenth-century gentry is a partial redirection of personal loyalty, from vertical commitment to a single lord in a hierarchical system to a more horizontal dispersal of loyalties among the members of one's own social group.

The Nature of Chaucer's Ties

Chaucer may, I believe, be regarded as one of the *mesnals gentils* in the 1390 statute. That phrase quite accurately conveys his relation to the household of Edward III between 1366 or 1368 and 1374, and suffices as a general characterization of his relations with Edward III and Richard II thereafter. As a *mesnal gentil* or a gentleperson "en service" he was bound to Richard by a tie that, while significant, differed in kind from traditional vassalage. As a gentleperson of the household, he appears never to have done formal homage—an understandable state of affairs, since household service was not necessarily connected with land tenure. (Successful household servants, such as John Beauchamp of Holt, might be richly endowed with lands or even ennobled, but such grants were a separate and extraordinary sign of royal favor.) Nor does he seem to have been subject to formal retention or indenture.[68] The language by which Richard confirmed Edward III's annuity in 1378 might seem to suggest that Chaucer has been retained ("prefatum Galfridum retinuimus"[69]), but this retention is probably only in that implied sense in which *anyone* receiving a life annuity may be considered retained. As with the *mesnals gentils* of the 1390 statute, Chaucer belonged to a group that was evidently seen as bound to good service without the formality of a contract. (The self-evident nature of this tie may, as N. B. Lewis has suggested, be connected with the venerability of the concept of household service, long predating the origin of the indenture system.[70]) Although not formally retained, as an esquire of the king's household Chaucer must have enjoyed a status equivalent to that of indentured members of the royal retinue who lived outside the household, and in some respects his position (solidified by a lifetime annuity) must have been more secure than theirs.

With his move to London and to customs in 1374, Chaucer left the ranks of immediate household familiars, but he remained an esquire in service to the king. Given-Wilson has argued that for nonresident esquires the possibility of continued connection to the court emerged only in the later 1370s,[71] and Chaucer appears to have been among the very first to take advantage of it. We cannot imagine him as one of those esquires described in Edward IV's household book, called to "occupie the Court," "in talking of Chronicles of Kinges, and of other Pollicies, or in pipeing or harpeing, songinges, or other actes marcealls."[72] Not only is this description, burnished with the mellow glow of old custom, anachronistic in the fifteenth century, but it would probably have been anachronistic in the court of Richard II.[73] The emptying of the royal (or baronial) hall was a social fact of the later fourteenth century, however one might wish to imagine otherwise.[74] Thus, while a single document of 1385 includes his name among select members of the household, most of Chaucer's duties would have involved special embassies and assignments, a few within the court but most far outside. These assignments were partly ambassadorial, partly clerical, partly diplomatic, partly ceremonial. Taken together, they demanded literacy, fluency in French (and, in cases like Chaucer's, languages such as Italian, Spanish, and Latin), and other formidable skills. No entertainers, Chaucer and his friends were clearly educated bureaucrats like those who concerned Thomas Wimbledon, when he complained in a contemporary sermon about those who had eschewed the study of philosophy or divinity and joined "the kyngis court to writen lettres or writis" in the hope "that thyse occupacions shul be euere menis to make hem grete in the world."[75] Chaucer's metier was as a literate and versatile civil servant of the king, carrying out a wide range of duties within, and then outside, the royal household.

Though neither sanctified by oath nor formalized by written agreement, Chaucer's relations to Edward III and then to Richard II should not be considered shallow or unimportant. Royal interest in the progress of Chaucer's career and his own reciprocal readiness to serve are evident in each stage of his life after 1366–1367. The move to customs that facilitated his transfer to London in 1374 was, after all, by royal appointment. This appointment was supplemented by a royal grant ("un picher de vyn a prendre chescun jour en port de nostre citee de Londres"), a rent-free house over Aldgate entered during the mayoralty of Adam de Bury (himself a member of the court party), as well as uninterrupted continuation of his life annuity—gestures that constitute a handsome send-off.[76] Richard not only continued the annuity but made Chaucer's professional situation a matter of early concern after resumption of full rule after 1389.[77] Richard even paid attention to Chaucer's economic problems in the years after 1391, when the latter's service to the crown had greatly diminished.[78] For his part, Chaucer continued to be available for royal service in a way that exceeded the definition of any particular post he occupied. Surviving records suggest at least a dozen journies across the sea—including trips to Navarre, France, Genoa, Florence, Flanders, and Lombardy—conducted before, during, and after his actual residence in the household. He participated in peace and marriage discussions, and engaged in other secret business on behalf of the king ("in secretis negociis regis" [79]). Other domestic charges also occurred at intervals: in 1376 he was sent on secret business with John Burley, and as late as 1398 he received a two-year safe conduct for the king's "ardua et urgencia negocia." [80] Such involvements occurred against a background of assumptions far broader than can be encompassed with a simple title such as "Clerk of Works" or even "King's Esquire."

Despite such evidence of reciprocal responsibility, the pattern of Chaucer's relations with the monarchs he served deviated considerably from the traditional relation of vassal to feudal lord. No longer based on a sworn oath, Chaucer's relation to his monarchs was essentially secular and contractual (whether the contract itself was real or, more likely, implied). No longer atemporal or permanent in its aspirations, his understanding with his sovereigns played itself out in "real" time. Though for the term of life ("ad totam vitam ipsius Galfridi"), his annuity was connected with services rendered ("pro bono servicio")[81]—and, as we know, annuities were notoriously subject to disruption.[82] His efforts were compensated by annuities and special grants—that is, by a salary.

Chaucer was still bound to his monarchs, but bound by the complex mixture of residual loyalty and unabashed self-interest that united lords and their followers within the bastard feudalism of the late fourteenth century. Most tellingly, his relation to his lords was no longer personal but was enacted within a much larger and looser coalition of individuals for the accomplishment of common aims. To understand the "postfeudal" implications of Chaucer's social experience, we must consider the network of relations within which it occurred: that social formation known in Middle English as the "retinue," in Old French as the *affinite,* and today as the "party."

2 The King's Affinity

WEBER situates status groups in the social order and classes in the economic order, but observes that "parties live in a house of power."[1] The party or faction, as an opportunistic and relatively nonhierarchical alliance of persons from different social strata to achieve common ends, surfaces in late fourteenth-century social commentary. Its importance may be briefly indicated in the multiplication of terms by which it was known: *conjuracion, covine, confederacie, bretherhede, fraternite.* Consider, for example, the blizzard of terminology stirred up in a bill promoted by Nicholas Brembre (himself no mean factionalist) in his 1383 mayoral term, in order to discourage John Northampton and his craftsguildsmen by forbidding "congregaciouns, conuenticles . . . assembles . . . alliances, confederacies, conspiracies . . . [and] obligaciouns, forto bynde men to gidre, forto systeyne eny quereles in lyuinnge and deyennge to gidre," and mandating arrest of "eny swich congregaciouns or covynes in gaderyng, or ygadred."[2] Of particular concern to contemporary commentators was the misuse by such associations of *conjuracion* or debased forms of oath taking to bind people on a nontraditional basis. The proper use of the oath, it was felt, was to secure orderly and hierarchical patterns of domination and subordination by reference to a transcendent and atemporal order. But emerging forms of association were using the oath in a new way: to sanction lateral involvement of persons "to gidre," in pursuit of temporary aims.[3]

These new associations were organizational counterparts to the shift from vassalage to contract service. Their most inclusive and characteristic form was the enlarged party or faction known by contemporaries as the *affinite* or by modern commentators as the "affinity group." This grouping was both product and producer of a new system of relations in which a king or magnate could unify the efforts of persons in the most varied social and occupational situations on a basis of common advantage. Its virtue was, of course, flexibility: by escaping the rigidities of strict hierarchy, in which both distinction and reward were based on an unwieldy system of land tenure, the affinity permitted a more flexible vocabulary of social relations, a widened array of rewards for specialized or temporary services.

The king or magnate was situated not (as in a hierarchy) at the *apex* of the affinity but at its *center,* with followers arrayed around him in a series of concentric circles, widening out to less and less defined forms of interdependency.[4] Richard's affinity consisted of at least three such circles: one of officers of state (including chamber knights), one of salaried servants (including chancery officials and sergeants-at-arms), and one of his general "retinue" (including king's knights and king's esquires).[5] There was, as Given-Wilson adds, "constant overlap and movement" among these groups. Taking Chaucer as a provisional example, we might observe that he was friendly with members of the first, a member of the second in 1368–1374 and 1389–1391, and spent the rest of his adult life as a member of the third.

This "sea of varying relationships"[6] is, then, the one in which we find Chaucer, sustained by complicated and often tacit ties of loyalty and self-interest. Twentieth-century literary historians have rather wishfully thought him apolitical, a free agent between parties or even wholly free of factional ties. But any freedom of personal choice or perspective he enjoyed was achieved from within the conditions imposed by his factional situation, not by ignoring them but by manipulating them with patience and skill. Sifted with care, the entries of the *Life-Records* offer fascinating glimpses of Chaucer within Richard's affinity. These glimpses suggest the broad extent of his participation in the politics of faction, as well as the prudence with which he managed that participation in difficult and dangerous times.

The Ricardian Faction

Richard's affinity functioned in the 1380s and 1390s not merely to magnify the royal splendor but to accomplish political aims. These aims varied, embracing what might be considered a royal program (such as peace with France, subjugation of Ireland) as well as more purely personal ends (security for the monarch, rewards for his followers). Associated within this faction were aristocrats like Robert de Vere and Alexander Nevill, wealthy urban merchants like Nicholas Brembre, William Walworth, and John Philipot, unlanded knights and esquires like Chaucer and his friends, and ambitious lawyers and aspiring politicians like John Blake and Thomas Usk.

Although some historians have shown no reluctance to treat Chaucer as a member of the royal party or Ricardian faction,[7] Chaucerians have been reluctant to draw that conclusion. Thus James Hulbert, evaluating Chaucer's associations with the Ricardians and their aristocratic opposition in 1386–1389, observes that "by far the greater number were in that of the King," but he still concludes that "too many things connect Chaucer with both parties to make his identification with either possible."[8] So too S. Sanderlin, emphasizing Chaucer's involvement with the royal faction, offers the indeterminate instance of William Beauchamp as the sole support of the conclusion that during the struggle with the aristocratic Appellants Chaucer "was a known associate of prominent men on both sides."[9]

This prevailing reluctance to imagine Chaucer as factionally committed may be a consequence of having met him primarily on a literary ground. Those who have experienced his broad-mindedness and capacity to entertain alternatives within the compass of his writings have been reluctant to imagine that he could ever commit himself to a single political perspective. But Chaucer's factional alignment need not be considered an embarrassment to his qualities of balance or good sense. As a person of his time and as a professional courtier and civil servant, he had no choice but to participate in factional politics. His particular habits of mind are indeed suggested by the choices he made, but they are revealed less in the avoidance of factional activity than in the particular form of his commitment and in the degree to which he kept the possibility of alternatives alive. As for his initial and enduring act of political choice, however, we can have little doubt: a review of his interactions with the members of the principal camps confirms his predominant connection with the royal faction, first under Edward III and even more emphatically under Richard II.

At the center of the Ricardian camp during the 1380s was that group of royal supporters charged with treason by the aristocratic faction (the Appellants) in 1387–1388. This central group, all of whom were ultimately condemned, consisted of five principals (Archbishop Alexander Nevill; Robert de Vere, Earl of Oxford; Chancellor Michael de la Pole; Chief Justice Robert Tresilian; and recent mayor and collector of customs Nicholas Brembre), four chamber knights (Simon Burley, John Beauchamp, John Salisbury, and James Berners), and the functionaries Thomas Usk (an earlier supporter of Northampton now recruited to the royal faction) and John Blake (a lawyer who had assisted Richard in framing judicial questions). To this group may be added a handful of chamber knights who managed to avoid the animosity of the Appellants but who were active in Richard's service throughout the 1380s, among them John Clanvowe, William Nevill, Philip la Vache, and Richard Stury.[10] The London group (something like an "aldermanic patriciate") with which this royal faction often cooperated included such merchant-capitalists as Brembre, Philipot, and Walworth (three mayors, all of whom were knighted for their support of Richard in 1381), as well as such supporters as Nicholas Exton and John Hende.[11]

Leading the opposition to Richard during the 1380s were the three principal Appellants: Thomas of Woodstock, Duke of Gloucester; Thomas Beauchamp, Earl of Warwick; and Richard, Earl of Arundel. Joining them briefly in 1387–1388 were Thomas Mowbray, Earl of Nottingham, and Henry, Earl of Derby.[12] Naturally a group so influential and so diverse also had connections within Richard's court. Chaucer's friend William Beauchamp, for example, was both Chamberlain of the Household (1378–1380) and the brother of Thomas Beauchamp. Arrayed against Richard's aldermanic supporters was John Northampton's group of lesser masters, ascendant during his mayoralty in 1381–1383, briefly active into 1384, and essentially ineffective (though by no means forgotten) thereafter.[13] Northampton's active allies, named by Usk in his Appeal of Northampton for treason in 1384, included John More, Richard Norbury (or Northbury), and William Essex.[14]

A final major faction was the Lancastrian interest, with John of Gaunt charting an independent course—sometimes anti-Ricardian (during the conflicts with Richard and his favorites in 1384–1385 and during Henry of Derby's brief alliance with the aristocratic opposition in 1387–1388) and at other times highly supportive of Richard and the crown.

Chaucer's contacts with members of the Ricardian faction were rich and varied. One might go so far as to say that he had few documented contacts that were *not* with members of this group. In the case of the eleven royal retainers condemned in 1388, for example, he had verifiable contact with at least eight and may have known the rest. Robert de Vere served as King's Chamberlain (hence Chaucer's superior in the household), and in that category endorsed and possibly personally signed Chaucer's 1385 petition for a permanent deputy in the office of controller.[15] While the connection may have been nothing more than official business, and Vere himself was more often than not absent from his post, he and Chaucer must have had some direct contact.[16] Michael de la Pole, as chancellor between 1383 and his impeachment in 1386, signed off on documents related to the 1383 appointment of a deputy controller,[17] opened the Parliament at which Chaucer served, and would in other ways have been a conspicuous figure. Robert Tresilian served as Chaucer's fellow justice of the peace for Kent between 1386 and his death, and must have been well known to him.[18] As collector of wool customs and Chaucer's immediate superior throughout most of the latter's term as controller, Nicholas Brembre had to be known as well.[19]

Chaucer was also linked with those chamber knights who were condemned for their treasonous association with Richard. The venerable and powerful subchamberlain Simon Burley, whose office under Vere placed him in effective control of the household,[20] held the concurrent position of constable of Dover Castle, which made him the supervisor of Chaucer's activities as justice of the peace for Kent.[21] He was the brother of John Burley, with whom Chaucer went on a mission in "secretis negociis . . . domini regis" in 1376.[22] Among the three additional chamber knights who were to die on May 12, John Beauchamp is listed with Chaucer as an esquire of the household in 1368,[23] and John Salisbury is listed with Chaucer in the same capacity in 1372.[24] Chaucer might not have known John Blake, but he would probably have had some contact with writer-conspirator Thomas Usk.[25]

Chaucer's contacts with the royal party were not, of course, limited to this group. Within the group of ten chamber knights in Richard's service both before and after 1387–1388 (a group to which I would add Lewis Clifford, whose documented service in that capacity dates from 1391 but who was active in and about the court well before then[26]), he had personal relations with at least five. Richard Stury was captured in France in the same campaign with Chaucer in 1359–1360, participated with him in an embassy to discuss marriage between Richard II and a daughter of the king of France, and headed a commission of which Chaucer was a member in 1390.[27] John Clanvowe wrote the Middle English poem that must be regarded as most attuned to Chaucer's artistry[28] and joined with his friend William Nevill as a witness to Chaucer's release in the affair of Cecily Champain. Philip la Vache is addressed through a play on his name in Chaucer's "Truth."[29] Lewis Clifford was Chaucer's intermediary with the

French poet Deschamps.[30] (As has often been noted, four of these five, excepting only Vache, were cited by Walsingham as among a group of "Lollard Knights"—and Vache might just as well be included; he was Clifford's son-in-law, and he and his wife were recipients of religious books, including a "Book of Tribulation," from Clifford's will.[31]) Not to prolong this discussion unduly, I would simply add that Henry Scogan, to whom Chaucer addressed his "Envoy," was also in Richard's service in the 1390s,[32] and that one Peter Bukton, possible dedicatee of Chaucer's envoy on marriage, was an esquire in the service of Queen Anne.[33]

Extending the circle of consideration outward to embrace Chaucer's working life, we encounter many adherents of the royal faction among his associates and contacts, and virtually no opponents. This is certainly comprehensible, since the majority of his business associates were, like himself, royal appointees. Some examples might help to convey the nature of these associations. Among the collectors of customs in the port of London from the beginning of Richard's reign until Chaucer's resignation, we find Brembre, Philipot, and Walworth. These staunch royalists were joined by John Organ, William More, and Nicholas Exton, all of whom may be considered at least nominal royalists, supporting Richard's policies through 1387 and then subsiding in the more dangerous year of 1388.[34] Also listed are John Churchman, an alderman of undetermined sympathies,[35] and one Walter Ralf. None may be regarded as supporters of Northampton (though Philipot and More, together with Richard himself, did briefly acquiesce in his reelection for a second term in 1382[36]); for a staunch supporter of Northampton—or at least a person who would become one—we must go back to the appointment of Richard Norbury in 1376.[37] Chaucer's fellow controllers were less conspicuous socially (being mainly merchants and not aldermen) and are thus harder to trace. But John Hermesthorpe, Chaucer's eventual successor in the wool custom, is known as a favorite of the king and evidently served for a time as his confessor[38]; he is cited as "king's clerk" in the Patent Rolls.[39]

Chaucer also found himself among fellow courtiers and royal supporters during his service as justice of the peace for Kent, 1385–1389. A peace commission, according to a statute of 1389, was to be composed of the most sufficient "Chivalers, Esquiers, & gentz de ley des ditz Countees" [40]—augmented, a statute of the following year makes clear, with lords assigned by parliament ("les seigneurs assignez en cest parlement").[41] The eighteen justices with whom Chaucer served were arrayed along such lines, including four lords, six lawyers (five of them sergeants-at-law), and seven or eight gentry (five knights, two esquires, and one wealthy burgess).[42] The justices of known political sentiment were all more or less Ricardian; division by political view is not so much between those for Richard and those against him as between vigorous and lukewarm supporters. Among the vigorous adherents of Richard must be numbered Simon Burley (head of the commission as constable of Dover Castle), Richard's former tutor and vice-chamberlain of the household, who was beheaded in 1388. Similarly committed were Robert Tresilian, chief justice of the King's bench, and Robert Belknap, chief justice of common pleas. Both were active in supporting Richard's judicial challenge to the Appellants in the summer of 1387.[43] Tresilian was among those executed in 1388, and Belknap was exiled to Ireland until his recall by Richard in 1397. Walter Clopton was appointed to succeed Tresilian as chief justice and found himself pronouncing sentence on Beauchamp, Berners, and Salisbury[44]—yet evidence suggests that his complicity was reluctant and against personal principle.[45] Still associated with the king, but chosen by the Appellants as members of the king's party with whom they would negotiate and cooperate, were two more justices, John Cobham and John Devereux; they might be regarded as something of a breakaway faction within the king's larger circle of adherents.[46] The political sympathies of the gentry on the commission are harder to trace, but their number included at least one energetic king's man in addition to Chaucer himself: this is Hugh Fastolf, wealthy burgess of Great Yarmouth and London.[47] In the course of his term as alderman and sheriff of London, he was denounced to the Parliament of 1386, which sought his removal on grounds of complicity with Brembre.[48]

In her study of an aristocratic affinity, Christine Carpenter places particular emphasis on the support available within the affinity for legal pleading and looks particularly to those connections "whose existence can usually only be inferred, principally from frequency of association on legal documents, but is sometimes confirmed by their appearance as co-defendants or fellow plaintiffs."[49] Another indication of Chaucer's involvement with the royal faction is his involvement in legal relations with other persons who possessed clear royal ties—relations involving surety, witnesses to his release in the matter of Cecily Champain, and those to whom he gave power of attorney before journeying abroad in 1378.

Two of the people for whom Chaucer was surety were family or

Kentish connections that cannot be traced here, but three offer significant insight into his affiliations: John de Romsey, treasurer of Calais, William Beauchamp, and John Hende, draper of London who would become mayor in 1391–1392.[50] William Beauchamp, whose complicated case will be discussed later, was a king's man when Chaucer met him in 1378. John de Romsey came, like Chaucer, from service in the household of Edward III and is listed as an esquire and esquire of greater degree in the accounts of the 1360s and 1370s.[51] His association with Chaucer in 1375 predates any relation to Richard, but he was definitely one of Edward's men. Chaucer's surety for Hende was given in 1381, well before he became mayor but after his elevation to aldermanic rank. Although a member of a nonvictualing guild, and thus a potential supporter of Northampton's attack on the fishmongers and other victualing guilds, Hende was among those who petitioned for the execution of Northampton.[52] Though among the aldermen who finally acquiesced in the death of Brembre,[53] he may certainly be considered a member of Brembre's group throughout the decade.

Witnesses of Chaucer's release in the 1380 case of Cecily Champain included William Beauchamp, John Clanvowe, William Nevill, John Philipot, and London grocer Richard Morel.[54] Richard elevated both Clanvowe and Nevill to chamber knight the following year. Philipot was already Chaucer's superior in customs, and his affiliations with the court are well known. Morel was to be elected member of the Common Council during Brembre's 1383–1384 term as mayor and may be considered a member of his faction. He was, for example, one of the group of aldermen and other prominent citizens of London summoned to the king's council at Reading to hear the case against John Northampton—a council heavily stacked with stalwarts of the Brembre faction such as William Walworth, Hugh Fastolf, John Hende, and Nicholas Exton, as well as other members of the faction such as John Hadle, Adam St. Ives, William Venour, and recent recruit Adam Bamme.[55]

In 1378, on the brink of his journey to Lombardy, Chaucer granted power of attorney to John Gower and Richard Forester.[56] Chaucer's fellow poet, we may say in simple summary of a complex body of evidence, was effectively nonaligned. A landed esquire of independent means who addressed admonitions and encouragement both to Richard and to Henry of Derby, Gower depended for his livelihood on neither.[57] Our sense of Gower's independence may be sharpened in contrast with the partisanship of his fellow dedicatee of *Troilus*,

Ralph Strode. An instance of Strode's involvement with Brembre's group is contained in *Letter-Book H*. There we learn that in December 1382, during the term of John Northampton, Ralph Strode has "of his own accord relinquished" his office as Common Pleader and hence entitlement to his mansion over Aldrichesgate. Yet we find in 1384, after the return of Brembre, that Strode is to receive four marks in annual compensation for the loss of the mansion, "which had been granted to him for life during a former Mayoralty of Nicholas Brembre . . . and from which he had been speciously ousted during the mayoralty of John Norhamptone."[58] Richard Forster, named with Gower as Chaucer's attorney, is a harder person to identify. He may be the Richard le Forester of Beckele, *valettus* and retainer of Edward III, mentioned in the Patent Rolls and named with Chaucer as an esquire of lesser degree.[59] Alternatively, he may be the professional lawyer mentioned in the calendars of rolls and assizes.[60] Either way, we know him as a factionalist: for a Richard Forster succeeded Chaucer in his mansion over Aldgate, by grant of Nicholas Brembre, mayor in 1386.[61] Whether civil servant or lawyer, this Richard Forester was a person acceptable to the king.[62]

Against this evidence of involvement with the royal faction and its London allies, the "aristocratic" group is very sparsely represented in Chaucer's circle of acquaintance. Though suggesting that Chaucer's associations were divided between the court party and the aristocrats, Hulbert offers only two examples from the latter group: Oton de Graunson and Henry of Derby.[63] Even these must be qualified severely. The Savoyard knight Oton de Graunson was indeed retained for life by John of Gaunt in 1374, and he joined Henry of Derby in his 1393 expedition.[64] But these Lancastrian contacts did not prevent Richard from granting him a handsome annuity of 100 marks a year in 1392.[65] The fact is that he seems to have gotten along well with both Richard and the Lancastrians—a plausible accommodation of which Chaucer also showed himself capable. In the list of members of Philippe de Mézières' Order of the Passion, he was inscribed as "monseigneur Othe de Granson, de la terre Savoye, chevalier d'onneur du roy d'Engleterre et du duc de Lencastre."[66]

Chaucer had no documented contact with any of the other major Appellants: Thomas of Woodstock, Duke of Gloucester; Thomas Beauchamp, Earl of Warwick; Richard, Earl of Arundel; or Thomas Mowbray, Earl of Nottingham. Gloucester was a person of considerable literary cultivation, and the account of goods forfeit at his death in 1397 includes a vast personal library consisting mainly of works written in French, including "Rimance de la Rose," "Tresor," prophecies of Merlin, "Beux de Hampton," "Launcelot," "Tretiz de Roy Arthur," and many more.[67] Beauchamp, less clearly literary, was nevertheless a patron of architecture and possessed tapestries at his death.[68] Still no records suggest that either knew or cared about Chaucer. Nor did Arundel or Nottingham, excepting only the evidence of some routine items of business involving Arundel during Chaucer's clerkship of works.[69]

Indeed, Chaucer appears to have had close and frequent contact with only one person who was close to Gloucester and the aristocrats, and that case turns out to be somewhat clouded. William Beauchamp—for whom Chaucer stood surety in 1378 and who witnessed Chaucer's release in the 1380 Champain incident—was chamberlain in 1378–1380 and might be considered a member of the young king's party at that time. He was subsequently appointed captain of Calais and served in that post in the troubled year of 1387. He was visited by Chaucer in the service of the king in July of that year,[70] and he was soon drawn into the conflict of the Appellants with the king. That his loyalties might have been mixed is no surprise; he was a younger brother of Thomas Beauchamp, one of the three principal Appellants. He seems nevertheless to have walked a careful line, at least in the accounts of the Westminster chronicler and of Walsingham. According to the former, in November 1387 William de la Pole fled to Calais to avoid the coming appeal of treason, when he was turned over to William Beauchamp, who returned him to England, although he escaped once again soon after his return.[71] Walsingham essentially agrees but adds that he was returned to the king and that the king granted him liberty.[72] Knighton, on the other hand, portrays Beauchamp as much more a partisan of the aristocrats, seizing letters of the king and forwarding them to Gloucester, refusing to relinquish custody of the city to Richard, being placed briefly in custody by the enraged king, and actively "capturing" the fleeing de la Pole.[73] The Knighton account may be somewhat exaggerated. Beauchamp assumed the title Baron Bergavenny without interruption in 1393 and, though not in apparent favor during Richard's remaining years of rule, escaped Richard's reprisals against the principal Appellants. In fact, Dugdale includes the curious detail that during his lifetime William Beauchamp offered a donation to the collegiate church at Warwick "for the good estate of King Richard the second and of Queen Anne his consort."[74] The extent of Beauchamp's anti-Ricardian involvement is, in short, anything but clear, and Chaucer's relationship with

Beauchamp need not have compromised his own commitment to the Ricardian faction.

Chaucer's Lancastrian Ties

Chaucer's contacts with Henry of Derby have been offered as evidence of his ties to the other "side,"[75] and we know that he and Philippa received annuities from John of Gaunt. Would not such involvements seem to contradict the notion that Chaucer was a king's man? The response to this question depends on two others: Was Chaucer, literally, a Lancastrian retainer? (I would reply, yes and no.) And did such a tie contradict his loyalty to Richard? (I would reply, not at all.)

Chaucer's wife Philippa was connected to John of Gaunt through her sister Katherine Swynford—damoiselle of the household, mistress, and eventual third duchess of John of Gaunt.[76] She is cited in the grant of a 1372 annuity from the duke for her services to Duchess Constance. Then, in 1374, Chaucer and Philippa received a further annuity as part of the arrangements facilitating his move from the king's household to the controllership in London.[77] In distinction from Richard's confirmation of Chaucer's annuity, which clearly specifies that Chaucer has been retained ("retinuimus"), the Lancastrian grant makes no reference to retention and refers only to service already done (rather than the alternative and common "fait et ferra en temps avenir"). Still, though he was not formally retained and no future services were evidently expected, Chaucer would no doubt seem by acceptance of his annuity to have accepted the protection of a second lord. So too in his relations with Henry of Derby in 1395–1396 he accepted a partially formalized tie somewhere short of actual retention. Evidences of these relations are the flamboyant detail of Henry's provision of fur for a scarlet robe in February 1395 and the delivery from the earl's wardrobe of £10, either (depending on the ambiguous wording) paid to Chaucer for the purpose of delivery to the earl's hands or paid to Chaucer directly.[78] Just as Chaucer's receipt of the 1374 annuity from the duke led to the erroneous conclusion that he was living at Savoy palace,[79] so have these details encouraged some to place Chaucer in the earl's retinue[80]—a conclusion that overstates what we know. Further evidence of a tie just short of formal retention is offered by Henry's prompt confirmation and supplementation of Chaucer's royal annuity upon accession to the throne. Even though it was one among many such confirmations, and even though Chaucer had some difficulty collecting the sums in question, some evidence of Lancastrian—now become royal—favor must be supposed. For by this action Chaucer continued as a king's esquire—though as esquire of a new king.

Let us say, then, that Chaucer did enjoy some kind of Lancastrian tie just short of formal retention in the years 1372 or 1374 until 1400. We must first realize that this additional affiliation would not have seemed nearly so strange to his contemporaries as to modern scholars—because of the frequency of divided allegiances within the period and also because Chaucer's contemporaries would have viewed his Lancastrian association from a different perspective. Our view of the Lancastrians is inevitably conditioned by our awareness of the usurpation of 1399. Despite this turn of events, however, John of Gaunt must be generally reckoned a supporter of the royal prerogative and the throne. Certainly the Commons were suspicious of Gaunt's designs upon the throne in the late 1370s, and Richard entertained his own definite suspicions in 1384–1385.[81] But, as Armitage-Smith points out, Gaunt's support of the royal prerogative underlay his conflict with the Good Parliament of 1376, and—despite rumors to the contrary reported by the St. Albans chronicler and others—he used the Parliament of 1377 and the coronation itself to affirm his loyalty to the young king.[82] Once rebuked in 1384–1385, he decisively shifted his ambitions away from England and toward the throne of Castile, embracing a military strategy against Castile in 1385 and absenting himself from England altogether in 1386–1389. Back to England as a close ally of Richard's fully restored monarchy in 1389, he became, and would remain, in McKisack's words, "the strongest pillar of the monarchy."[83]

A similar pattern may be traced for Henry of Derby, who briefly joined the Appellants against Richard and his courtiers in 1386–1388, but soon returned to a posture of loyalty that prevailed until (and even in the early stages of) his banishment. Actually, as Tuck has shown, he was always in the moderate faction of Appellants, joining Nottingham and the queen to plead for the life of Simon Burley and in other ways showing himself cool to Gloucester's more ambitious designs.[84] He fell away early from the conspiracy and in 1397 joined his father in assisting Richard's reprisals against Gloucester and the senior Appellants, becoming Duke of Hereford as a reward.[85] In short, the actual pattern of relations between the Lancastrians and the crown would have given contemporaries little cause to see a contradiction in Chaucer's divided loyalty. His dual service would probably have been viewed rather matter-of-factly, as when Philippe de Mézières styled Oton de Graunson "chevalier d'onneur de roy . . . et du duc."

Even recognizing that multiple affiliations would not have appeared strange to Chaucer's contemporaries and that ties to John of Gaunt would not necessarily have contradicted ties to the king, the fact remains that Chaucer did acknowledge a second and alternative lordship throughout most of his career. This alternative loyalty did not, I firmly believe, compromise his identity as a king's man. Still, the Lancastrian tie probably did contribute an additional measure of independence to Chaucer's already independent cast of mind, by providing him with another footing in the rough terrain of factional politics in the last quarter of the fourteenth century. For Chaucer did limit his commitment to the king in ways that others like Brembre and Usk did not. Chaucer's restraint in factional intrigue was probably a result of his own calculation rather than any outward encouragement—but his Lancastrian connection must have provided both material and emotional support to his own tendency to limit his involvement in factional affairs.

The Limits of Faction

Chaucer's relation to the king was, as we have seen, neither bound by oath nor secured by land tenure; it was a relation based on mutual interest and thus open to constant reevaluation on both sides. Chaucer's management of his career suggests that he exercised this prerogative and that he adjusted the extent of his own factional involvement according to circumstance. A number of episodes in Chaucer's career support an estimate of his good judgment in precarious circumstances. One such episode is his shift from the court to London in 1374, during Edward III's senility and in the midst of the uncertainties about succession that accompanied the illness of the Black Prince. Another is his increased involvement with Henry of Derby in the mid-1390s, during the development of Richard's absolutist strategy. My particular interest here, however, is in Chaucer's modification of his relations with the court during that charged period of the mid-1380s, when the Appellants were challenging Richard's sole rule and seeking the death of so many of Richard's (and Chaucer's) closest associates.[86]

Chaucer might have observed evidence of mounting dissatisfaction with Richard's rule as early as the parliamentary session of November-December 1385, which adopted a series of measures opposing royal patronage and household extravagance, and suggesting ways of increasing revenue. One proposal he might have taken to heart requested the appointment of customs officials only upon the advice of the king's council (rather than "par . . . desir singuler"), their remuneration according to merit, and their service without deputies.[87] Implementation of this bill was apparently neglected.[88] Nevertheless, a reading of the possible impact of this and other measures would have lain well within Chaucer's often-demonstrated powers of political analysis.

Chaucer appears to have responded to these stirrings by strengthening his Kentish connections. This strategy is by no means unambiguous, since his first involvements in Kent are very much as a king's man—first through appointment with Tresilian and other royalists as justice of the peace and then by acceptance of election as shire-knight to what became the "Wonderful Parliament" of 1386.[89] In this very parliament, however, additional steps toward limitation of the royal prerogative were taken—steps that probably encouraged Chaucer further to limit his royal ties. Among other moves against Richard, he would have witnessed the appointment of Gloucester and others as a "graunt & continuel Counseil" charged "de corriger & amender totes les defautes, de ce que vre Corone est tant emblemy,"[90] the impeachment of de la Pole, and the presentation of a petition of Commons deeply embarrassing to his own situation. This petition asks that all controllers appointed by the king for life be removed because of their "grauntz oppressions & extorcions."[91]

Chaucer appears not to have been directly affected by the 1386 petition. His was not a life appointment in the first place, and he might have been shielded in any event by Richard's temporizing reply that the controllers would be examined before his council, with the good kept and the bad removed. Yet the chronology of events suggests that the petition did precipitate a precautionary action on Chaucer's part. On November 19, letters patent gave effective control of the kingdom to the antiroyal Continual Council.[92] On November 28, Parliament itself ended. On December 4 and 14, successors were appointed to Chaucer's controllerships of the wool and petty customs.[93] No particular pressure seems to have been brought against him to resign his posts.[94] Brembre, a more ardent factionalist than Chaucer ever was, continued beyond 1386 in his collectorship, and Chaucer's ultimate successor in the post was very much a king's man.[95] Chaucer's action, in other words, seems to have been voluntary, resulting not from a purge of Richard's adherents but from his private decision to scale down his visibility as a member of the royal faction.

A similar effort to lessen his royal commitment is suggested by an apparently voluntary step taken in response to an action of the Merciless Parliament of 1388. That Parliament is remembered mainly for condemning a number of the king's intimates for treason. It also sought, however, by a series of petitions to circumscribe Richard's authority, including a purge of the royal household and a wholesale voiding of royal annuities. The petition calling for a purge of the household evidently never came to much.[96] A good deal closer to Chaucer was a petition calling for nullification of all those annuities of Richard, his grandfather, or his father that included the phrase "Quousque pro Statu suo aliter duxerimus ordinand' " in all cases where the recipients had accepted subsequent grants from the king.[97] Chaucer's annuity might have fallen into this category. Crow points out that it contains the indicated wording and that conversion of his wine grant into an exchequer annuity might have applied the enactment to his case.[98] In any event, he granted his exchequer annuities to John Scalby on May 1, 1388—a date that probably fell between the first promulgation of the petition and the adjournment of Parliament on June 4.

As an old court hand, Chaucer probably knew that he stood a good chance of weathering the petition with his annuity intact. Despite Richard's agreement to the petition, no general nullification of annuities or large-scale transfer of annuities seems to have occurred.[99] But the resignation of his annuity may be seen as a step consistent with a long-term policy of moderating his royal ties during the period between November-December 1385 and May 1389.

That this policy was justified seems amply demonstrated by the condemnations of spring 1388. When we compare the behavior with respect to preferment of those chamber knights who perished in 1388 and those who survived, a persuasive pattern emerges. Those who died—Burley, Beauchamp, Berners, and Salisbury—harvested patronage throughout the decade and with accelerating intensity in those critical years when Richard sought to confirm old supporters and reward new ones. Burley, already ensconced in the highly lucrative position of constable of Dover Castle and warden of the Cinque Ports, engaged throughout 1385–1387 in a long series of real-estate deals.[100] John Beauchamp became stewart of the household on June 8, 1387, and Baron of Kidderminster—the first baron created by royal patent—on October 10, 1387. James Berners received a substantial grant on November 6, 1387, even as the Appellants were gathering in arms. John Salisbury received nothing in 1386–1387 but had been given two major preferments in 1385.

In contrast, the active chamber knights who survived—Clanvowe, Nevill, Stury, and Vache, together with household knight Clifford—appear to have distanced themselves from Richard by strategies very similar to Chaucer's. They kept a low profile in terms of patronage. Lewis Clifford received no significant grants after 1384. A grant enrolled on September 28, 1385, carries a notation that it was vacated by surrender; an action of June 18, 1387, merely involves details of an earlier grant. Philip la Vache, Clifford's son-in-law, is cited in the rolls only for his withdrawal from affairs; on August 28, 1386, a grant from Edward III was revised and subsequently surrendered; on October 20, 1386, he surrendered his custody of the king's park at Langley. William Nevill received a grant on January 9, 1386, but only in place of an earlier arrangement. John Clanvowe received a grant on March 7, 1386, but none in succeeding years. The only exception to this general pattern is Richard Stury, who did receive a grant in the course of the dangerous summer prior to the Merciless Parliament, enrolled on May 24, 1387. Taken together, though, these rewards are routine, and truly modest compared with the staggering self-aggrandizements of Burley and Beauchamp during the same period.

Just as these knights close to Chaucer showed restraint in regard to rewards, so did they reduce their activities on behalf of the crown in the crucial period between the impeachment of de la Pole in 1386 and the Merciless Parliament of 1388. Lewis Clifford, who had served the Black Prince and then Edward's widow Joan, became active in Richard's service only in 1391, when he appears among several "viri valentes et famosi" chosen to treat with the French.[101] Clanvowe treated with the French in February 1386[102] and went with Nevill to survey the endangered port of Orwell in September 1386,[103] just prior to the opening of the Wonderful Parliament on October 1. He then disappears from the rolls and chronicles until November 1388, five months after the end of the Merciless Parliament, when he was named with a politically varied group of distinguished knights to talk to the French. Nevill manifests himself in a curious and oddly timed way: in April 1388, with Burley and the other chamber knights on the brink of condemnation and with others (Elmham, Trivet, Dagworth) in peril, he obtained the king's pardon for the thief of a silver bowl in the verge of Westminster.[104] Otherwise Nevill was inactive before his departure with his friend Clanvowe on their journey abroad in 1391. Vache kept the lowest profile of all; his resignation as keeper of the king's park in October 1386 occurs in the first month of

Gloucester's period of control, and he is not to be found again until April 2, 1390, when he is mentioned as captain of one of the king's forts in Picardy.[105] Only Stury is, again, an exception. Walsingham mentions him in the critical summer of 1387, as one of the favorites of the king (along with Vere, de la Pole, and Burley) who envied the military successes of Richard, Earl of Arundel.[106] Nevertheless, he seems not to have been very active in 1387, and his gift for survival is pronounced; by action of June 8, several days after the end of the Merciless Parliament, he was included in a commission for defense of the Marches of Scotland.[107]

The wisdom of these associates, as well as Chaucer himself, in withdrawing from the affairs of court during a period of trouble is confirmed not only by their survival but by positive developments in their careers after 1389.[108] Stury had an active old age, treating for peace in France in 1394 and welcoming his old friend Froissart to the court in 1395.[109] Clanvowe and Nevill would undoubtedly have continued to flourish, if not for their untimely deaths in Constantinople in 1391.[110] Vache, in the words of Edith Rickert, "grew steadily in honor and in wealth" between 1390 and the end of Richard's kingship, and he had the satisfaction of joining with three other knights as "plegges de pursuer" in the bill of appeal against Gloucester in 1397.[111] His father-in-law Clifford became a Knight of the Garter in 1398, and he joined the order in 1399. Chaucer was one of the very first of the "old courtiers" to be given preferment after Richard's reassertion of control in May 1389;[112] he was appointed Clerk of Works in July 1389, with other appointments to follow.

Most of those chamber knights and others in comparable service who perished (Burley, John Beauchamp, Salisbury, Berners) as well as Chaucer and those close to him who survived (Clanvowe, Nevill, Stury, Vache, Clifford) were of the middle strata, and that particularly volatile segment of nonaristocratic gentlepersons "en service." All may be seen as subject to both the temptations and the dangers of careerism, and all were careerists to one degree or another. Yet the former group (along with merchants like Brembre and urban intellectuals like Usk) seems to have lost a sense of proportion along the way, while the others retained some equilibrium. To put it differently: all were king's men, but Chaucer and his associates managed to be king's men in a less rushed, less greedy, more circumspect, and more thoughtful way.

Part of Chaucer's success may have been based on an ability to mobilize in his political choices those qualities that readers have found in his literary choices, including even-handedness and receptivity to opposed points of view. Analogies between Chaucer's social perspective and the way he views the content of his poetry seem to me both reasonable and valid. Confining ourselves here to his political choices alone, we can associate his success with his receptivity to distinctive possibilities inherent in the new forms of social relations current in his day. Chaucer was true not only to his own characteristic moderation but to the presuppositions of bastard feudalism when he tempered his loyalty to the king with a second, Lancastrian tie; so too when he remained a member of the king's party but calibrated the intensity of his activity according to the shifting fortunes of the king; so too when he sought and accepted the benefits of Richard's lordship, even while his closest bonds appear to have been less to his lord than to associates and friends in situations close to his own on the social scale.

Chaucer's Circle

Donald Howard once observed to me that, considering the varied worlds in which Chaucer moved, we should speak of his "circles" rather than his "circle." He was of course quite right, and a number of such circles can be described according to geography (Westminster, London, Kent), vocation (courtiers, merchants, bureaucrats), or social rank (the aristocrats with whom he was connected through marriage, the gentry with whom he served the king, the citizens, burgesses, and artisans he met as controller of customs and clerk of works). This being said, the recurrence of certain names in the *Life-Records* would seem to argue for a loosely defined group of people, situated mainly though not exclusively within the king's affinity, known to Chaucer and to each other in ways that would justify their designation as his particular "circle." In drawing the boundaries of this circle, however, we must take care not to abuse the resource afforded by the *Life-Records* by claiming that each person with whom Chaucer had dealings was a close friend. We must consider those people mentioned often, or consequentially, as a pool within which friendships were formed, and seek further the criteria by which such relations might be recognized.

Several overlapping but distinct categories have already been noticed within the life-records: people who shared Chaucer's political affiliation, those who enjoyed similar social standing, and those who displayed an enthusiasm for literary works. But not all can be called friends. Chaucer had extensive professional and factional dealings with Nicholas Brembre, for example, but I would hesitate to suggest that the two were close; Chaucer's social experiences were undoubtedly quite remote from those of the merchant-oligarch, and nothing disposes us to think Brembre literary. The aristocratic chamber knight Montagu was praised by Christine de Pisan as a lover of poetry and a "gracieux ditteur,"[113] but his poetry was probably written in French for a circle more socially elevated and more focused on the Continent than Chaucer's own,[114] and no specific evidence links him with Chaucer. Thomas Usk managed to crash the Brembre faction and to become a sergeant-at-arms of the king just before his condemnation in 1388, and the praise of Chaucer in his *Testament of Love* and his apparent access to a manuscript of the *House of Fame*[115] may suggest special contact; yet Chaucer more likely regarded him as an unsavory opportunist than as a friend. Since Usk's prevailing mode was one of self-nomination, he might be seen as a self-nominated associate of Chaucer, but we need hardly think of him as a trusted companion. Chaucer's verse compliment to the French poet Graunson ("Complaint of Venus," line 82) goes well beyond the perfunctory and may indicate a friendship dating from the mid-1380s or 1390s, but its context remains unclear. Civil servant Thomas Hoccleve claims to have known Chaucer personally (*Regement of Princes,* lines 2077–2107), but he was a much younger man and the claim cannot be verified.[116] Even after such exclusions are made, however, the contours of an amicable circle may still be traced in the cases of several people whose lives touched Chaucer's at more than one critical point. Such a "core" might consist of several knights in royal and civil service whom Chaucer knew in the 1370s and 1380s, including William Beauchamp, Lewis Clifford, Philip la Vache, John Clanvowe, William Nevill, and Richard Stury; London acquaintances of the 1380s, including Ralph Strode and (with certain qualifications) John Gower; and newcomers of the 1390s, including Henry Scogan and Peter Bukton.

The most obvious link between these people is their involvement with the affairs of Richard II. Most belonged to Richard's affinity, not just as an expression of political sympathy but as a source of livelihood and a way of life. Gower must be excepted from this generalization in several respects, including his independent livelihood and his shift to the Lancastrians in the 1390s; yet he appears to have found some merit in Richard through at least 1390–1391, the date of the initial dedication of his *Confessio*.[117] William Beauchamp must also be excepted, since he began his career as a Lancastrian retainer and leaned toward the Appellants after 1386; yet he was a perfectly good Ricardian between 1378 and 1386, the years of his apparent friendship with Chaucer.[118] Scogan would later become tutor to the sons of Henry IV, but—like Chaucer—he seems to have maintained an essential loyalty to Richard until his actual deposition.[119]

The members of this group occupied social positions like Chaucer's own. All are from one echelon or another of the middle strata. All—excepting only Ralph Strode who, as a prominent lawyer and possibly as a former academician, had his own basis for prestige—may be considered gentle. None—excepting only William Beauchamp in the last decade of his life—was aristocratic or baronial. In a society of hereditary position, each seems to have prospered mainly as a result of his own exertions, and all—excepting only John Gower—were in the service of lords or parties greater than themselves.

Even the socially prominent William Beauchamp spent most of his years in royal service, before his accession to the estates of the Earl of Pembroke in 1392.[120] Among the chamber knights, Nevill was a younger brother in a baronial family including Alexander, Archbishop of York (one of Richard's principal supporters, appealed for treason in 1388), and his career was undoubtedly advanced by his connections.[121] But he remained of knightly rather than baronial rank, and his own career and associations were in the household. Clanvowe, Clifford, and Stury all enjoyed career patterns similar to Chaucer's, though at a more prominent and lucrative level. According to McFarlane, they "sprang from the lesser gentry and made their way more slowly by their wits . . . with some help from connection and some from marriage."[122] Vache can hardly be said to have moved from rags to riches; he inherited land from his father, a garter-knight prominent in the service of Edward III.[123] But even Vache's successes of the 1390s were built on a typical foundation of long service (he was in the chamber by 1378) and a good marriage (to Elizabeth Clifford, herself a landowner of some substance). Scogan's career was much like Chaucer's. Though he inherited manors in 1393, he was also in military and other service as an esquire of the king from 1394 on.[124] The debate as to whether Chaucer's Bukton was Sir Robert or Sir Peter need not be continued here, except perhaps as a cautionary reminder of the frail evidence upon which any analysis of Chaucer's social position must depend. We would obviously like to know more, but Pace and David make the crucial point: "It does not matter which Bukton was the recipient of the poem. What *is* significant is that Bukton belonged to the same class as Chaucer himself, a class that found rapid advancement in the service of the high nobility."[125]

As a London lawyer and possible fellow of Merton College before 1360, Strode might be thought to have followed a different track. But evidence suggests that Strode's position as Common Pleader was a patronage position, related to his involvement with the Brembre faction, and that he was himself involved in providing service to the king or supporters of the king. Only Gower stands outside this prevailing pattern of service-related careers. Although Gower's rank of esquire was nominally the same as Chaucer's, the two titles actually mask a distinction explored in the previous chapter: the manors and the £100 this "esquire of Kent" bequeathed to his wife suggest that he was one of the propertied esquires (and perhaps even among the upper tier of esquires) mentioned in the 1379 poll tax, while Chaucer at his most affluent would certainly have been included among the esquires "en service."[126]

Finally—to draw together some observations made piecemeal in this chapter—most members of this group show some degree of literary predisposition, either as owners of books, as addressees in contexts that suggest their capacity for appreciation, or as writers in their own right. Clifford was Chaucer's intermediary with the poet Deschamps. Clifford's son-in-law Vache is addressed in a play on his name in "Truth." Similarly, but more extensively, implicated in Chaucer's verse are Scogan and Bukton, addressed by Chaucer in friendly epistles.[127] John Clanvowe wrote a secular poem (*The Boke of Cupide*) much in Chaucer's debt, and a devotional treatise ("The Two Ways") that stands as far from that work in form and voice as does the *Parson's Tale* from the secular tales of Canterbury.[128] William Beauchamp may have been interested in "The Two Ways" more for religious than literary reasons, but he still took pains to have the work copied as part of a devotional and mystical compilation.[129] "Moral Gower" and "philosophical Strode" are linked as dedicatees of Chaucer's *Troilus,* in a context suggesting that each will bring to the poem certain qualities of grave insight. For all the difference between the two poets' sensibilities, Gower shared with Chaucer certain broad points of literary agreement, including his decision in favor of the English vernacular over earlier choices, his experiments with framed narration, his secular use of religious forms, his choice of a middle way between earnest and game, and his occasional (though far from exclusive) addresses to the great. Ralph Strode of London was probably no poet, but (assuming him to be the Oxford philosopher of the same name) we might note that the fifteenth-century "Vetus Catalogus" of the fellows of Merton College glosses his name with the surprising suggestion that he was a poet and author of a work entitled

"Phastasma Radulphi."[130] Even the courtier Stury turns out to have been a person of some literary aptitude, not only assisting Froissart in presenting Richard with a volume of his amorous poems but also possessing his own copy of the *Roman de la Rose.*[131]

If this process of "triangulation" involving class perspectives, factional loyalties, and literary sympathies has yielded some probable friends of Chaucer, other conceptual difficulties must cause one to hesitate before styling them a "circle." Most obviously, they could never have been assembled together in one place, since they (or, at any rate, their friendships with Chaucer) belong to different decades. Chaucer seems to have made the acquaintance of several of the Lollard Knights—Clifford, Vache, Stury, Clanvowe, Nevill—in the 1370s and early 1380s; although his conduct in the trying period 1386–1389 reflects the same discretion as theirs, he seems not to have seen much of them during his time in Kent. The dislocations of these years were consequential in other ways as well. Chaucer and William Beauchamp, finding themselves on different sides of the Ricardian divide in those years, seem not to have resumed their friendship, and Beauchamp's lordship in 1392 would have accentuated the social gulf between them. I have not treated Usk as a full-fledged member of Chaucer's circle, but his execution in 1388 did have the effect of removing from the London scene a probable aspirant to such membership. Other London-related friendships seem not to have survived this period: Strode died in 1387, and—whether for political reasons or simply through lack of personal contact—Chaucer's friendship with Gower appears to have declined after 1385–1386.[132] Others mentioned as members of Chaucer's circle must be considered late "recruits." Chaucer certainly could not have known Scogan before the mid-1380s and probably did not know him much before his appointment as esquire to Richard in 1394.[133] Chaucer's jesting references to himself as a formerly married man in his epistle to Bukton must certainly stand some years subsequent to Philippa's death in 1387, and most commentators would date that poem (the sole evidence of Chaucer's friendship with Bukton) to the mid-1390s.

Chaucer's most intimate circle must therefore be imagined as a constantly shifting group. But a continuing process of separation and alienation, on the one hand, and recruitment and renewal, on the other, may in fact argue for rather than against the existence of a supportive circle. Seen in this light, the addition of new members like Scogan and Bukton argues for Chaucer's continuing power to define new and appreciative addressees, even in unpropitious circumstances formed by his removal from city and court, his continuing economic duress, and his advancing age. The apparent continuation of a circle of gentle civil servants and littérateurs contrasts strongly with the decade after Chaucer's death, when his own absence from the scene and the Lancastrian redefinition of the household seem to have resulted in the disappearance not only of Chaucer's circle but of *any* such circle.[134] One is struck, for example, by the apparent artistic isolation within which Hoccleve, Chaucer's closest fifteenth-century follower, pursued his erratic writing career. If Chaucer dealt, as we all deal, with estrangement and loss, his own resources and his milieu afforded him the possibility of seeing such losses at least partially repaired.

Chaucer's realization of himself as a social being occurred primarily within the supple bounds of the king's affinity. Furthermore, the relatively free-wheeling social circumstances of the affinity appear to have encouraged horizontal ties based upon common interest, even at some expense to the vertical ties associated with more hierarchical formations. Chaucer availed himself of the opportunity to form continuing associations with a circle or group-inside-a-group, consisting mainly of fellow gentlepersons in the king's service. One of the defining characteristics of this circle is literary proclivity, and we would not go far wrong in treating it as coextensive with his principal literary audience. The situation of address in Chaucer's poetry is, however, complex and constantly shifting, and will require separate consideration before a firm connection between his circle and his audience can be drawn.

3 ⊠ Audience

THE IDEA of art without audience would probably have seemed either contradictory or absurd to Chaucer, if in fact he could have entertained it at all. The word "audience," as he uses it, remains close to its etymological sense of "those within hearing," and his own poems almost always contain references to those who "hear" or "harken" or to whom he is "telling" his "tale." [1] Even in his later works, when listeners begin to yield to page turners who "see" his meaning written out rather than hear it read, these absent readers are as much the objects of admonition and address as if they were literally present. For, whether Chaucer seeks literal audience from listeners or figurative audience from an emerging reading public, the consequences of losing audience would be devastating; in a view that he repeats several times, the narrator who fails to hold the attention of those he is addressing might as well not speak or write at all. In the *Tale of Melibee,* for example, one of the "olde wise" gains audience or hearing but then loses the attention of the group he wishes to sway: "alle atones bigonne they to rise for to breken his tale, and beden hym ful ofte his wordes for to abregge." Chaucer as pilgrim-narrator observes that, "whan this wise man saugh that hym wanted audience, al shamefast he sette hym doun agayn. / For Salomon seith: 'Ther as thou ne mayst have noon audience, enforce thee nat to speke'" (VII. 1037, 1042, 1045–46). A similar moment is about to occur on the pilgrimage itself. The Monk's "hevy" recital of tragedies is interrupted by the Knight, who is in turn seconded by Harry Bailly: "Whereas a man may have noon audience, / Noght helpeth it to tellen his sentence" (VII. 2801–2). The sentiment is of course a commonplace. The spurned counselor of *Melibee* and the narrator's accompanying observation are taken directly from the *Livre de Melibe* of Renaud de Louens,[2] and

Harry Bailly's remark has its source in Ecclesiasticus 32.6. Such insistence on the indispensability of attentive hearing to meaningful discourse is commonplace because it was one of the cornerstones of a rhetorical system, elaborated in various places including medieval treatises on preaching, in which Chaucer's work remains securely lodged.[3]

The notion that discourse assumes its full significance—perhaps its only significance—in interaction with an audience has certain corollaries, one of which is that artists should not simply hope for good audition but should shape their discourse with the needs and capacities of an intended audience in view. As Petrarch observes to Boccaccio, in a somewhat condescending explanation of his decision to countenance the free humor of the *Decameron,* the style and language of that work may well be suitable for those who are likely to read such tales. "It is important," he continues in a more general vein, "to know for whom we are writing, and a difference in the character of one's listeners justifies a difference in style."[4] Chaucer's own allegiance to this precept is not only suggested by his poetic practice but is embodied in words presumably close to his own voice when he states his tactical decision to avoid complex argumentation and to reiterate hard points in explaining the astrolabe to little Lewis: "curious endityng and hard sentence is ful hevy at onys for such a child to lerne . . . me semith better to writen unto a child twyes a god sentence, than he forgete it onys" (45–49). A similar tactical decision is made, but announced less discreetly, by the Eagle when he lectures Geffrey about the nature of sound: "so I can / Lewedly to a lewed man / Speke" (*HF,* 865–867). Such examples might be continued almost indefinitely. Their common denominator is simple: a successful artist adapts both content and style to the requirements and capacity of the intended audience.

Critics have not given much weight to the communicative dimension of Chaucer's work. The formalist or explicatory critics who have produced the largest volume of commentary on his work over the last three or four decades regard his oeuvre as autonomous, as a system of signs with no important referents outside itself. More recent criticism, written under the influence of Foucault and other French theorists, has been even more emphatically focused on the textual surface of the poetry and insistent on its status as discourse in a world of discourse, rather than as a form of utterance in a communicative situation.[5]

Other critics have followed the different lead of reception theory, abandoning the assumption that Chaucer's writing is self-contained and concerning themselves with its impact on auditors or readers, whether historical or current. Still, even while acknowledging a communicative dimension to Chaucer's work, these critics tend to view his communication with his audience as proceeding in one direction only: from author to audience. However active the audience's participation in the ultimate determination of meaning, it is presumed to be on the far side of a communicative divide that precludes its influence on the form of the work. Jauss' initial formulation of the matter seems to promise an expanded acknowledgment of the audience's impact at all stages of the creative process, as when he argues that "in the triangle of author, work, and public the last is no passive part, no chain of mere reactions, but rather an energy formative of history."[6] But he goes on to restrict the audience's influence to works yet to be created. In his scheme the work enters history only after its production, when the audience's experience of the work issues in new norms and new transgressions; underestimated is the contribution of the artist's understanding of an audience to the very form of the work.[7]

The medieval sense that the requirements of an audience might influence literary creation deserves consideration within the framework of a theory that grants its possible legitimacy. Such a theory would assign to the audience, and to the author's sense of audience, a role not simply founded on passive consumption but on active participation, in determining textual meaning and in influencing the form of texts. One such body of theory exists in the writings of Bakhtin and his collaborator/surrogates Voloshinov and Medvedev. The importance of Voloshinov's sociolinguistics and Medvedev's recasting of formalism in a social context is that these works give full weight to the importance of communicative context for the *formation* of utterances. The utterance, according to Voloshinov, is a "two-sided act . . . the product of a reciprocal relationship between speaker and listener, addresser and addressee."[8] As such, it is to be regarded as the sole property neither of the speaker who frames it nor of the listener who receives it, but as their common property. This is because the utterance is formed and received within the larger social milieu that embraces both speaker and listener and the more particular social relationship that exists between them; the organizing center of the utterance thus lies in the social circumstances and purposes of the discourse.

Literary works cannot, of course, be treated simply as utterances or speech acts.[9] Medvedev and others have long recognized that the literary text is hardly a fresh or pure creation of a speaker and an addressee, but that it represents an artist's selection of an appropriate genre from within a previously existing system of literary possibilities, a system through which any communicative intent is "refracted" in extremely subtle ways.[10] While the literary work remains a highly specialized form of communication, a communication mediated through the spectrum of existing generic possibilities (for the writer) and generic expectations (for the audience), it remains a form of communication nonetheless. Medvedev's contribution to Voloshinov's theory of the utterance is to argue that the artistic work, like every other form of utterance, "is a communication, a message, and is completely inseparable from intercourse."[11] The text is not transmitted from the author to the reader, but is constructed between them as a kind of ideological bridge.[12]

Persuasive as this formulation of the audience's contribution may be in theory, however, its implications for the understanding of particular works of literature are less easily explored—particularly in a case like Chaucer's, where the composition of his actual audience remains a matter of uncertainty. The most plausible supposition about Chaucer's audience is that it consisted mainly of those gentlepersons in service who, together with a few London intellectuals, I have identified as Chaucer's social and literary circle. Owing to the perplexing nature of the available evidence and the peculiarities of the circumstances, however, this conclusion cannot be reached in a straight argumentative line. We must pause at every point to evaluate the character of the evidence itself and its relation to Chaucer's own circumstances.

Starting with the assumption that Chaucer addressed much of his poetry to a circle of social equals and near-equals, I wish to give fair weight to a number of countervailing considerations. We have, for one thing, already seen that the membership of this group was in constant flux and that it played a variable role in his life. To address such a group would have meant one thing in the 1360s and early 1370s, when he was very much a member of a court circle; a somewhat different thing in the period 1374–1385/86, when associations with members of the royal household were supplemented by involvements with London intellectuals; quite another thing after 1386, when political friction and Chaucer's removal from Westminster-London would have complicated communications among such a circle; and yet another thing after his return to a reconstituted circle in the fall of 1389.

Not only did this group shift in composition throughout Chaucer's career, but it vied with other groups for his attention. At times he addresses other groups altogether; a poem of clear-cut advice to princes, "Lack of Steadfastness," is a case in point. This poem, together with works like *Boece* and *Melibee,* stands as an apt reminder that, although he rarely if ever wrote for patronage, Chaucer conformed in some ways to the career of "court poet." Although current consensus regards Chaucer as writing mainly for social equals,[13] we would, as Elizabeth Salter reminds us, be wrong to deny him any audience in the inner circles of the court.[14] At times, too, Chaucer undoubtedly worked concurrently on poems for more than one kind of audience within a single period of his career. The years after 1387, for example, probably involved some simultaneous work on a poem for the most broadly conceived of his audiences (the *Canterbury Tales*) and for one of his least socially diverse (the *Legend of Good Women*). Another competing audience, increasing in importance throughout Chaucer's career, is his audience in posterity. The *Canterbury Tales* numbers people like Bukton and Scogan among its hearers or readers, but they must share his attention along with a larger audience of imagined page turners, encountering Chaucer's work beyond his control.

I do not, in other words, mean to argue that Chaucer addressed one audience alone. In a sense, the thesis of this chapter might be served simply by attributing a communicative aspect to his poetry and tracing it through varied situations of address and varied groups of addressees. But the shifting body of social equals and near-equals I have identified as his core audience continues to stand in *some* relation—however tacit or indirect—to most of his major work. Without exaggerating this audience's role, I will nevertheless trace its continuing importance throughout Chaucer's career by concentrating on several instances from different stages of his career: the *Book of the Duchess,* a poem addressed to a social superior in which this core audience is evoked as a kind of "secondary" addressee; *Troilus and Criseyde,* in which this audience vies for narrative attention with a host of other implied and intended auditors; the *Canterbury Tales,* in which traces of this audience are practically lost between the vividly inscribed pilgrim audience on the one hand and an imagined future audience on the other; and a cluster of short poems (and works written under Chaucer's influence) in which the importance of an audience of friends and equals most vividly shows through.

The "Book of the Duchess" as Social Communication

The *Book of the Duchess* is securely grounded in communicative situations, both within the poem (as the grieving Knight in Black pours out his sorrows and recollections to a narrator marked either for his obtuseness or his extreme tactfulness) and beyond the poem as well (in the presumed connection of the Black Knight with John of Gaunt and that of the narrator/dreamer with Chaucer himself[15]). I do not say "presumed connection" because Chaucer's referential motives are in any serious doubt. Nothing could be more reasonable than the supposition that the young courtier Chaucer between 1368 (the death of Blanche) and 1371 (Gaunt's marriage to Constance of Castile and his assumption of the title "King of Castile")[16] should write a poem directed to a social superior who was in a position to do favors for him and his wife.[17] Still, certain considerations argue against an exact correspondence between the Black Knight and Gaunt, the dreamer and Chaucer. Commentators wishing to firm up the connection have been forced to some ingenuity by the fact that the Black Knight's age is not right,[18] and the dreamer seems less closely identified with Chaucer's own person than is a narrator such as Geffrey of the *House of Fame,* who makes "rekenynges" by day (653) and has a weight problem. The relation of the narrator and the Black Knight within this poem is, then, less a replication of that between Chaucer and his eventual patron than a restatement of it, a counterpart refracted through the available literary tradition of the Old French love vision. With this modest distinction, I would argue for a very broad application of the poem to Chaucer's relations with John of Gaunt: that the dream is not only a consolation to John of Gaunt for his loss of Duchess Blanche, but an exploration of Chaucer's own existing and potential relations with Gaunt, in a form at once tactful and quietly self-promotional.

The debates about the dreamer's therapeutic strategy—whether he is obtuse or is giving the Knight a chance to vent his sorrows and replace them with fond memories—are essentially beside the point. The dreamer tells the Knight outright that "to make yow hool, / I wol do al my power" (553–554), and whatever its motivation and source, his persistent interrogation of the Knight certainly promotes a series of healing recollections. More interesting here is Chaucer's subtle delineation of the Knight's and the dreamer's respective social positions. At every point in their interaction, we are reminded of a certain amicable equity, on the one hand, and of a considerable social gulf on the other; of a polite egalitarianism in that both are gentlepersons and a decided limitation of egalitarianism in that one is an aristocrat and the other is not.

The dreamer is the most gentle of any of Chaucer's narrators. He tells us that, unable to sleep, he "bad oon reche me a book" (47), a book not only bespoken from a servant in the voice of one accustomed to obedience, but also a book elected from among other gentle leisure-time activities such as "ches or tables" (51). Once within the dream, he conducts himself as one accustomed to participating in the hunt, addressing a huntsman with a confident, " 'Say, felowe, who shal hunte here?' " (366). The Black Knight recognizes his station, warmly addressing him as "goode frend" (560). But the social divide between them is acknowledged in a number of ways. Having first greeted the Black Knight as best he can, the narrator waits patiently before him, head uncovered, presumably out of respect not only for his grief but for his superior social station ("y stood / Before hym and did of myn hood"—515–516). As Alfred David points out, the Black Knight addresses the dreamer with the informal "thee," while the dreamer retains the more formal "ye" or "yow" appropriate for a social superior.[19] The Black Knight's civility is ultimately marked by social condescension; the dreamer's evident pleasure in the fact that the Black Knight addresses him without difficult verbal formulas or verbal artifice ("He made hyt nouther towgh ne queynte," he gushes—531) measures both their proximity and their considerable social distance.

The actual relations of Chaucer and John of Gaunt would presumably have been marked by a similar mixture of equity and inequality. On the side of equity, we may note that Chaucer, as a newly appointed esquire of the king, was a gentleperson and hence a member along with Gaunt of the broadly conceived fellowship of gentlepersons and clerks that R. T. Lenaghan has described as embracing all the members of the household and court, from the civil servant most recently elevated to gentle status to the king himself.[20] Moreover, Chaucer was recently married to Philippa, either newly appointed or soon to be appointed as lady in the household of Gaunt's second wife Constance.[21] Eventually, by virtue of Gaunt's third marriage to Philippa's sister, Chaucer would even become a kind of brother-in-law to Gaunt. Yet, on the side of inequality, we must remember that, during the period in which Chaucer's poem was probably composed, John of Gaunt was arguably the most powerful man in England. With his marriage to Blanche in 1359 and her inheritance of 1362, he gained title to the most extensive duchy in the country. With his marriage to Constance in 1371, he gained additional claim to the throne of Castile. With the illness of the Black Prince after 1367, he became the most authoritative of young Richard's uncles and in some ways overshadowed the aged and infirm ruler. Lenaghan reminds us that relations within the court were not only lateral but decidedly hierarchical, and, within the society of gentlepersons constituting the court, Gaunt was situated near the very top and Chaucer near the very bottom.

We cannot know what Chaucer might or might not have felt himself able to say to John of Gaunt in real life, but the poem as a whole and particularly the dream provide a forum within which it can be shown that Chaucer is a fit interlocutor—at once a gentleperson worthy of intimacy and friendly exchange, and a person of discretion who can be trusted not to forget aspects of social difference (including the ultimate separation of the Knight and the dreamer into their respective worlds, as "this kyng" [1314] returns to his castle and the dreamer to his bed). Chaucer found his format in the love visions of Machaut and Froissart, and he learned much from them. To our relief, he also manages to avoid the pitfalls of bathetic excess, as in Machaut's "Dit de la Fonteinne Amoureuse," in which the patron falls asleep with his head in the narrator's lap and the two experience temporary obliteration of social difference by dreaming the same dream.[22] As in Machaut's *Dit,* however, the poem itself—and especially the dream within the poem—provide an imagined arena where some ordinary restraints on the interaction between socially unequal parties may be set aside.

While modeling Chaucer's relation with John of Gaunt in its dream, the *Book of the Duchess* is nevertheless simultaneously addressed to a larger group that the narrator describes collectively as "ye" or "yow." Not only are these people presumed to be auditors of an oral narration rather than readers of a text ("Ryght thus as I have told hyt yow"—271), but certain shared understandings are taken for granted ("And wel ye woot"—16) and certain allusions presuming special knowledge of Chaucer's personal state are addressed to them ("there is phisicien but oon / That may me hele"—39–40). Our sense of this enlarged but familiar audience is sharpest in the frame of the poem, as opposed to the dream with its focus on the narrowed situation of address, and this broadened situation of address permits poetry of correspondingly greater range and tonal variation. Present in the framing narrative of Seys and Alcyone, for example, are shifts in perspective and tone missing in the conscientious and respectful dialogue of the dream, including alternation between serious attention to Alcyone's loss and the buffoonery of the messenger's approach to Morpheus, between the implied consolation for those who know the ending of the Ovidian tale and the narrator's own sly refusal to tell it, between the narrator's presumed reason for choosing a tale of bereavement and his trumped-up suggestion that he has recounted Alcyone's plight because it gave him the idea of praying to Morpheus for sleep.

Chaucer's address to this larger audience also suggests that its membership is encouraging to a new dimensionality in subject matter and tone. Although the composition of this audience cannot securely be known, the confidence with which Chaucer approaches it would argue for relatively greater social equality than that existing between Chaucer and John of Gaunt. In the late 1360s and early 1370s, such an audience could most likely be found among fellow knights and esquires of the household and ladies of equivalent station—persons like Richard Stury, for example, listed with Chaucer in 1368 along with other members of the household of Edward III,[23] someone well situated to appreciate his transformations of poems by Machaut and Froissart.[24] Other evidence of the composition of this enlarged public, with its seemingly expanded capacity for tonal variation, will be pursued in the discussion of Chaucer's subsequent poems. We can certainly say for now that the increased expansiveness in content and tone that marks Chaucer's address to this larger audience suggests his early recognition that alternative situations of address can open alternative narrative and stylistic possibilities.

The Audience of "Troilus and Criseyde"

Troilus and Criseyde exemplifies a dazzling array of situations of address. Within this one poem we encounter a plethora of temporary (and presumably fictional) addressees, briefly evoked in order to provide an orientation for particular perspectives that Chaucer wishes to employ in the process of his narration; references to real listeners or readers who provide the ideal audience-within-an audience for particular aspects of the poem; and an implied audience of unusual acuity and sophistication.

Chaucer's use of fictional audiences within his poem may be seen as the complement of his flexible use of his own narrative position. We have all benefited from E. T. Donaldson's discussion of Chaucer's manipulation of the narrative voice within the poem,[25] and his formulation has been extended by Derek Brewer, who has argued for a multiplicity of vague narrators whose voices "surge up and fall away" within the boundaries of Chaucer's text.[26] These multiple narrators find their counterparts in Chaucer's tactical evocation of appropriate addressees to hear them out. These fictional addressees are not, by the way, simple extensions of the narrator's outlook; integral as they are to an utterance, they may fulfill their role by virtue of their very difference from the narrator's speaking voice. Dwelling on his own "unliklynesse" (I. 16) in the opening lines of the poem, the narrator imagines himself speaking to an audience composed of "loveres" (I. 22) who rarely fail and who are unacquainted with pain or woe. Several hundred lines later we hear a new narrative voice, as the speaker adopts tones of lofty disdain to comment on the deserved subjugation of those who scorn love. His imagined audience also shifts, to embrace a cohort of these proud and scornful persons:

> Forthy ensample taketh of this man,
> Ye wise, proude, and worthi folkes alle. (I. 232–233)

Another voice, issuing from a more inclusive view of human experience, belongs to the historically conscious narrator of book II, who understands that human behavior remains essentially the same, despite changes in customs and speech ("and yet thei . . . / spedde as wel in love as men now do"—II. 25–26). The imagined auditors of these remarks are thought essentially to agree with him, but possibly to include the odd skeptic, who "wondreth" at Troilus' customs (II. 34). The presence of at least a few people who nurse small reservations is suggested in the next book, where the narrator pauses to explain his omission of some details of Troilus' and Criseyde's looks, conversation, and voluminous correspondence; while assuming that most members of his audience understand his practice, he says that "som man" may expect a more detailed recounting (III. 491). Any suggestion that the audience might harbor skeptics is, however, abandoned as the time for consummation of Troilus' and Criseyde's love draws near. The narrator now associates himself and all of his audience with Pandarus' preparations: "Us lakketh nought but that we witen wolde / A certeyn houre, in which she comen sholde" (III. 531–532). For the remainder of the book, the zealous narrator and his audience are one.

Corresponding with the narrator's own uneven and uneasy disengagement from the substance of his narration in books IV and V are several kinds of estrangement of the presumed audience from the plight of the lovers. The immediate, aural audience presupposed in the opening books (as in I. 52, 154) is replaced by a more remote "redere" (V. 270), with the aural audience not to reappear until late in the poem (V. 629, 637). When this audience does reappear, it is—needless to say—no longer an audience of lovers, successful or otherwise. Instead we encounter different auditors chosen to complement the different kinds of agitation that have overcome the narrator of the poem. We encounter, for example, a group consisting of "every lady bright of hewe, / And every gentil womman" (v 1772–73) that the narrator nervously assumes to be inclined toward blame for his treatment of Criseyde. He gives these ladies no satisfactory answer—or rather too many answers, including an explanation that he was dealing with received subject matter, a promise to do penance by writing something like his eventual *Legend of Good Women,* a somewhat fishy attack on false men, and an antic claim that only he among all men is to be trusted ("Beth war of men, and herkneth what I seye"—v. 1785).

Narrative voices and tones of voice multiply in the closing stanzas of the poem, but (as Donaldson has pointed out) the most decisive shift is when the narrator takes Troilus' own advice to eschew "The blynde lust, the which that may nat laste" (v. 1824) and launches into his own fervent rejection of the world. Summoned to hear this rejection is an audience well suited to profit by it, composed of "yonge, fresshe folkes, he or she" (v. 1835). Yet these young folks do not endure for long. Chaucer shifts to a more general address in his bemused assault on rascally pagan gods and (apparently) on those poetic sources that got him into this trouble in the first place (v. 1849–55). Finally, ending in utmost seriousness with a prayer for mercy, Chaucer addresses God, establishing his utterance as, for once, wholly fervent by directing it toward an auditor who subsumes all previous audiences and surpasses them in ability and inclination to perceive devotional intent ("And to the Lord right thus I speke"—v. 1862–69).

Also addressed in the poem's closing stanzas are two persons drawn from Chaucer's circle of actual acquaintance, "moral Gower" and "philosophical Strode," whom he urges on the basis of their "benignities and zeles goode" to correct his book as need be (v. 1856–59). Coming as they do within a succession of fictional and hypothetical addressees, these two historical persons plainly represent a special opportunity for added insight into the composition of Chaucer's actual audience, and this opportunity will be pursued below. For now, though, they may be seen as a partial vindication of Walter Ong's observation that "the writer's audience is always a fiction," [27] since they are used for the same purpose as Chaucer's more obviously fictional addressees, that of orienting address to an audience able to comprehend its intended meaning.

However variously critics might apply Chaucer's concluding stanzas to the interpretation of the poem as a whole, we can hardly disagree that he has chosen to end with strong emphasis on the instability and false felicity of earthy attachments. "Moral Gower" clearly belongs to a segment of Chaucer's audience well suited to hear and respond to this point of view. Gower is, as John Fisher has shown us, the preeminent moral poet of Chaucer's day, in the sense in which Chaucer would have used the word, to describe an interest in the principles of human conduct.[28] And, as Fisher also reminds us, Gower brooks no illusions about the durability of earthly love. The opening lines of his earlier *Mirour* remind us that worldly delights pass like a dream ("Car s'un soul homme avoir porroit / Quanq'en son coer souhaideroit / Du siecle . . . / Trestout come songe passeroit") and that secular love must finally pass to nothingness ("l'amour seculer / En nient au fin doit retorner").[29] When Gower himself will write of Troilus in his *Confessio,* we will find him "hevy chiered" in the parade of lovers viewed by the aged Amans as he takes leave of earthly love at the end of his poem, for he knows that he has been supplanted and that his love has failed (VIII. 2531–35).[30] Gower may or may not have been thinking of Chaucer's poem here; certainly his own previously written reflections on love would have disposed him to such a view. We are reminded of Gower's persistent skepticism about earthly love when his Amans bids his final farewell to such love, choosing—as in Chaucer's final stanza—the love of God:

> So that above in thilke place
> Wher resteth love and alle pes,
> Oure joie mai ben endeles. (VIII. 3170–72)

The identification of Gower as ideal auditor confirms a moral emphasis within Chaucer's concluding stanzas. Assuming, provisionally, that Strode the Oxford philosopher and fellow of Merton College (before 1360) and Strode the London lawyer and factionalist (who died in 1387) are one,[31] the commendation of the poem to "philosophical Strode" would seem to assert the importance of a philosophical dimension as well. The most evident moment of overt philosophizing within the poem occurs in Troilus' meditation on necessity (especially IV.953–1085).[32] In these lines Troilus embraces Boethius' arguments against human freedom (based on *Boece,* V.2–3), but omits Lady Philosophy's more encouraging rejoinder (*Boece,* V.4–6). The point of this passage would seem to reside less in what Troilus reasons out—that deeds are subject to God's prescience—than in what he mistakenly omits—that God's prescience is conditional and does not constrain choice. Seen in this way, Troilus' speech seems to require some knowledge of Boethius or some general philosophical understanding for correct interpretation. Even knowing Boethius, Thomas Usk gets the passage wrong, citing it as a basis for his declaration that Chaucer is "the noble philosophical poete in Englissh" (III.iv), but erroneously applauding it for resolving a question it does not address, that of God's apparent sufferance of evil in the world. "Philosophical Strode" would, however, have been well equipped to read the passage correctly. In fact he contended with Wyclif on this very question of free will. While his own critiques of Wyclif's early work are lost, two surviving responses by Wyclif suggest that Strode protested against Wyclif's necessitarianism.[33] Strode's position on free will fitted him well to penetrate the weakness of Troilus' halfway argument, a weakness attributable to Troilus (rather than to Chaucer[34]) and to his attempted self-exoneration for those same worldly attachments condemned in the last stanzas of the poem.[35]

In Gower and Strode, Chaucer invokes what might be considered a special "interpretive community" within the larger community comprised by his whole contemporary audience. The two are a particular subset of his larger audience, designated to reinforce or complete a meaning that Chaucer wishes his passage to have. Here, concerned to advance a moral/philosophical perspective from which Troilus is seen as free to choose divine love over earthly pleasure, Chaucer finds "audience" by directing his words to those members of his circle most likely to understand his words as he wants them understood.[36]

As in the case of the *Book of the Duchess,* however, this poem clearly has an even larger circle of addressees than those persons fictional or actual who are named or directly addressed within the poem. Auditors with a still larger range of response are constantly presupposed or implied. Both speaker and addressees are, for example, represented to us as polished courtiers, in the narrator's nicely turned compliment to Queen Anne ("Right as oure firste lettre is now an A"—I.171).[37] At other times the narrator shares with his audience observations about love suggesting that both he and they are more mature and knowledgeable than either the "clerc" of love (III.41) who narrates parts of the story or the audience of "loveres" that harkens to him. "Blissed be Love, that kan thus folk converte!" (I.308) exclaims the narrator over Criseyde's first effect on Troilus—remaining within the speaker's credulous voice, but also offering his audience something of the bemusement with which the mature Theseus comments on the plight of Palamon and Arcite ("How myghty and how greet a lord is he!"—I.1786). Sometimes, in fact, the narrator's word choice and tone suggest a bemusement that he and his audience share. This tone is fleeting early in the poem ("God leve hym werken as he kan devyse," the narrator observes as Troilus rehearses his speech while awaiting Criseyde at Deiphebus' house—III. 56). As the poem progresses, and as attitudes toward Troilus' love multiply, we encounter moments of outright flippancy ("But Troilus, thow maist now, est or west, / Pipe in an ivy lef, if that the lest!"—V. 1432–33). Other remarks presuppose a speaker who is slyly flirtatious, if not a downright rake, and an audience that is knowing in this regard. Quite different from the tone of modest credulousness adopted by the narrator of the opening books is this sly innuendo, unmistakably underscored in its closing line:

> To God hope I, she hath now kaught a thorn,
> She shal nat pulle it out this nexte wyke.
> God sende mo swich thornes on to pike! (II. 1272–74)

We are certainly dealing with a sexually aware narrator who, at the moment Criseyde "heals" Troilus' pain with her love, twits the women in his audience and no doubt overjoys the men, with the suggestion that "take every womman heede / To werken thus, if it comth to the neede" (III. 1224–25).

Implied by such narrative sallies is the presence of an audience broader in its perspective and more sophisticated in its responses than are any of the particular fictional audiences addressed within the poem. One constantly has the sense of an audience addressed in temporarily narrowed ways, but actually possessed of a more inclusive point of view. Some narrative observations imply the audience's entire sympathy with Troilus' predicament ("lith Troilus . . . / Ibounden in the blake bark of care"—IV. 228–229), while others, in nearly adjacent passages, imply that his sorrows might be overblown or partially self-inflicted:

> A thousand sikes, hotter than the gleede,
> Out of his brest ech after other wente,
> Medled with pleyntes new, his wo to feede. (IV. 337–339)

Even at the end of the poem, important passages about "feynede loves" (V. 1848) are closely juxtaposed with passages so hectic in tone as practically to require a sophisticated audience ("Lo here, of payens corsed olde rites"—V. 1849).

Among the different sorts of sophistication evidently expected of his audience is an implied literary "horizon" of some refinement. Within the poem itself, Chaucer gives us a model of the integration of literature into a certain kind of gentle life. Criseyde, hearing a romance of Thebes, summarizes its plot to the visiting Pandarus, up to the disappearance of the bishop Amphiorax through the ground into hell (II. 100–105). Pandarus assures her that he knows the story too. His motives are colored by his objective of getting Criseyde to set aside her book, but we have no reason to doubt the truth of his claim. The work in question appears to be a "romaunce" similar in nature to the French *Roman de Thèbes,* as would befit persons with ties to the royal family, slightly more elevated in social position than those at the heart of Chaucer's own audience. Yet the notion of literary pleasure, and knowledge, in integration with the details of daily living may surely be permitted to stand as an emblem of Chaucer's own expectation.

Of course Chaucer stops short of any expectation that his hearers are littérateurs or mythographers, choosing a reasonable middle course in what he expects them to know. Difficult paganisms are glossed, as in "Thesiphone . . . thow goddesse of torment" (I. 6–8), or "Herynes, Nyghtes doughtren thre" (IV. 22). So that the audience will not miss the irony of Criseyde's exchange for Antenor, his ultimate betrayal is carefully explained ("For he was after traitour to the town / Of Troye"—IV. 204–205). On the other hand, Chaucer feels no need to gloss the first appearance of major figures like Hector (I. 110), and I should be very surprised if his audience were not included in the humor of his jesting reference to the supposed Lollius (I. 394). This audience certainly has a sufficiently developed sense of literary tradition to permit Chaucer to frame even more elaborate jests upon the literary afterlife of his characters. Like characters in postmodern fictions, the protagonists of *Troilus* seem constantly on the brink of discovery that they are characters in a book. Pandarus, ignorant of the fact that his reputation has preceded him, speculates that if his intrigues were known, "al the world upon it wolde crie" (III. 277). Troilus, in his extremity, sees his troubles in narrative form (as a "proces"—V. 583) and wonders if his plight might not have literary potential ("Men myght a book make of it, lik a storie"—V. 585).

Appreciative of ironic interplay between a character's life in tradition and particular realization in a story, this audience is no less capable of recognizing the different generic patterns within which a narrative may be cast. For much of the challenge and narrative excitement of *Troilus* is Chaucer's play on his audience's previous expectations. Telling us from the outset that his poem will end with Troilus "out of joie" (I. 4)—that is, in a form that his audience would recognize as tragic and that he finally does label "tragedye" (V. 1786)—Chaucer sets about to deflect his audience's attention from this announced pattern by signaling all sorts of other generic possibilities. Troilus, for example, falls in love like Amans in the *Roman de la Rose* and the heroes of several dozen chivalric romances, wounded through the eye into the heart: "he felte dyen, / Right with hire look, the spirit in his herte" (I. 306–307). No sooner, though, does the audience begin to accept its entry into the world of amorous romance than it is confronted by other, conflicting characteristics: as in a history, sentiment is to be eschewed and sources are to be weighed (II. 13–14); room is to be made for philosophical "argument" (IV. 956); songs and epistles are embedded throughout; in the end, the audience is sermonized. This constant clash of codes within the larger framework of a Christian tragedy would be rich in literary excitement for an audience aware of the genres and generic features in question, and very confusing for an audience ignorant of them. Evidence of early reception suggests that Chaucer was probably regarded as a somewhat difficult poet,[38] but not so difficult that he would depend heavily upon systems of literary expectation beyond the recognition of his audience.

The room is beginning to fill up with audiences—fictional, actual, and implied. Fictional audiences of lovers, scoffers, historians, those unsophisticated in history, ladies and gentlewomen, and young people on the brink of love jostle with actual (though exemplary) addressees in Gower and Strode, and also with implied audiences of courtiers, mature people able to keep love in perspective, rakes, embarrassed or vexed women, flirts, devout moralists whose devotion is nevertheless constrained within human limits . . . and closer analysis of the poem at the level of individual lines would enable us to extend this list. We might now be gaining enough sense of these audiences to frame a crucial question: taken together, do these addressees somehow add up to Chaucer's "real audience"? Not quite. Some of these fictional and implied audiences must be seen as ephemera, in the sense that they exist as temporary ways of orienting discourse or even as products of the discourse itself. We might, for example, want to assign such figmentary status to the "man" (III. 491) who expects every word of every letter exchanged between Troilus and Criseyde to be reported verbatim (permitting Chaucer, in return, to explain his principle of selectivity). In many cases, though, we can reasonably assume that fictional and implied audiences are employed to facilitate communication between Chaucer and his real audience, and that their attitudes stand in some tactical or referential relation to attitudes characteristic of the audience of the poem. Proceeding on this assumption, we might seek cautiously to locate these fictional and implied audiences within a historical frame by connecting them to the ultimate audience with which they seem designed to provide communication.

Chaucer's poem presupposes an audience capable of embracing a mixture of styles and tones of voice and of managing abrupt transitions between them. It presupposes an audience able both to inhabit and to stand outside a particular point of view. (It seems able to view ardent secular love both as admirable and as rather foolish; to believe that only divine love as embodied in God's sacrifice is stable and trustworthy, but that there are many paths to Rome and we have much to learn from pre- or non-Christian attempts at understanding.) It presupposes an audience that can simultaneously entertain different perspectives and tolerate a high degree of contradiction between them. (Privy at the outset to the knowledge that Troilus' love will fail, the audience is then treated as a group of accomplished lovers who hope for his success; urged to join Troilus in rejecting the world, it is tantalized by fleeting reminders of the world Troilus has lost.[39]) It presupposes an audience of some literary sophistication, which shares literary expectations formed not only by the experience of the work at hand but also by acquaintance with other major texts and genres of antiquity and the newly flourishing vernaculars.

God save such an audience! It deserves our admiration.[40] Yet we have progressed very little in connecting the traits of this audience with its actual membership. If we pause, however, to reflect on the fact that the poem was completed in or about 1385,[41] we will gain some important clues into the rich sense of audience conveyed by the poem. The period culminating in 1385 was not only the period of greatest stability in Chaucer's life, it was the period in which he would have come closer than ever again in his career to participation in a stable social and literary circle. Still in close touch with the court, he enjoyed continuing contact with such persons as Stury (the literary courtier who befriended Froissart), Clifford (whom we recall as Chaucer's intermediary with Deschamps), and Clanvowe (author both of a Chaucerian love vision and a devotional treatise in prose). Now resident in London, he enjoyed added scope for acquaintance with such citified intellectuals as Gower and Strode. There he could hardly avoid crossing paths with such other interesting persons as the shifty politician and author Thomas Usk, who mentions *Troilus* in his *Testament of Love*.[42] Common sense supports the likelihood that this Westminster-London audience of gentlepersons and clerks was at the heart of Chaucer's public. For such an audience—with its verifiable acquaintance with literary tradition, its inclusion of several fellow poets, and its simultaneous interest in the secular and the divine—has much in common with the audience that is fictionalized, implied, and (in the cases of Gower and Strode) directly cited within Chaucer's *Troilus*.

The Pilgrims as Fictionalized Response

If implication and direct invocation suggest for *Troilus* an audience drawn from a circle congruent with Chaucer's own, our sense of the importance of such an audience will gain little added support from the *Canterbury Tales*. Despite the many signs of its provisional and unfinished nature, that work nevertheless possesses a degree of creative autonomy that, as one commentator has properly concluded, "makes it almost impossible to talk about the 'historical' audience of the *Canterbury Tales* on the basis of internal evidence."[43] An element of this autonomy is Chaucer's remarkably complete effacement of evidence bearing on contemporary reception. This effacement is facilitated by the development of an internal communication system that permits Chaucer to orient narrative within fully realized conditions of telling and hearing without leaving the boundaries of his work. His masterwork thus teems with fictional pilgrim tellers and hearers, and contains no references at all to a real audience.

Chaucer's emphasis on the responses of a fictional pilgrim audience seems to leave little space for history, in the form of contemporary engagement with an actual public. Yet history has its own trick of covertly reentering discourse precisely at its point of exclusion, sometimes even in and around our understanding of the *act* of exclusion. In the case of the *Canterbury Tales,* Chaucer's own obliteration of the evidence of actual reception can itself be historicized in several different and revealing ways. His effacement of history can, in the first place, be seen as historically conditioned, in its relation to known features of his own career. And his creation of a fictional audience can, in the second place, be seen as an enabling device, a vehicle for communication with a contemporary audience that, while unrepresented, remains important to him.

Chaucer's interest in inscribed situations of telling and hearing is apparent at every stage of his career, but never so vividly as in the realization of his *compaignye* of pilgrim-narrators. Although this elaborate fictionalization of narration and response occurs in a plainly aesthetic register, it may still have been encouraged by developments in his own career in the years after 1386. As we have seen, the period between 1386 and 1389 posed substantial obstacles to Chaucer's continuing interaction with members of his circle. In 1366–1374, when he composed the *Book of the Duchess,* Chaucer had been a member of the royal household, with opportunities for intermittent contact with powerful figures like Gaunt and for more regular contact with people like Clifford, Vache, and Stury. In the period 1374–1385/86, culminating in the completion of *Troilus and Criseyde,* he was settled in London with opportunities for continued communication with the court. Several events, including his service at Parliament and his testimony in Scrope-Grosvenor, would have had him in London throughout 1386. But, after the relinquishment of his Aldgate house and full withdrawal to Kent in 1386, many of his associations must have been interrupted. Between fall 1386 and fall 1389, he seems to have lived in virtual estrangement from both court and city. The *Canterbury Tales* were, in short, launched in a situation that permitted much less direct address to an intimate circle than the one to which he had been accustomed. Given Chaucer's tendency to conceive his work as communication, we may understand his deliberate enhancement of a fictional situation of telling and reception as a way of "staging" his work during a precarious time, in the absence of a stable communicative situation.

The same point may be made of Chaucer's heightened tendency to look beyond the present, to an audience of distant and future readers. The idea of such a readership emerged as a matter of mingled aspiration and unease at the end of *Troilus,* where he aspired to launch his book into a timeless realm of "alle poesye" but unsettled himself by reflecting on the interpretative disasters (including not only problems of transmission but outright failures of understanding that might attend circulation of his work in written form). Such a remote readership, rather than the more familiar circle implied in the *Book of the Duchess* or *Troilus,* now seems to be addressed in the "yow" of the General Prologue and in the *Parson's Tale* and the Retraction. Those so addressed are, we learn on several occasions, a reading audience, which will draw its conclusions in private, away from any possibility of Chaucer's intervention. To such readers, encountering his poetry through the medium of a bound manuscript, he refers in the Prologue to the *Miller's Tale:*

> . . . whoso list it nat yheere,
> Turne over the leef and chese another tale. (I. 3176–77)

His relative remoteness from this audience is registered in the absence of familiar banter (in the vein of his "Beth war of men" in *Troilus,* V. 1785). His admonitions to this audience have a tone of generality and seem—if anything—to convey a certain unease about how his poetry might be received. Lines that might be confidently read as jocular in address to a present public seem somewhat more defensive or even apologetic in a written text:

> But first I pray yow, of youre curteisye,
> That ye n'arette it nat my vileynye,
> Thogh that I pleynly speke in this mateere. (I. 725–727)

This same observation may be made of the Retraction, in which he seems at pains to clarify his "entente" (X. 1083) to an audience of whose understanding he does not seem completely certain.

Other references to audience inside the *Tales* add little to our understanding of their contemporary reception. Once we move from the frame of the *Canterbury Tales* to the body of the work, references to any audience external to the work itself come to an end. A disclaimer addressed to "every gentil wight" at the threshold of the *Miller's Tale* and a vagrant reference to "yow that reden" in the Prologue to the *Second Nun's Tale* (VIII. 78) do little to enstate the rich sense of context we have previously observed, and most other alleged references to groups outside the poem—such as to those "lordes" whom the Nun's Priest warns against flattery (VII. 3325) or the "chanons" whom the Canon's Yeoman takes time to reassure (VIII. 992)—are simply instances of apostrophe, without a point of contact in groups of real auditors.[44] Although discourse within the *Tales* retains a firm audience orientation, that orientation is now located inside the poem, and the "lordynges," "wise wyves," "ladyes," "sires," "lordes," and "goode men" addressed in individual Canterbury narratives are imagined to exist within the pilgrim company rather than outside it. By no means wholly to be explained as a mere function of Chaucer's personal circumstances, this remarkably self-contained quality, this nearly complete absence of external reference, may be connected with the relative social isolation in which the *Tales* were begun.

The estrangement of 1386–1389 was soon moderated by Chaucer's appointment as Clerk of Works in the fall of 1389 and his return to something like a literary circle—an altered and diminished circle, to be sure, but one nevertheless subject to reconstitution and one he probably had a hand in reconstituting. Strode had died in 1387. Chaucer seems not to have resumed active contact with Gower and

Beauchamp after the events of 1386. Aspirant-to-membership Thomas Usk had died, along with others, in 1388. Clanvowe and Nevill were on the scene but left in 1391. On the other hand, Chaucer's poem to Vache (possibly 1386–1389) and his epistles to Scogan and Bukton (in the 1390s) suggest both his continuing commerce with old friends and his ability to recruit to his literary audience new, younger persons. Some of these new interactions probably involved the reading or loan of portions of the *Canterbury Tales*. Partly as a result of his own exertions, Chaucer would appear once again to have found some measure of "audience."

The question I wish to pose now concerns the relationship of Chaucer's inscribed audience of Canterbury pilgrims to the actual audience I am suggesting he reconstructed as he wrote the *Canterbury Tales*. The one observation to be made with certainty is that this relation is *not* the one we might spontaneously suppose: one in which the pilgrim audience might be taken as a representation, or at least a refracted version, of Chaucer's contemporary audience. We may, for example, note from the outset that Chaucer's pilgrims represent neither an accurate cross-section of late fourteenth-century English society nor an accurate cross-section of his possible audience. Compared with fourteenth-century society as a whole, the Canterbury pilgrimage is deficient in representing the two ends of the social scale, as comprised by those landholding aristocrats and knights who monopolized the attention of conservative theorists like Bracton and by the multitudes of free and unfree who worked the land. The landholders, while numbering less than 1 percent of the populace, certainly loomed large in people's awareness. Yet, on the pilgrimage, they are represented by a single knight, and not necessarily a landholding knight at that. Also represented by a single individual are the 90–95 percent of the populace who earned a livelihood by various forms of free and bonded agricultural labor.

Present in vast disproportion are people from the "middle strata." Yet, although the pilgrims come from what Brinton sees as a fairly spacious midsection of the body politic, they come from different parts of that section than those probably occupied by Chaucer's actual audience; not from the right hand where the knights are located, but from the left hand ("mercatores et fideles mechanici") and the heart ("ciues et burgenses"). In the terms of the Statute of Apparel, this band of pilgrims slights the various categories of gentlepersons, esquires, and knights, instead inclining heavily toward those nongentle persons of the middle strata described as "Marchantx, Citeins &

Burgeis, Artificers, gentz de Mestere." The pilgrims' tilt away from Chaucer's circle is most vividly revealed in the four categories of the 1379 poll tax, the first of which consists entirely of *gentils* down through the rank of esquires "en service" and the other three of which include sergeants at law, attorneys, aldermen, merchants, sergeants, franklins, pardoners, summoners, and others. Chaucer's actual audience would have been concentrated largely in the first of these four groups; the pilgrims are drawn mainly from social and occupational groupings described in the other three.[45]

Of course, as Jill Mann has definitively shown, Chaucer was obliged like any other artist to work through existing models of representation.[46] Even so, he shows little impulse to put forward his pilgrims as persuasive representations either of his society as a whole or of his particular social group. Their composition is determined less by motives of historical or social representation than by a more immediate and more literary imperative, which is to create a socially diverse group drawn from the most dynamic fourteenth-century social strata, whose social and vocational conflicts will provide good possibilities for staging a diverse collection of tales.

The historicity of the pilgrim audience lies less in the fidelity of its social representations than in its effectiveness as a constitutive strategy enabling Chaucer to produce a new kind of tale collection, some of whose aesthetic features themselves bear an historical charge. The "newness" of Chaucer's collection is expressed in its unusual generic and stylistic diversity, a diversity that departs emphatically from the precedent of previous medieval collections.[47] What Chaucer appears to have grasped so firmly in his creation of his pilgrim tellers and hearers is the inseparability of the different elements of the communicative situation: a generically diverse collection requires a diverse group of tellers and hearers as well.[48]

The inextricability of the connection between Chaucer's mixed circle of tellers and hearers and the mixed genres of his collection—as well as its sheer originality—may best be understood against a background of customary medieval practice. Boccaccio's *Decameron,* for example, draws its novelle from sources as diverse as fabliaux and pious exempla, but seeks to refine these differences away and to treat all its subject matter in an even style that is likened to a *piano* or plain;[49] so too does he create an ideal body of tellers and listeners who are uniformly gentle and who differ only in modest respects. Gower's *Confessio Amantis* attains stylistic evenness by assigning all its narratives to Genius, a single-voiced and authoritative teller.

Chaucer himself experiments in the *Legend of Good Women* with a generically uniform collection, recounted in a single narrative voice (however internally varied that voice might be) and aimed at a very limited segment of his possible reading public.[50]

In contrast with such uniform audiences as the gentle hearers and tellers of the *Decameron* and the royal couple of the *Legend* we can appreciate the diversity of Chaucer's body of pilgrims.[51] Chaucer in fact seizes on every pretext to emphasize divergence in outlook and literary taste. Only at rare moments do we encounter consensus, such as when, stirred by the Prioress' miracle, "every man / As sobre was that wonder was to se" (VII.691–692) or when, the end of the journey drawing near, the "Hoost hadde the wordes for us alle" (X.67). More often we encounter every species of disagreement, fostered by Chaucer's insistence on the divisive impact of social position and vocational role upon literary taste.

One of his bold strokes is to divide his pilgrims into different literary camps on the basis of their social position—most noticeably, into *gentils* and *cherls*. (The exact membership of these two groups is never specified, though we may assume that the *gentils* include the Knight, the Squire, the Prioress, possibly the Monk, and—in spirit if not in fact—the Franklin and the Man of Law; explicitly identified as *cherls* are the Miller and the Reeve, and we may assume that they are joined by the Cook and a number of other pilgrims as well.) This polarization is introduced immediately after the first tale, when we learn that everyone likes the Knight's narrative on general grounds as a "noble storie" (I.3111)—that is, as a narrative that is historically verifiable or is so venerable and edifying that it might as well be—but some like it better than others. Liking it most are the "gentils everichon" (I.3113). Less persuaded is the Miller, whose own "noble tale" (I.3126) will be no "storie" but a narrative out of oral tradition that parodies aspects of the *Knight's Tale* ranging from derisive echoes of its most serious lines through its plot configuration to its premises about necessity and choice. Further, Chaucer implies that the Miller's revolt is socially based, identifying him as a *cherl* who will tell a "cherles tale" (I.3169). Then, reaching beyond the created audience of pilgrim tellers and hearers, Chaucer reinforces his point by suggesting that his reading public (or at least a faction of *gentil wights* within it) may, by reason of its own social position, prefer to choose other, more "storial" tales involving "gentillesse, / And eek moralitee and hoolynesse" (I.3179–80). Opinion is in fact divided after the *Miller's Tale* ("Diverse folk diversely they seyde"—I.3857), though we never learn the details of the *gentils'* response. They will, however, rise once more as a group in the prologue to the *Pardoner's Tale,* provoked either by Harry Bailly's request for "som myrthe or japes" (VI. 319) or by the Pardoner's intention of stopping for a drink:

> But right anon thise gentils gonne to crye,
> "Nay, lat hym telle us of no ribaudye!
> Telle us som moral thyng . . ." (VI. 323–325)

We know that this dichotomy—between *gentils* who want moral content and *cherls* who want as much harlotry as they can get—is mostly pretense. Modern scholarship confirms that a romance might be "chivalric" or "popular"; a fabliau might be aimed at a courtly audience (in the instances cited by Nykrog[52]) or a bourgeois audience, or even (in the adaptations cited by Rychner[53]) successively at each kind. But, even if the social basis of literary judgment is far more complex than Chaucer chooses to pretend, his pretense can be embraced as one that (in conjunction with a socially mixed body of tellers and hearers) permits a tale collection of unprecedented internal diversity.

Equally a matter of pretense is Chaucer's assertion of an occupational or vocational basis for his tellers' selection of tales. Many of his assignments are based on premises—like the attraction of knights to *storial* romances and *cherls* to low tales—that were not really operative in the later fourteenth century. And he is fairly casual even about the realization of these premises, assigning his Knight an elevated *storie* but then granting him a down-to-earth narrative perspective (as in I. 886–887) and assigning his Miller a tale of village life that is then told from a decidedly haughty point of view (as in I. 3268–70). The legerdemain lying behind even the most plausible assignments is evident in the tales of such religious pilgrims as the Prioress, the Monk, the Second Nun, and the Parson. Nothing could seem more reasonable on its face than the assignment of religious tales to religious people, but Chaucer nevertheless puts this premise under some strain. So plausible is the assignment of a miracle of the Virgin to the Prioress, for example, that we hardly pause to reflect that evidence of manuscript ownership and popular taste suggests that such miracles (and especially such miracles in vernaculars) were almost exclusively the province of lay audiences and an object of popular circulation rather than reclusive or contemplative devotion.[54] The Monk's *tragedies* are not at all the kind of thing that a monk would be expected to have lying around his cell, but were in the 1380s the province of an international and Latinate literary elite of the highest order of humanistic pretension, and the assignment of tragedies to the Monk would itself have been a subtle literary joke.[55] The Second Nun's impeccably devout tale of St. Cecilia is based on a tradition of hagiographical narrative derived from the *Legenda aurea* and employed from the very beginning for purposes of lay piety.[56] Even the *Parson's Tale* is less the popular sermon of a country preacher than a learned treatise suited for an audience that must be supposed highly educated if not academic.[57] But the point is finally not whether we believe in every one of Chaucer's assignments, or even whether we believe any of them; the point is the kind of diverse collection enabled by these assignments, and in this sense we can regard them as a literary strategy of consummate worth.

Detached as they might seem from history in the sense of immediate reception, the aesthetic choices involved in launching this literary strategy nevertheless have an important social aspect. For the apparently aesthetic choice of a tale collection varied in style and genre gains social implication in the likelihood of its attractiveness to a particular social group. Even in some of its most accessible features of stylistic variousness, multiple perspective, and mixed tone, the poetry made possible by Chaucer's diverse pilgrim tellers is of a sort likely to be particularly attractive to the social group I have described as his core audience.

The idea that certain highly contrastive poetic features are likely to appeal to those in ambiguous social situations would appear to be one that must be accepted or rejected on grounds of personal belief. But, fortunately, available evidence does permit us to form some opinions about the kinds of poetic features that addressees like Scogan, Bukton, and Vache, and fellow writers like Usk, Scogan, and Clanvowe, did in fact like.

Other Evidence of Social Interaction

Chaucer's short poems to Scogan, Bukton, and Vache might be thought "familiar" in their intimate and frequently jocular form of address, but they are additionally revealing of what Chaucer expected in the way of literary competence from members of his circle. These poems as a group might be contrasted with other of Chaucer's short poems, such as "Lack of Steadfastness," in their relatively high demands for attentive response.

These familiar poems ask much of their hearers, in their manipulation of voice and other aspects of literary form and their mixed perspective on the subjects under discussion. Portentous statements are made and then undercut by new tones of voice suggesting new attitudes. Traps are suddenly sprung, revealing alternative interpretative layers beneath authoritative statements. Hearers are asked to think two things or to juggle different voices in simultaneous conflict. Knowledge of Chaucer's previous poetry is assumed, and assumed to be available for use. Taken as a group, these poems move beyond mere amicability to require of their readers such additional qualities as a nimble response to changing tone, an ability to hear opposed voices and to sustain mixed attitudes, and a readiness to follow complex textual choreography.

These poems have been sensitively analyzed on several occasions.[58] Of interest here is the subtlety of some of the demands they make upon their audiences. All presuppose a single speaker and a single addressee, but each is actually multivoiced in the sense of shifting rapidly among different perspectives, and each appears to be addressed simultaneously to its intended listener and to an enlarged—though still intimate—group.

"Scogan," for example, imagines a seemingly straightforward situation of address between a single speaker and his "friend" Scogan, but actually draws its hearer through a rapid succession of alterations in voice and points of view. The bold certainty of its opening lines ("Tobroken been the statutz") gives way to the quavering uncertainty with which the stanza concludes ("I deye almost for drede"). The bathetic reference to the tears of Venus yields to a jocular accusation that Scogan is the offender. Scogan is charged ("Hastow not seyd . . ."), but we are then given cause to suspect that in giving his lady up for lack of responsiveness to his overtures he might have some common sense on his side. The jocular fear that Cupid might have revenge on both of them (by withholding his arrows) gives way to a part jesting, part serious retreat from the poetic fray that in turn yields to a rather melancholy reflection on time and succession ("But al shal passe that men prose or ryme; / Take every man hys turn, as for his tyme"). The envoy shifts ground again, to a request for Scogan's intervention on Chaucer's behalf ("Mynne thy frend") and then returns to the poem's central jest ("never eft Love dyffye").

Scogan remains the object of this varied address, and the easy tone of the poem leaves us no doubt of the sincerity with which Chaucer describes Scogan as his friend. But we are also left with a sense of a slightly expanded public for this poem, a larger listening circle of friends who appreciate Chaucer's association of Scogan and himself as aging and portly lovers with fears of being left out of Cupid's sphere altogether.[59] This expanded public is also called upon to resolve yet another dilemma. Scogan's offense turns out to be intriguingly two-sided in import. By giving up his lady for failing to respond to his appeals, he has undoubtedly offended the "lawe of love," but his down-to-earth attitude would certainly have its defenders elsewhere in Chaucer's poetry. One thinks, for example, of his worm and water fowl, including the goose ("But she wol love hym, lat hym love another"—*PF,* 567) and his like-minded associate the duck ("That men shulde loven alwey causeles! / Who can a resoun fynde or wit in that?"—*PF,* 590–591). Is Chaucer suggesting that Scogan has blundered or that he makes a great deal of sense? The verdict appears to lie with the circle of friendly associates implied by the poem. "Scogan" reveals itself as open in form, as willing to pose both formal and substantive problems, trusting the ability of its audience to resolve them or to accommodate their contrariety.

"Scogan" tests its hearers' capacity for adjustment both in its opening stanzas and later. But "Bukton" turns its corners even more quickly. The speaker tells us at the outset that, no more truthful than other men, he must now break an earlier promise to describe "the sorwe and wo that is in mariage." He dares not write any wickedness about marriage, "Lest I myself falle eft in swich dotage"—meaning that he might be punished for his words by an obligation to remarry? That if he remarried, his wife's tongue might cause him to suffer for what he has said? As the Variorum editors note, "The logic in the introductory stanza is by no means clear."[60] But the hearer does feel sure of one thing: the speaker will guard his words. In the next stanza, though, while seeming to be cautious in utterance ("I wol nat seyn how that yt is the cheyne / Of Sathanas"), the speaker takes a strong position: anyone, once out, would be a fool to expose himself to marriage again. Might Bukton, like the speaker, have placed one marriage behind him and be considering another? Or is the speaker thinking mainly of himself? No matter; we are at least certain now of the speaker's opposition to marriage. But hearers are to be surprised once again: the speaker cites Corinthians, proposing that Bukton take a wife after all ("lest thow do worse, take a wyf"). Does he mean it? If so, only in a sense more fatalistic than the apostle's own, because he goes on to predict on the basis of authority and experience that "thow shal have sorwe on thy flessh, thy lyf." And, instead of seizing the occasion of the envoy to relent, he cites an ultimate authority (the Wife of Bath) on the problems of bondage. In "Scogan," the audience was asked to entertain different attitudes about love. Here the audience is asked to revise, and then to revise again, its attitudes about what the speaker is likely to say next—even to a mild surprise when, in the envoy, the speaker does *not* change his ground.

"Truth" would pose no such interpretative problems, were it not for the single manuscript of the poem that attaches an envoy. The body of the poem without envoy is a single-voiced and unambiguous injunction to an undefined (but presumably broad) audience, urging it to "Flee fro the prees and dwelle with sothfastnesse." Questions of interpretation have, however, multiplied, ever since Edith Rickert explained that the "Vache" addressed in the first line of the envoy is not just the beast of the earlier "Forth, beste, out of thy stal," but a double reference to the sluggish beast of the body of the poem and to Chaucer's acquaintance and probable friend Philip la Vache.[61] We evidently have at least two audiences here: the general audience of the gnomic poem as circulated without the envoy and (if we can assume that the addition of the envoy represents some intention of Chaucer's, and not simply an editorial intervention or chance association) the more particular audience of Vache, and perhaps a few friends, who received the altered version. But questions do not cease here. Would members of the general audience, stumbling upon the envoy, have read it "straight," as Chaucer critics did before Rickert? Would injunctions like "leve thyn old wrecchednesse," amusing in address to a friend and fellow gentleperson, have seemed appropriately generic and Boethian to those who did not catch the "Vache" reference? And, more perplexing still, how are readers of the Vache envoy to take the earlier, gnomic stanzas? Can lines like "Forth, beste, out of thy stal" still be read without mirth? Or is there such a thing as *retrospective* comedy? In presenting Vache with this envoy, Chaucer would also have presented him with an interpretative bind that would not easily have been resolved, with a problem that both recognizes Vache's friendship and builds some presumptions (about patience, good will, and ability to handle ambiguity) upon it.

Special relations between Chaucer and his addressees are implied by all these poems, and many problematic passages would undoubtedly be clarified if we could know them: whether Chaucer has a particular favor in mind when he asks Scogan to "mynne thy frend," what larger audience is implied in Chaucer's epistle to Bukton, whether the envoy to Vache was prepared for Vache's private reading or was circulated among a larger group. Even as the poems stand, though, they are replete with hints of shared understanding. When

Chaucer professes to "deye almost for drede" in the first stanza of "Scogan," one senses that he is invoking a narrative persona with which his audience is already well acquainted. When he speaks to Bukton of the "wo that is in mariage," one senses that his echo of his own Wife of Bath (IV. 3) is meant to be recognized—even before his subsequent mention of her name.

Whatever their ostensible subjects, these poems can also be appreciated as solidifications and celebrations of the relations that made them possible. As R. T. Lenaghan has said of "Scogan," "The statement of the poem is not, 'Renew my pension,' or 'Don't defy love'; rather, it is something closer to 'We are friends, we react the same way to matter of love.' "[62] Chaucer also, in my estimation, celebrates the high expectations he is able to entertain of these friends as addressees of his poems—expectations of their capacity for mixed perspectives and open forms, their ability to enjoy his abrupt shifts of direction and tone, their willingness to rethink and revise prior interpretations. One has in reading these poems a sense of symbiosis: a sense that Chaucer demands more of these friends and social equals than of his other possible audiences and that he gets more from them; he addresses them through poems that speak well for their qualities and capacities, and their availability as sympathetic respondents helps to make such poems possible.

THE FAMILIAR poems addressed to Scogan, Bukton, and Vache imply that Chaucer's poetry was comprehended sympathetically by members of his circle, but they include no conclusive evidence of reception. For this, or at least evidence more specific than general encomia to Chaucer as translator, philosopher, and rhetorician,[63] we do have access to an underutilized source of information in the form of several passages and poems written under Chaucer's influence, two (by Usk and Clanvowe) from his lifetime and one (by Scogan) from the months or years immediately after.[64] The lessons to be learned from these three passages differ, but each in its own way confirms one point: at least some of Chaucer's contemporaries did read his work attentively and with keen comprehension.

Thomas Usk might conceivably have heard Chaucer's works read, since he was in and about London in the 1380s, was hand in glove with Brembre (after 1383), and even gained provisional and ill-fated admission to the royal faction between autumn 1387 and his death in 1388. More probably, though—given his role as a rather shadowy and Pynchonesque inhabitant of what Chaucer probably considered a political demimonde—he encountered Chaucer's works in manuscript form. While working on his *Testament of Love* between late 1384 and mid-1387, he may have had access to Chaucer's *Boece* (though this notion has been challenged[65]), and he refers to Chaucer's *Troilus* in his *Testament of Love* (III.4, 248–258).[66] His unmistakable encounter with Chaucer's text occurs, however, in his use of the passage preceding Dido's complaint in the *House of Fame* (269–360). His adaptation of this passage in his *Testament* (II.3, 45–81) shows that he was well able to apprehend Chaucer's sense and even to embellish it on some occasions.

Chaucer's narrator denounces Aeneas' adoption of a fair outward manner to deceive Dido (269–285); Usk assigns similar sentiments to Love, who visits him in confinement and denounces the tendency of men to display feigned goodness in order to win women's grace (45–58). Chaucer encapsulates his point in a proverb:

> . . . lo, thus yt fareth:
> "Hyt is not al gold that glareth."
> For also browke I wel myn hed,
> Ther may be under godlyhed
> Kevered many a shrewed vice. (271–275)

Usk's lines are parallel and—contrary to what we normally suppose of him—somewhat more direct: "For every glittring thing is nat gold; and under colour of fayre speche many vices may be hid and conseled" (47–49). In fact, Usk not only catches Chaucer's sense in an economical way but goes on to embroider it sympathetically. Nearing the end of this section, Chaucer notes that a man tends to make a fair outward show until he has "caught" what he sought (280–282). Usk, adopting the same point about outward show, then expands upon the latent implications of "capture" by introducing the metaphor of the fowler, his whistle and net: "Lo! the bird is begyled with the mery voice of the foulers whistel. Whan a woman is closed in your nette, than wol ye causes fynden" (54–56). I have discussed elsewhere Usk's keen attentiveness to Chaucer's verse, but the brief examples given here should confirm his ability to read Chaucer with care even as he bent him to his own uses.

Written between Chaucer's death in 1400 and Scogan's own death in 1407, Henry Scogan's "Moral Balade" is literally a poem of advice to princes. "To the Kynges sonnes," the heading of Shirley's Ashmole MS 59 declares, and the text that follows is addressed to "my noble sones and eek my lordes dere."[67] This poem functions as a communicative "bridge" between Scogan and his young charges by mixing deference and pedantry in reasonable proportion to the mixture of social inferiority and tutorial authority within the relationship itself.

The poem's solemnity may argue for the power of genre to constrain utterance, for Scogan's adaptation to his tutorial role, or possibly for the fact that Scogan (whose literal-mindedness is implied in Chaucer's epistle) was solemn all along. Despite his narrowing of Chaucer's tonal range, however, Scogan amply demonstrates the intimacy with Chaucer's poetry that our poet seems to have expected from members of his circle. He echoes the *Wife of Bath's Tale* and "Gentilesse" with some subtlety, he borrows from the *Monk's Tale,* and he finally quotes "Gentilesse" outright and in full. Some recollection of lines 1119–22 of the *Wife of Bath's Tale* and lines 16–17 of "Gentilesse" is embodied in Scogan's remark that virtue may not be inherited:

> He sayde, the fader whiche is deed and grave,
> Biquath nothing his vertue with his hous
> Unto his sone . . . (67–69)

A subsequent use of the *Wife of Bath's Tale* is so dutifully exact that it moves editor Skeat to quotation marks:

> Thus "by your eldres may ye nothing clayme,"
> As that my mayster Chaucer sayth expresse,
> "But temporel thing, that man may hurte and mayme." (97–99)

Consistent with his argument is an enumeration of princes that "cam fro povertee to hy degree" (167), and his positive citation of Tullius Hostilius and Julius and his negative mention of Nero, Balthasar, and Antiochus seem based entirely on precedents provided by Chaucer—the first from the *Wife of Bath's Tale* and the other three from the *Monk's Tale.* His comment on Antiochus and his chair ("Loke how Antiochus fil fro his char, / That he his skin and bones al to-tar!"—177–178) seems a direct echo of Chaucer's lines in the *Monk's Tale* ("For he so soore fil out of his char / That it his limes and his skyn totar"—VII.2610–11). But his ultimate act of deference to Chaucer's work is undoubtedly the inclusion of a complete (and carefully transcribed) text of "Gentilesse" within the body of his poem, dutifully marked off with "and of this thing herke how my mayster seyde" (104). Nor is Scogan's use of Chaucer's poem unconsidered; he shows some talent as an interpreter of Chaucer's poetry. Modern critics have disagreed about whether the "first stok, fader of gentilesse" with which Chaucer's poem begins is God (Christ) on the one hand or a worthy human ancestor on the other.[68] Scogan takes a clear and persuasive position, explaining within the body of his verse that "than is god stocke of vertuous noblesse" (100).

For all his deference, Scogan shows himself willing in the final analysis to alter Chaucer's meaning to suit purposes of his own. Even though Chaucer's poem contains virtually nothing about youth (touching upon it only obliquely in reference to inheritance), Scogan characterizes it as a complaint on "the losse in youthe of vertue" (128), to further his own motive of persuasive address to the young princes. He is closely acquainted with Chaucer's poetry, and he is prepared to open his poem to Chaucer's voice and to credit his master extensively for his borrowings. He seems a good deal less interested, however, in responding to Chaucer's actual sense, or to such formal traits as openness to generic mixing, shifts in tone, rejection of the singular authority of monovocalism in favor of multivocalism, or the reconciliation of competing voices. For evidence of a thoroughgoing appreciation of these and related elements of Chaucer's poetry, we must turn to another member of his circle: John Clanvowe.

The most "Chaucerian" of fourteenth-century poems, the *Boke of Cupide* is labeled "Explicit Clanvowe" in the colophon of one mid-fifteenth-century manuscript.[69] Fifteenth-century attributions are notoriously fanciful, but I am inclined to take this one seriously and to connect it with John Clanvowe, Chaucer's known associate in the Ricardian faction. Several considerations support his authorship. His dealings with Chaucer would have permitted him access to Chaucer's poetry of the mid-1380s, especially to two poems from which borrowings abound in the *Boke of Cupide*—the *Parliament of Fowls* and the *Knight's Tale*. John Clanvowe is known to have been an author, since the devotional treatise "The Two Ways" is almost certainly written by him.[70] Finally, arguments for the only other Clanvowe seriously advanced as a candidate, Thomas, have proven unsubstantial.[71] The principal argument for John Clanvowe—his involvement with Chaucer in the matter of Cecily Champain suggests a degree of involvement that could extend to literary discipleship, and his literary discipleship argues that his surety for Chaucer was undertaken from friendship rather than as a routine factional assignment—may be admitted to have a certain circularity. Still we should make what we can of the few facts available to us, and, circular or not, the conjunction of the facts that John Clanvowe was an associate of Chaucer and a likely author in his own right would seem legitimately to support the proposition that he is the one.

Unlike the *Testament of Love* (which cites Chaucer in III.4) and the "Moral Balade" (which lauds Chaucer as Scogan's "mayster"), the *Boke of Cupide* refrains from mention of Chaucer by name. Yet, while Usk and Scogan eulogize Chaucer and use his works in particular ways, neither seems to have explored in depth the formal or stylistic precedents offered by his major works. Clanvowe, mentioning Chaucer not at all, shows in his poem a deep level of assimilation of Chaucer's poetic accomplishment in such major poems as the *Parliament of Fowls* and the *Knight's Tale* and a deep level of artistic response to that achievement—so deep a response that the *Boke of Cupide* may be read not simply as a poem that stands in Chaucer's debt for particular lines and phrases, but as a virtual meditation on Chaucer's artistic example.

The question of the poem's deliberateness in evoking Chaucer and his poetic accomplishments is raised in its very first lines, which are quoted verbatim from Theseus' ironic praise of love:

> The god of love, a! benedicite,
> How myghty and how grete a lord is he!

This couplet has, as John Scattergood has pointed out, the look and feel of a piece of sententious or proverbial lore, a fact that raises in turn the possibility that Clanvowe has no intention of invoking Chaucer, meaning only to launch his own poem with an anonymous apothegm.[72] But any such deliberate suppression of Chaucer as his source is belied by the next lines of the poem, which use the succeeding lines of Theseus' speech in an unmistakable way. Theseus continues in his speech that love "can make" of each heart whatever he can devise (I.1789–90). Clanvowe picks up this phrase and proceeds to give us examples of love's impressive but unsettling power: it "can make" low hearts high and high ones low, sick well and well sick, wise folk silly and irresolute folks moral, and so on.

Theseus' lines, moreover, offer a particularly apt point of entry to the consideration of issues central to Chaucer's *Parliament of Fowls* and the *Knight's Tale*. For Theseus' speech in Chaucer is double-voiced, purporting to praise the god of love but actually (as we learn later in his speech when he comments more directly on love's irrationality and folly) mocking love's potential to turn followers into fools. The irony is double in the sense that it places two contradictory propositions before us: love *is* great, but great in its capacity to make fools of its servants. This sense—that a certain kind of passionate love is at once solemnly important and wildly irrational—underlies many of the formal dichotomies of Chaucer's poetry of the 1380s, including the contrasts between Venus' and Nature's gardens and between the avian factions respectively favoring *fin amour* and procreative love in the *Parliament,* the contrast between Troilus' idealistic intensity and the fallible earthy object toward which he directs it, and the degree to which Palamon and Arcite's hot pursuit of Emily blinds them to the capricious workings of destiny in spheres beyond human control.

In launching his poem as he does, Clanvowe has not simply seized upon a neatly self-contained maxim, but has chosen a couplet charged with implications that touch large formal and conceptual issues. Nor does Clanvowe fail to see the possibilities that attend his choice; he explores the contradictions between views of love as both admirable and destructive in the debate of his nightingale and cuckoo. One can hardly maintain that every use of a contradictory position to generate poetic debate is specifically Chaucerian, since the *debat/conflictus* tradition in both Latin and Old French poetry by far antedates either Chaucer's or Clanvowe's poems.[73] Yet Clanvowe's own urbanely impartial attitude toward the respective poles of his debate, and his extension of the debate into such correlative subjects as the social basis of the relation between attitudes, artistic styles, and issues of reception, have a flavor that—for all the looseness with which we usually use the word—seems particularly Chaucerian.

Clanvowe's nightingale and cuckoo embrace polar attitudes toward love, the former believing it to be the source of "al goodnesse, / Al honour and al gentilnesse" (151–152) and the latter regarding it as the source of "disease and heuynesse, / Sorow and care and mony a grete seknesse" (171–172). The complexity of their debate is enhanced, however, by its extension into thematically related areas. As in the *Parliament of Fowls,* the different views of love are seen as socially based; the nightingale expects her views on love to appeal to everyone "that gentil ys of kynde," and accuses the cuckoo of revealing a "cherles herte." Most appropriate in a poem that I have already characterized as being "about" Clanvowe's relations with literary tradition generally and the example of Chaucer in particular, the two views of love are linked to matters of art and aesthetics. The nightingale's voice is "clere" (99) while the cuckoo's is "foule" (94); the nightingale's song is stylistically intricate or "queynte" (123) while the cuckoo's is direct or "pleyn" (118); in addition to being bloody-minded, the nightingale's cry of "ocy! ocy!" or "kill! kill!" (124) is characterized by the cuckoo as elitist and obscure—"Who myght wete," he asks, "what that shulde be?" (125).

The debate is terminated rather than resolved. The nightingale, having argued that love rewards "whom him likes," finds herself unable to reply to the cuckoo's charge that love is diverse and willful, and her anger and frustration silence her ("I can for tene sey not oon worde more"—209). Hearing her wish to be revenged upon the cuckoo, the narrator lurches into action, driving him away with a stone. The narrator's actions place him emphatically in the nightingale's camp, as have his words and actions throughout, but—as in the comparable poems of Chaucer—we cannot arrive at a final judgment of his position without noting his decided limitations. Far too obtuse to command or hold our respect, he has already earned a year's bad luck in love by hearing the song of the cuckoo before that of the nightingale, and his own ally has no more comfort to give him than the rather cryptic assurance that the god of love will send "As mekil ioy . . . As euer yet he eny lover sende" (254–255)—a consolation already somewhat tainted by the revelations of the cuckoo. He seems fatally injured by the parting taunt of the cuckoo ("Farewel, farewel, papyngay"—222) and weakens himself still more by seeming unsure of whether he has been insulted ("As thogh he had scorned, thoghte me"—223). This limited and enfeebled promotion of the nightingale does little to turn our sympathies her way. In fact, the nightingale has—if anything—lost the debate and is less than successful in convincing the other birds to sustain her complaint against the cuckoo (they decide instead to hold a parliament, at which the cuckoo will be allowed to speak).

The use of an evidently limited narrator is not of course strictly "Chaucerian," but rather the common property of an entire tradition that reaches at least as far as Boethius, with his need for Lady Philosophy's advice, and is elaborated by the poets of the French love visions. Closer still to home is the bedazed and obtuse Amans of Gower's *Confessio,* and with respect to his example Clanvowe's narrator might well be considered at least as "Gowerian" as "Chaucerian." But Clanvowe's handling of his narrator within the total framework of his poem does have still more in common with the example of Chaucer, when we consider the absence of *other* authoritative voices from his poem. Gower's *Confessio* introduces the decidedly authoritative voice of Genius, which resolves differences and effects the reformation of Amans, resolving the issues of the poem and transforming it into a unified and ultimately monological statement. The *Boke of Cupide* offers no voice more authoritative than that of its fallible narrator, allowing him to report the multiple voices of his dream but finally denying him the prestige or cogency to reconcile them or to resolve the multiple issues of the poem. This use of the narrator as a way of maintaining the open form of the poem and a competition of values within the world of the poem may not be uniquely Chaucerian, but it is certainly consistent with distinctively Chaucerian strategies as we have come to know them.[74]

These passages by Usk, Scogan, and Clanvowe remind us that, however fictionalized the devices by which Chaucer reaches out to his audience, the audience itself was not a fiction. Three real authors are listening attentively, adapting lines from Chaucer, and—in Clanvowe's *Boke of Cupide*—assimilating central devices as well. With respect to Clanvowe, and with respect to Scogan and Bukton and Vache as addressees of Chaucer's familiar poems, we are given the unique opportunity to link poetic devices and strategies to particular persons who received (or who were expected by Chaucer to receive) them sympathetically. These devices have already been broadly characterized as including the mixing of generic expectations, shifts in perspective and tone, rejection of a singularly authoritative narrative voice in favor of multiple voices, and a willingness to leave such voices in competition—qualities characteristic of what might be considered open rather than closed and hierarchical poetic forms. From the evidence of Chaucer's familiar poems and Clanvowe's poem, we may conclude that these characteristically Chaucerian devices were received with particular warmth by his rather close social counterparts. Putting it slightly differently, Chaucer's familiar poems and Clanvowe's poem may be viewed as held in common by speakers and by addressees who are their near-social equals, depending on and celebrating certain capacities for delight and habits of mind: nimbleness, alertness to tone, ability to entertain multiple points of view, and sensitivity to the social relatedness of seemingly literary address.

The sense of an immediate audience dims within the *Canterbury Tales,* even as Chaucer's sense of an audience in posterity seems to grow. At times he seems to turn away from his core audience altogether, as when he shapes poems like "Lack of Steadfastness" and "To His Purse" toward royal addressees or advises princes in the *Tale of Melibee.* Yet, as we have seen, Chaucer expected Bukton to know the *Wife of Bath's Tale,* and we know that Scogan knew it well and that Clanvowe not only knew the *Knight's Tale* but incorporated some of its elements into his own verse. Such incidental and accidentally preserved scraps of information remind us that—even as the membership shifted within Chaucer's core audience and even as the vicissitudes of his career raised obstacles to regular contact—such an audience did not cease to exist for him as an inspiration and an animating ideal.

The supposition that Chaucer's poetry normally enjoyed at least some exposure to a reasonably congenial contemporary audience invites us to consider its reception within a historical frame. I will return now to the poetry itself, viewing it as a socially conditioned bridge between Chaucer and a similarly situated audience. So considered, certain of Chaucer's themes—particularly those involving hierarchy and community, human ties, and the bonds that sustain them—gain special immediacy as charged social communication. So too will some of the more apparently formal or aesthetic aspects of his work gain added implication as products of socially conditioned choice and bearers of socially determined meaning.

4 ⊠ Selflessness and Selfishness

PARTIALLY lost to us, but available to members of Chaucer's immediate circle, is the social comedy inherent in the clash of characters who entertain different assumptions about social hierarchy and social responsibility.

Jostling both as tellers of Chaucer's narratives and as persons within them are characters with the most divergent views of themselves and their relation to society. Some behave as if the traditional ordering of estates within a hierarchical frame is undisturbed, as if they are still bound by sacral ties of obligation to their superiors and to the maintenance of the system as a whole. Others seem wholly emancipated into a relatively uncharted area, in which an absence of established obligations permits them to form associations designed to further personal agendas or special interests. Characters of the more traditional sort tend to shape their behavior toward transcendent principles and designs, deferring to the influence of an order that is unseen but deeply felt. The other sort, often members of more recently emergent social groups and in any event possessed of a sensibility rarely encountered in earlier medieval centuries, tend to live very much in this world and to shape their behavior toward the attainment of material goals. The former seem unhurried and barely aware of time. Disposed to static "stances," [1] they barely interact with the people around them, except when their own sense of social obligation is activated by the need to play an adjudicative or mediative role. The latter display endless bustle and activity, a constant and almost excruciating awareness of the people around them, and a penchant for easy and opportunistic entry into lateral relations of fraternity with their social equals. The more traditional characters have a special attraction to oaths and sworn relations, with their implied promise that worldly relations can be rescued from contingency and fixed in some meaningful relation to an unseen world of transcendent values. The more worldly characters have their own kind of attraction to oath taking, and in fact engage in it at the drop of a hat, but they are likely to manipulate the forms of the chivalric oath or vow for their own cynical and decidedly short-term purposes.

Socially Defined Behavior on the Pilgrimage

One thing that unites the traditional characters is a willingness to efface the claims of self in favor of a transcendent ideal. This selfless tendency is embodied most clearly in the three most traditional characters of the Canterbury pilgrimage—the Knight, the Parson, and the Plowman—who are of course drawn from the three recognized orders of feudal society.[2]

All the pilgrims are to one degree or another exemplary of the estates from which they are drawn,[3] but each of these three characters collaborates in an energetic presentation of himself as an exemplar of certain transcendent values. A character's "port" or bearing is a matter over which he or she exercises a certain amount of control; for example, Shame in the *Romaunt of the Rose* believes herself to have trespassed and thus deliberately adopts a humble "port," choosing to wear a nun's veil instead of a wimple as an outward manifestation of her inner feeling (3861–65). So too does Chaucer's Knight carry himself in a fashion that assures us that his inner thoughts will never lead him to abuse his chivalric skills, presenting to the world a "port as meeke as is a mayde" (I.69).

The Knight's bearing is borne out both in what he does and in what he does not do. Notable among his achievements are his fifteen "mortal batailles" (I.61), which establish him as a knight who is doing what he ought to do, eschewing domestic quarrels and profit-making pursuits in order to engage in strenuous activity abroad.[4] Equally notable, though, are those acts and ostentations that the Knight deliberately avoids. As Chaucer asserts in emphatic quadruple negative, he refrains from speaking any kind of rudeness to anyone at all: "He nevere yet no vileynye ne sayde / In al his lyf unto no maner wight" (I.70–71). In keeping with his self-imposed restraint is the modesty of his retinue; he is accompanied only by his son (an esquire of the traditional sort—that is, a young man engaged in military support services prior to his own assumption of the responsibilities of knighthood) and by one yeoman.[5] The Knight's decision to ride with a single servant is—as we are to learn in the portrait of the Yeoman—a matter of free choice rather than of military or social necessity, presumably conditioned by the spiritual aims of the pilgrimage itself: "A yeman hadde he and servantz namo / At that tyme, for hym liste ride so" (I. 101–2).[6] The fact that the Knight has curtailed his retinue voluntarily suggests that he has further resources on which he might have drawn—resources derived either from possession of his own lands and rents or at the very least from a secure relation to his lord (I. 47). Whether bound by the most traditional ties of vassalage or simply of lifetime indenture, he nevertheless stands in a firm rather than ephemeral relation to a hierarchy of earthly attachments.

The Knight's fixed position in the earthly hierarchy is of importance to his whole portrait, which resolves varied impulses into a single stance exemplifying the ideals to which he has committed himself. Although Jill Mann, noting Chaucer's emphasis on the Knight's attachment to chivalric virtues "fro the tyme that he first bigan / To riden out" (I. 44–45), points to a "time dimension" in the portrait,[7] the actual effect of Chaucer's treatment of time is to dissolve chronological differences. Chaucer's "fro the tyme" suggests that the Knight has not developed or changed, but has been this way from the very beginning of his career. Also fortifying this suggestion of persistence in virtues is his invariable choice of battles against pagans instead of the more urgently publicized and frequently more rewarding national campaigns against French, Castilian, or Scottish Christians urged throughout the second half of the century. The campaign list itself, stretching as it does over nearly five decades, finally tumbles together places and dates in a fashion that defeats any impression of linear time, suggesting that the important thing is not so much the particular campaigns as the permanent ideals manifested in their selection. The "holy" emphasis of the Knight's campaigns, an attire and equipage so simple and practical as to be virtually ascetic, his haste to commit himself to a pilgrimage upon his return to his native land—all suggest what Mann identifies as a religious dimension to his role, a sense in which service to an earthly lord is ultimately coextensive with a lifelong, unvarying commitment to a divine lord.[8]

Even more completely shaped to the contours of a transcendent ideal is the conduct of the Parson, whose devoted services as shepherd to his fold offer a virtual type of Christ.[9] His whole life is an enactment of Christ's lore, embodied in pastoral deeds before it is taught in any more abstract way (I. 497, 528). The narrator, himself aware of (and actually overwhelmed by) the exemplary importance of the Parson's conduct, drives the point repeatedly home, stressing the "noble ensample" he gave to his sheep (I. 496), his "ensample" of personal purity (I. 505), and his effort to draw folk to heaven "by good ensample" (I. 520). The exemplary value of the Parson's life is not, however, simply in the eye of the beholder. The Parson chooses, in the terminology of the narrator, to "give" a noble example to his parishioners (I. 496), recapitulating over and over again the essential lesson of Christ's charity. For all its diligent activity, the Parson's life is finally static and iconic in its rejection of the variation or change inherent in earthly time.

Also shaping his life to reflect his devotion to a transcendent and permanent ideal is the Plowman. He is evidently the Parson's "brother" (I. 529), both by birth and in the mutuality of their determination that an inner attachment to God's love be reflected in acts of charity and Christian obedience. As with most of his fellow *cultores* in the second half of the fourteenth century, the Plowman enjoys an element of personal choice in the use to which he puts his labors. He is evidently a freeholder (one of Bracton's *liberi)* rather than a villain or bondperson *(villani)*, or, if he is still in some sense bound, his opportunity to work for "hire" (I. 538) suggests at least his ability to arrange the commutation of duties by cash payment.[10] Though free to work for wages, however, he eschews the opportunity for individual profit, working instead "withouten hire" for the truly poor. Possessed of modest goods (of *catel* in the form, presumably, of produce and livestock), he freely and obediently takes these possessions into account in the computation of his tithes (I. 539–540). Such is the power of Chaucer and Langland to create tradition that Chaucer's obedient Plowman is sometimes taken as an expression of established tradition of "sancta rusticitas"—but in fact the plowmen of satiric poetry were often depicted as lazy, irreligious, and greedy.[11] Rather than drawing upon an established commonplace, Chaucer gives us a new kind of plowman, one freed from the self-indulgence and the restless covetousness of his time.

The repose achieved by each of these three characters cannot be confused with sloth. Each is among the least idle on the pilgrimage, deeply involved in the kind of "leveful bisynesse" or permissible activity that will be contemplated by the Second Nun (VIII. 5). Yet each is free of the self-aggrandizing restlessness exhibited by so many of the other pilgrims. Each is untroubled by desire for anything that anyone else on the pilgrimage has the power to give, and hence is essentially self-contained, with no need to make himself agreeable to anyone.

The Parson is even prepared to be downright unmannerly when his values are threatened or ignored. We learn in his portrait that he is perfectly ready to "snybben" or rebuke spiritually obstinate persons, whether "of heigh or lough estat" (I.521–523). We encounter just such a rebuke in the canceled epilogue to the *Man of Law's Tale,* when the Parson responds sharply to Harry Bailly's invocation of "Goddes bones" (II.1166, 71), and his preference for unmediated doctrine over fabulous or invented narrative causes him to be equally abrupt in his response to Harry's eventual request for a fable (X.29, 31).

Less severely tested but still aloof in his own way is the Knight. Consistent with all we know about him, he shows good grace in launching into his tale, "obedient / To kepe his foreward" (I.851–852). Well mannered as he is, though, his conduct here and elsewhere on the pilgrimage seems an extension of his social role; his interventions are never acts of self-assertion but seem motivated by continued respect of the "foreward" (I.848) that all the pilgrims have made. His interruption of the Monk's lugubrious and potentially protracted narrative is surely a socially responsible act.[12] And certainly his reconciliation of the Pardoner and Harry Bailly is responsive to the venerable tradition that knights fulfill their civic responsibility by protecting the social order.[13]

In short, the behavior of the Parson and the Knight among their fellow pilgrims offers exemplary testimony to the transcendent values toward which each life is oriented. The same may, to strain a point, be said of the Plowman's silence: although his tale is not yet included within Chaucer's design, and we thus cannot know exactly what Chaucer might have intended for him, we can be rather certain that it would not have involved a high degree of loquacity or conviviality. For, like the Knight and the Parson, he conducts himself in ways that seem not to require the approval of others. His attention is finally oriented away from his fellows—whom he loves "for Cristes sake" rather than for themselves alone (I.537)—and toward God.

Still the orientation toward transcendent values exhibited by these representatives of the three traditional social estates is liable to appear in debased or less attractive guises. Their selflessness is susceptible to confusion with less commendable forms of self-sufficiency. The Prioress, for example, gives even more thought to matters of "port" than does the Knight, a point emphasized by the narrator's comment that she "peyned" herself to imitate the manners of court and to be stately and worthy of reverence (I.138–141). But her pains are finally directed toward the fine details of her own behavior rather than toward a transcendent code, seigneurial or divine. This same motive of projecting an idea of the self may appear elsewhere on the social scale, as in the case of the Merchant, who has adopted a solemn manner of speech in order to encourage potential investors ("His resons he spak ful solempnely, / Sownynge alwey th'encrees of his wynnyng"—I.274–275).[14] Of course, adopted only for such a limited purpose, the Merchant's veneer of solemnity lacks the depth or resonance of the stances adopted by the Knight, the Parson, and the Plowman; so we cannot be surprised when he launches into his emotional, self-lacerating, and ultimately quite unsolemn account of his trials in marriage.

The Merchant's idea that he might increase his winnings by portraying himself as a person of solemn reserve may represent one of the frequent cases described so well by Sylvia Thrupp in which the ideals of the more prosperous merchants and the new gentry interpenetrate. The Merchant's assumed solemnity separates him from the more boisterous and convivial conduct of most representatives of newly emergent middle strata on the pilgrimage. The aloofness and other-worldliness that give the Knight, Parson, and Plowman so detached and self-sufficient an air gives way in the cases of most of the pilgrims to a decided penchant for involvement and engagement, an intense and continuing interest in each other. If the attention of the Knight, Parson, and Plowman is directed away from the pilgrimage, that of most of their fellows is very much directed toward experience in this world.

So worldly, in fact, is their interest that their very conviviality may often be seen as connected with motives of advancement. Advancement is palpably the aim of the Guildsmen, for example, who are of considerably lesser stature than the Merchant but whose level of accomplishment in lesser guilds encourages them (and their wives) to aspire to aldermanic status (I.371–378).[15] If the Knight, Parson, and Plowman are to some degree "types," each nevertheless engages in an individual form of striving distinctive to his social station; the Guildsmen have become alike in their pursuit of a common earthly goal. The Knight, Parson, and Plowman are finally solitaries, while the Guildsmen are literally indistinguishable in their submergence in the worldly ambitions peculiar to their particular social station. Their aspiration toward a socially defined and collective goal is finally embodied in their adoption of "o lyveree" (I.363), the identical costume of a parish guild or "solempne and a greet fraternitee" (I.364). Normally drawing their membership from a single class or stratum,[16] such guilds tended to represent a collective impulse toward the "comune profyte" of their members—profit, in this case, more material than spiritual.[17]

Other pilgrims also shape their behavior toward selfish objectives, in less structured and still more opportunistic ways. Notable among them is the Friar, who, "ther as profit sholde arise," makes himself "curteis . . . and lowely of servyse" (I.249, 250). Comparable is the behavior of the Reeve, who finds ways to "plesen subtilly" his lordly employer for his own profit, combining apparent friendship with finance through gifts and loans with capital taken from the lord's own substance. Similarly suspect motives underlie the behavior of the false canon of the *Canon's Yeoman's Tale* who "semed freendly" in order to extort sums from his victims, though actually was "feendly" in his motivations (VIII.1302–3).

Harry Bailly's ideal for the company of pilgrims is to sustain a fellowship without "debaat" (III.1288), in the spirit of the guild ordinances that seek to encourage amity in the interest of the profit of all members.[18] Needless to say, the pilgrims repeatedly fall short of this ideal, lapsing—for all their knack of serviceability—into wrangles and personal quarrels that reverberate through their conflicting narratives. Yet these quarrels actually issue from the same proclivities as their capacity for bonhomie. For their quarrels are, like their friendships, primarily intended to project a certain "estaat," a certain professional or vocational position, a potentiality for productive (and usually profitmaking) activity in the world. This is the affirmative sense in which the land-buying Sergeant of the Law and the landholding Franklin are knit in a vocational/ideological commonality of purpose (I.331) and also the sense in which the Summoner and Pardoner, as two scammers who play for their own advantage upon people's spiritual hopes and fears, are united as apt "compeers" (I.670). This is also the negative basis of the "territorial" struggles of the deceitful Miller (I.562) and the deceitful Reeve (I.604), and of the mutual accusations of those two rivals in extortion, the Summoner and the Friar. As Jill Mann has shown, Chaucer's Prologue presents us with "a society in which work as a social experience conditions personality."[19] Once we have ventured beyond those comparatively reserved characters whom I have called "traditional," we find ourselves in a world in which the possibility of profit in the exercise of a worldly vocation encourages a high velocity and intensity of interaction, whether amiable or contentious in nature.

Unlike the sworn and permanent relations by which such characters as the Knight and the Parson orient themselves to a world of timeless values, the more temporary alliances that draw other characters into association need constant priming, furbishing, redefinition, and reward. We have seen that, in later fourteenth-century society generally, sworn and theoretically permanent relations of vassalage were rapidly being replaced by more temporary and more opportunistic forms of alliance. And so too does Chaucer's poetry acknowledge a debasement of traditional relations and their replacement by a variety of other forms, all of which are less securely situated within a vertical hierarchy, are freer-floating and more opportunistic in their very nature.

The Debased Language of Sworn Relations

Chaucer's works are marked by a continuing conflict between the relative selflessness of characters oriented to transcendent ideals and the selfishness of characters who find their objects of aspiration in this world. The spiritual and ethical question of the ends of human aspiration is in some respects fought out in the struggle for possession of the terminology of sanctified relations—of sworn homage, of oaths taken and received, of *trouthe* in all its ramifications. Whether these terms are to remain fixed in their traditional meanings, or are to be appropriated to debased ends, is a constant theme and a significant social question in its own right.

Much poetry of the thirteenth and fourteenth centuries depends on the relations of vassalage as an undiminished reservoir of precedent and meaning. A particularly common instance would be those amatory poems in which the lover is represented as a feudal vassal, paying homage either to love itself or to the object of his love. A representative case, with which Chaucer himself would undoubtedly have been acquainted,[20] is that moment in Guillaume's section of the *Roman de la Rose* at which the lover enters the "servyse" of the god of love. The relation between the god of love and the lover begins as one of conquest, with the lover's resistance having been weakened by the transforming assault of Cupid's arrows and the god of love requiring his submission. When the god of love discovers the lover's gentility by his speech, however, he offers the opportunity not of simple submission or coerced service but of service based on full homage:

> . . . now I wot wel uttirly
> That thou art gentyll by thi speche.
> . . . I wole that thou obay

> Fully, for thyn avauntage,
> Anoon to do me heere homage. (1986–87, 1996–98)

The lover's homage is conceived and represented with full tradition. He first kneels "with hondis joynt" (2037), as he would in fulfillment of the vassal's role in the ceremony of *immixio manum*—a gesture ordinarily completed when the lord enclosed the vassal's hands within his own.[21] An even more venerable gesture follows, patterned on the *osculum,* in which the lord places a kiss upon the mouth of his follower.[22] In this case, however, the roles are reversed, with the servant planting the kiss, in suggestion of his eager predisposition to place himself in the service of love (2039–40).

This act of homage is in no simple sense "about" feudal relations in thirteenth-century France—yet it does ultimately depend upon a perception of feudal relations. As with any metaphorical utterance, this one draws on two semantic domains (the one, of course, pertaining to relations of lordship and vassalage and the other pertaining to the lover's submission to strong feelings of love and loyalty toward his love object).[23] At an earlier point in the development of literary theory, one might have said that the text is only ostensibly about the domain of feudal relations and is actually about the domain of love relations. Such an assertion might have used the terminology of I. A. Richards: the language of feudal relations provides the "vehicle" of the metaphor, but its "tenor" has to do with love.[24] Recent theory suggests, however, that so hard and fast a distinction between the two semantic domains cannot finally be maintained. The instability of reference common to all language and particularly characteristic of poetic language argues that the passage is not just about homage or about love, but that it is about *both* homage and love. In what sense may vassalage be said to be present in the poem? Not simply as objective social "fact," for the treatment of vassalage in this poem is no less "literary" than its treatment of love. (The custom of the *osculum* had fallen into disuse in thirteenth-century France, as had the custom of *immixio manum* in fourteenth-century England; the meaning of the lover's kiss now lies as much within literary as social tradition.[25]) Like all components of literary meaning, however, the lover's vassalage depends on the audience's extraliterary experience. Even though the facts of vassalage as presented in Guillaume's *Roman* may no longer be strictly current, the metaphor still depends for its viability on an audience that imagines at least the possibility of a feudal relation. Guillaume reconstitutes and partly idealizes the idea of feudal vassalage in the language of his poem, but he depends upon its survival as a dream, a "type" of earthly relations, a reservoir of social meaning on which he can draw with some confidence.[26]

Yet Chaucer's use of vassalage as a component of metaphorical meaning suggests that the concept itself is under more severe challenge than we would imagine from reading Guillaume. Neither Chaucer's nor Guillaume's metaphorical uses of vassalage can be taken as direct social data. But Chaucer's more equivocal evocations of vassalage ultimately suggest growing trouble for the social institution on which they depend.

Although Chaucer's poetry includes many would-be vassals of love, the nature of their commitment is invariably called into question. We are presented with a host of false swearers, such as Jason in the *Legend of Good Women* or Arcite in *Anelida and Arcite* or the shifty tercelet in the *Squire's Tale*—opportunists who cannot wait to subscribe to any oath that will advance their temporary interests, but who have no intention of engaging in the protracted responsibilities of true vassalage. When we do encounter serious vassals of love, such as the tercel eagles in the *Parliament of Fowls,* the social utility of their commitment is challenged by other poetic voices and perspectives. The royal tercel of the *Parliament* certainly cannot be faulted for his constancy. His perseverance in service, even if unrequited, is central to his plea, as in his emphatic rejection of the notion that service might have an outer limit: "Ne nevere for no wo ne shal I lette / To serven hire" (439–440). This view is, however, watered down with the less-patient pleas of the other tercels and ultimately assailed by the down-to-earth lower fowl, who see the protracted nature of the tercels' pleading, and the pledge of unvarying service upon which it is based, as an impediment to "comune spede" (507). The lower fowl push for a verdict, a more practical recognition of the necessity for concluding arrangements in chronological time. Still, though the royal tercel does not win the debate, he does not lose it either.[27] He finds his apologists ("'Nay, God forbede a lovere shulde chaunge!' / The turtle seyde"—582–583), and his persistence may finally be taken as an oblique compliment to the persistence of the ideals he espouses. More telling still are those passages indicating change in the very institutions of vassalage and their lessened availability as stable objects of reference.

As I have suggested, the ties binding the feudal retinue were attenuated in the later fourteenth century, with the aspiration to permanence embodied in sworn vassalage replaced by a variety of looser and more frankly self-interested affiliations. These changes did not escape the explicit notice of the poets. Langland, for example, emphasizes the role of meed or false reward in retinue building and in legal maintenance:

> Emperours and Erles and alle manere lordes
> Thorugh giftes han yonge men to yerne and to ryde.
> The Pope with hise prelates presentz vnderfongeth,
> And medeth men hymseluen to mayntene hir lawes. (III.213–216)

Gower argues, conversely but just as damagingly, that the knightly retinue is now composed of simpleminded rich people who buy their way in:

> Cils qui sont povres indigentz
> Ne sont pas de sa retenue;
> Ainçois les riches innocentz,
> Qui font a luy les paiementz,
> Itieux pour son proufit salue. (*Mirour*, 23744–48)

And Chaucer's Parson, agreeing with the thirteenth-century *Tractatus de Viciis* that the holding of large "meynee" is evidence of prideful superfluity and lack of social utility,[28] broadens his critique in several directions. Exploitation of the people and civil extortion may, he suggests, underlie the practice, when "that meynee is felonous and damageous to the peple by hardynesse of heigh lordshipe or by wey of offices" (x.437). And some lords, he hints, may sell positions in their retinues for personal profit, in which case "swiche lordes sellen thanne hir lordshipe to the devel of helle" (x.438).

A consequence of such social turbulence, and its entry into literary discourse, is that even Chaucer's most metaphorical uses of the language of vassalage recognize a shift in the referential ground under his chosen semantic field. Consider, for example, the "Complaint unto Pity," in which the narrator represents himself as a faithful retainer, seeking to deliver a "bille" to Pity. His intent has been to deliver a traditional complaint, emphasizing his "trouthe" and his long service. Arriving, he finds that Pity has been supplanted by Cruelty, and that Cruelty has formed a new affinity in which she has enlisted Beauty, Jolity, Youth, and other crucial followers, "confedred both by bonde and alliaunce." Cruelty has not refrained from deception in forming this new grouping; she has operated "under colour of womanly Beaute" and her ultimate object is to expel Pity from her "heritage." This new affinity means trouble for Pity's old and faithful retainers, who would remain obedient:

> . . . but ye the rather take cure
> To breke that perilouse alliaunce,
> Ye sleen hem that ben in your obeisaunce.

For his part, the narrator will persevere in loyal service:

> . . . yet my trouthe I shal sustene
> Unto my deth, and that shal wel be sene.
> . . . my spirit shal never dissevere
> Fro youre servise for any peyne or woo.

The "Complaint" merges two semantic domains—one drawn from the language of service and another drawn from amorous relations, with the emphasis falling now on the one domain ("breke that perilouse alliaunce") and now on the other ("Let som strem of youre lyght on me be sene"). The emphasis on love is of course consistent with the thrust of the poem as a whole, and the poem is about love in that sense. But, as in Guillaume's earlier and more traditionally conceived treatment of the vassalage of love, the "Complaint" is also about what has happened to the language of relatedness in the last decades of the fourteenth century. Chaucer gives us a full experience of the instability of relations in his day and uses that very sense of instability as a component of meaning. His narrator is, if not a feudal vassal, at least a retainer of the most traditional sort, one who has no intention of altering his allegiance in the face of unfavorable circumstances. Much of the energy of the poem derives from the ways in which Cruelty's new affinity forces the narrator to confront emergent concepts of alliance and the deceptive and opportunistic practices that underlie them. I do not mean to be too solemn in my analysis of this poem, which is finally graceful and witty in the elaboration of its conceit. But the conceit itself depends on the emergence of new and unstable forms of relationship which are offered for our disapproval.

The replacement of stable lordship by shifting alliances is not the only degradation of traditional ties embodied in Chaucer's metaphorical register. Just as lordship may be treated as a temporary condition, subject to rearrangement, so may the traditional vertical direction of loyalty to one's lord be subject to horizontal redirection, toward one's fellows in a particular social situation. The concept of "brotherhood in arms" was, as Maurice Keen has shown, a potentially exalted alternative to relations of vassalage in the later middle ages.[29] Yet, when all its reverberations are considered, the commitment to fraternal relations for purposes of common profit turns out to be considerably more suspect than we might initially suppose. While the profession of brotherhood to one's immediate peers or social group might well seem to us more egalitarian than a commitment to traditional hierarchy, it held for the medieval sensibility a possible implication of connivance and dubious alliance, of self-advancement that neglects the total Christian community.

A modest but revealing case in point occurs near the end of the *House of Fame*. Describing the House of Rumor, the narrator reports instances when "at ones / A lesyng and a sad soth sawe" (2088–89) sought to exit simultaneously from a small window. Struggling between themselves for precedence, they agreed on a mutually advantageous compromise:

> . . . ech of hem gan crien lowde,
> "Lat me go first!" "Nay, but let me!
> And here I wol ensuren the,
> Wyth the nones that thou wolt do so,
> That I shal never fro the go,
> But be thyn owne sworen brother!
> We wil medle us ech with other,
> That no man, be they never so wrothe,
> Shal han on [of us] two, but bothe
> At ones . . ."
> Thus saugh I fals and soth compouned
> Togeder fle for oo tydynge. (2096–105, 2108–109)

Chaucer's ultimate source here is Virgil's description of Fama as "tam ficti pravique tenax quam nuntia veri" (IV.188), as much committed to the false and depraved as she is a messenger of the truth. But he elaborates his source by associating Rumor with certain established and extraliterary characteristics of sworn brotherhood: that such relations are essentially opportunistic, trumped up in response to an occasion rather than from acknowledged social necessity; that their opportunism is a source of social havoc; that the use of a sworn oath in so dubious a situation constitutes an abuse of a legitimate means of harmonizing social practice with God's larger plan.

Opportunistic Brotherhood

Chaucer's poetry not only presents a society in which vassalage has been replaced by an array of more casual relations epitomized by sworn brotherhood, but includes a critique of those relations. At the center of this critique is his repeated representation of situations in which the oaths that support sworn brotherhood are entered into casually or even cynically, with what might in earlier feudal contexts have been referred to as "mal ingan." So frequent are such transgressions that a member of Chaucer's audience soon learns to regard a character with a propensity for oaths with special suspicion, as a likely manipulator of the forms and phrases by which good faith has traditionally been affirmed.

Chaucer's concern with the subject of false swearing is textualized in the Parson's discussion of Jeremiah's stipulations on permissible swearing (in matters involving *trouthe,* judgment, or righteousness)—itself a modest expansion of the relevant sections of the *Tractatus de Viciis.*[30] But his most trenchant examinations of the practice link false swearing with the falsification of human ties, as in the *Pardoner's Tale.* There Chaucer produces a travesty both of brotherhood and of the oaths that support it, in the distorted ceremony by which the three revelers agree to seek "this false traytour Deeth":

> Lat ech of us holde up his hand til oother,
> And ech of us bicomen otheres brother . . . (VI.697–698)

This holding up of hands, while something short of *immixio manum,* is nevertheless a gesture toward solemnization. The initial gesture is further shored by a plighting of *trouthe,* by assertions that sworn brotherhood is equivalent to relationship by birth, and by those violent, gratuitous oaths on Christ's body that the Parson so deplores:

> Togidres han thise thre hir trouthes plight
> To lyve and dyen ech of hem for oother,
> As though he were his owene ybore brother.
> . . . And many a grisly ooth thanne han they sworn,
> And Cristes blessed body they torente. (VI.702–704, 708–709)

The language of brotherhood, of course, abounds within the relations of the three, as does the linked and ultimately incompatible suggestion that the purpose of such association is singular or selfish profit. ("Thow knowest wel thou art my sworen brother," says one conspirator, in broaching his plan to slay the youngest reveler and divide his gold. "Thy profit wol I telle thee anon"—VI.808–809.) In the apocalypse of self-seeking with which the tale ends, we find ample assertion of the instability of such profit-based confederacies and the baselessness of such "nedelees" oaths.

The Friar's and Summoner's tales likewise deal with the debasement of sworn brotherhood, but within a more particularized historical frame.[31] Embedded in each are feudal concepts and norms, invoked not with nostalgic but with ironic intent, to underscore their supplantation by more self-interested alliances. The Summoner of the *Friar's Tale* is, for example, situated within a mock-feudal retinue. His "lord" is an archdeacon, "a man of heigh degree" (III. 1302), and the Summoner is his retainer, ever "redy to his hond" (III. 1321). Yet, although in service, the Summoner does not lack retainers of his own; at his bidding is his own "retenue" (III. 1355), and he employs its members in his enterprise of collecting the "rente" owed to his lord as his "duetee" (III. 1390–91). The effect of this language is to present the Summoner "as a type of feudal bailiff," faithfully collecting his fief-rent.[32] In fact, the patent misapplication of the images and terms of feudal vassalage to the avaricious Summoner offers the reader a way both of measuring the Summoner's own transgression and the extent of his perversion of a venerable ideal. The feudal retinue, imagined in the *Knight's Tale* to consist of gentle knights served by squires (I. 2502) and in the *Clerk's Tale* to consist of Walter's "bachelrye" (IV. 270) or household knights of highest station, here consists of "bawdes" (III. 1339) and "wenches" (III. 1355). They are not his honorable servants in peace and war, but his "approwours" (III. 1343). "Approwours" are, in the broadest sense, from Old French *apprower* (to profit), those who look after the profit or interest of an employer. Yet the term also possesses a specifically legal sense, appropriate to the Summoner's own vocation, in its application to an informer.[33] The Summoner's "approwours" are therefore confederates of a particularly shifty sort, those who thrive by denying bonds of trust. The Summoner's devotion to extortion rather than to honorable service is spelled out in other displacements of traditional meaning. The "duetee" he seeks to collect is hardly the debt of loyalty owed by the vassal to his feudal lord, the "moral, religious, social, or legal obligation" contemplated in the most traditional senses of the word.[34] Rather, the duty in question is the first occurrence in English of a new meaning of the word—more economic than sacral or social—as "a tax, fee, rent, or service."[35] Further, the particular "rente" the Summoner seeks to collect is hardly the fief-rent of feudal tradition, but merely a shakedown or "extorcioun" of a few pence (and ultimately a pan) from an impoverished widow. His service to his lord is, needless to say, only a pretense; like his fellow "baillif," he keeps for himself all that he can extort (III. 1426–34).

The Summoner places "bretherhede" before faithful service to a lord (III. 1399), and the kind of brotherhood he espouses is far from that chivalric form identified by Keen. "Thou art a bailly, and I am another" (III. 1396), the devil tells him, offering the likeness of their situations as one reason for entering into relations of "bretherhede," and then goes on to specify the motive of personal profit underlying their proposed compact: "I have gold and silver in my cheste" (III. 1400). They swear, enacting (like the revelers in the *Pardoner's Tale*) a kind of debased version of *immixio manum:* "Everych in ootheres hand his trouthe leith, / For to be sworne bretheren til they deye" (III. 1404–5). Nor is the Summoner rattled to learn that his counterpart is a fiend from hell ("though thou were the devel Sathanas, / My trouthe wol I holde to my brother, / As I am sworn"—III. 1526–28). The language of sworn brotherhood seems intended only to facilitate the actual purpose of the arrangement, which is the equitable sharing of profit:

> Taak thou thy part, what that men wol thee yive,
> And I shal myn; thus may we bothe lyve.
> And if that any of us have moore than oother,
> Lat hym be trewe and parte it with his brother. (III. 1531–34)

No division of spoils will finally be necessary, since the Summoner's intransigence ("the foule feend me fecche / If I th' excuse"—III. 1610–11) finally delivers him and the disputed pan wholly into the hands of a devil who has been less his "temptour" (in the Friar's own inadequate resume—III. 1655) than his similitude, his brother in self-interest.

Opportunistic brotherhood is also a subject of scrutiny in the *Summoner's Tale,* with the Friar seeking gain from his "leeve brother" (III. 2089) Thomas. Thomas has been enrolled in the order's lay confraternity or spiritual brotherhood, and the Friar attests to this membership with his assurance that "I took oure dame oure lettre with oure seel" (III. 2128).[36] The sharing of material fortunes within this opportunistic brotherhood is, in a sense, Thomas' satiric target when he premises his flatulent gift on a "condicion" (III. 2132) of equal sharing. As in the *Friar's Tale,* though, the debased brotherhood the Friar offers Thomas is not merely criticized from the standpoint of its own shortcomings, but from the standpoint of a more traditional norm of good service implied by the imagery of the tale. The Friar himself is at least dimly inclined to invoke traditional concepts of service within an ordered hierarchy, supporting his own "meynee" (III. 2156), denouncing Thomas in terms of social degree ("false cherl"—III. 2153), and appealing for redress to the lord of the village's own manorial "court" (III. 2162). The Friar's appeal to such norms inevitably backfires. The lord, in fact, savors Thomas' sleight in inner monologue ("O nyce, proude cherl"—III. 2227), and the lord's retainer

Jankyn will offer the definitive appreciation of Thomas' gesture. Jankyn, "the lordes squier at the bord, / That karf his mete"—III. 2243–44), is for all his playfulness an apologist for the established order, and his prescription for the division of Thomas' fart by the thirteen friars confirms the Friar's isolation from the traditional community comprised by "the lord, the lady, and ech man, save the frere" (III. 2287).

The tales of the Pardoner, Friar, and Summoner all suggest that the driving force behind the debasement of sworn relationships is the allure of singular or personal profit. Most unsparing in its exposure of the impulse toward such profit is the *Shipman's Tale,* with its suggestion of an inextricable melding of human and monetary values, of the commodification of exchange relations in both the human and material spheres, of the extension of a mercantile ethos to all spheres of activity.[37] Here too, and perhaps even more explicitly than in the tales just considered, sworn ties are seen as wholly subject to negotiation in the quest for personal aggrandizement.

The commodification of human relations is established immediately in the tale, with the narrator's observations about the "cost" of maintaining wives, with the observation that Daun John always gives gifts to the lord and to his household when he comes to visit ("For which they were . . . glad of his comyng"—VII. 50), with the fluent negotiation by which Daun John and the Merchant's wife agree to exchange "frankes" and "flankes" (VII. 201–202). While most of the relations of the tale, including the marriage relation, are presented as economically motivated, one relationship first appears to have some potential for escaping this simple equation.

The friendship of Daun John and the Merchant predates any obvious avenue to personal advantage (they were "bothe two yborn in o village"—VII. 35) and is secured by reciprocal ties of figurative relationship ("The monk hym claymeth as for cosynage, / And he agayn"—VII. 36–37). Moreover, they have entered into what appears a long-standing relation of sworn brotherhood:

> Thus been they knyt with eterne alliaunce,
> And ech of hem gan oother for t'assure
> Of bretherhede whil that hir lyf may dure. (VII. 40–42)

However "eterne" the aspirations of this relationship, though, it is eligible for quick renegotiation once the Monk and the Merchant's wife enter into their innuendo-laden conversation. This conversation, the sexual undercurrents of which have been analyzed elsewhere,[38] is spiced throughout with self-interested oaths. The Monk begins, proposing an oath upon his breviary that he will not betray her counsel (VII. 131–133). She reciprocally swears, by the breviary and by God for good measure (VII. 134–135), disclaiming the shoddy motives that actually drive her conduct ("cosynage" and "alliance"—VII. 139) and claiming motives of a more elevated sort ("love and affiance"—VII. 140). The effect of the cynicism of these conspirators is to degrade every concept they touch, including the potentially elevated ideal of *affiance*. Derived from Old French *afiance,* or verbal reassurance that a promise will be kept, the Middle English term in the later fourteenth century generally suggests a bestowal of confidence or trust; Gawain, for example, places his *afyaunce* in the five wounds of Christ (642–643). Yet in the ethical world of this tale *affiance* seems flimsy, less trustworthy than more publicly sanctioned bonds.

Similarly unpersuasive is the barrage of oaths that now ensues. The Monk is moved by the promise of sexual favors to rewrite the history of his friendship, claiming ("by Seint Denys of Fraunce"—VII. 151) to have entered into alliance with the Merchant only to meet his wife ("This swere I yow on my professioun"—VII. 155). After a pious digression on the duties of wives, she reciprocates by denying her husband the value of a fly ("As helpe me God"—VII. 170), though she must nevertheless continue to array herself for his honor ("by that ilke Lord that for us bledde"—VII. 178). She will repay a loan from the Monk ("And but I do, God take on me vengeance / As foul as evere hadde Genylon of France"—VII. 193–194). A casualty of this barrage of oaths is, of course, the prior alliance of the Monk and the Merchant, and its basis in sworn kinship; the Monk swears ("by God and Seint Martyn") that "He is na moore cosyn unto me / Than is this leef that hangeth on the tree!" (VII. 148–150).

To suggest that the Monk and the wife are "newe Genylons," betraying their sacred ties with her sworn husband and his sworn brother, would be too elevated an interpretation of the motives at work. In fact Ganelon, or at least his era, emerges as an object of nostalgia here. The wife's Ganelon reference cuts with unintended irony, measuring the facility with which these glib oathtakers have debased the verbal currency in which they deal. It reminds the audience of a previous era in which the sacred bonds of vassalage were secure enough to permit spectacular and damnable transgression, and not simply cynical refashioning of the sort we encounter here. Like the ironical references to feudal structures and value systems buried in the tales of the Friar and the Summoner, a reminder even of a great forswearer of the past serves to reveal the shabbiness of these new forms of arrangement.

"Trouthe" in a Postfeudal Society

From the experience of these tales, we would not be far off the mark in concluding that oaths have become the exclusive tactic and refuge of scoundrels. Yet, like most social practices treated in Chaucer's poetry, the swearing of oaths is also subject to more complicated consideration, as a matter of admirable but finally untenable human aspiration and as a social institution that requires thoughtful redefinition.

Although everyone in *Troilus and Criseyde* takes oaths, fervently and with apparent sincerity, the oath's aspiration to transcend the vicissitudes of earthly time lends it perfectly to Troilus' love-struck desires. Troilus is always ready to affirm the durability of his intentions with binding oaths. He is not content, for example, just to swear secrecy to Pandarus "by that God . . . / That, as hym list, may al this world governe" (III.372–373). He goes on to swear that, rather than betray his love, he would lie "stokked in prisoun, / In wrecchidnesse, in filthe, and in vermyne" (III.380–381). And, pushing beyond words to deeds, he proposes to Pandarus that they spend the next morning making the rounds of all the temples in town, repeating his oath in each of them:

> And this in all the temples of this town
> Upon the goddes alle, I wol the swere
> To-morwe day . . . (III.383–385)

Troilus is in a fevered state, as revealed by his shocking offer to procure for Pandarus "my faire suster Polixene, / Cassandre, Eleyne, or any of the frape" (III.409–410). But, however much this uncharacteristic and decidedly impractical offer tells us about his state of mind, it need not cause us to doubt his word.

Pandarus takes the more pragmatic view of oaths that we have already encountered: his oaths are uttered in contexts that reveal their true purpose, which is invariably to achieve a practical objective. With Pandarus on the brink of informing Criseyde of Troilus' love, Chaucer takes care to emphasize the conscious artfulness of his approach ("he gan right inwardly / Byholden hire"—II.264–265) before relating his patently insincere assurance that he loves her honor and renown, "By alle the othes that I have yow sworn" (II.299). Pandarus' willingness to use oaths tactically is best illustrated in his design to bring Criseyde and Troilus together at his house. When asked by Criseyde if Troilus will be present, he first swears not (III. 570), then hints at the possibility (III. 571–572), and then—learning that Criseyde might still be concerned about appearances—frames a wide-ranging and grisly oath:

> He swor hire yis, by stokkes and by stones,
> And by the goddes that in hevene dwelle,
> Or elles were hym levere, soule and bones,
> With Pluto kyng as depe ben in helle
> As Tantalus. (III. 589–593)

Our estimate of the veracity of Pandarus' oath depends on our sense of what he is actually promising—whether that Troilus is out of town or only that all will be well. Either way we can be sure that his oath is tactical in nature, designed for the temporary objective of bringing Criseyde and Troilus together.

Troilus' oaths are fervent and impractical in their disregard of time and change; Pandarus' are calculated and shaped toward particular ends; Criseyde's are heartfelt, but subject to practical alteration according to circumstances. A case in point is the wildly inclusive oath she swears in order to affirm her *trouthe* to Troilus, unpeopling heaven, hell, and the classical kingdom of nature to persuade him that he need not execute his rash plan to steal her away:

> And this on every god celestial
> I swere it yow, and ek on ech goddesse,
> On every nymphe and deite infernal,
> On satiry and fawny more and lesse,
> That halve goddes ben of wildernesse;
> And Attropos my thred of lif tobreste
> If I be fals! Now trowe me if yow leste!
>
> And thow, Symois, that as an arwe clere
> Thorugh Troie rennest downward to the se,
> Ber witnesse of this word that seyd is here:
> That thilke day that ich untrewe be
> To Troilus, myn owene herte fre,
> That thow retourne bakward to thi welle,
> And I with body and soule synke in helle! (IV. 1541–54)

The very fervor of this oath reveals its essential unreliability. Even the often-credulous narrator of the poem more than once expresses skepticism about the sincerity of such promises. When Troilus faints beside Criseyde's bed, she revives him with "many an . . . oth"

(III. 1111), and once he has revived she restores his spirits with "swiche othes as hire leste devyse" (III. 1143). Yet the narrator here urbanely notes that the oaths are but a verbal pretext for the actual dynamics of the situation, in which "meaning" will work itself one way or another:

> Yet lasse thyng than othes may suffise
> In many a cas . . . (III. 1146–47)

Betraying Troilus, Criseyde will realize that "now is clene ago / My name of trouthe in love" (V. 1054–55). But she does not for that reason forgo the swearing of oaths. Instead she accommodates herself to the passage of time and to new circumstances by finding an object of *trouthe* closer at hand:

> But syn I se ther is no bettre way,
> And that to late is now for me to rewe,
> To Diomede algate I wol be trewe. (V. 1069–71)

Learning that Criseyde must leave Troy, Pandarus suggests to Troilus that relations succeed one another in time: "seur as day comth after nyght, / The newe love . . . / Don olde affecciouns alle over-go" (IV. 421–422, 424). Pandarus is talking "for the nones" (IV. 428), the narrator explains on his behalf, but we never doubt that he lives in a time-bound world in which commitments are subject to renegotiation as new facts emerge. We find to our sorrow that Criseyde finally lives in such a world as well. But Troilus' commitments are indivisible and eternal, aspiring to transcend time and circumstance. As he replies to his friend, "syn I have trouthe hire hight, / I wol nat ben untrewe for no wight" (IV. 445–446). Change is, for Troilus, neither desirable nor even possible; as for Pandarus' suggestion that he love another, he answers frankly that "it lith nat in my power" (IV. 458). His whole inclination is to assume an unvarying stance toward an earthly love, even though this project turns out to be impractical in the extreme. Only from the standpoint of the eighth sphere of heaven will Troilus find the eternal fixity that had previously eluded him among the "erratik sterres" (V. 1812), that "pleyn felicite" (V. 1818) he had sought vainly to constrain within the frail boundaries of earthly promises. "Who," he cries, when finally persuaded of Criseyde's betrayal, "shal now trowe on any othes mo?" (V. 1263)—and his disillusionment seems inevitable, for oaths cannot finally regulate human desire in a world ruled by time and change.[39]

Although implicated in the degradation of the sworn relations by which it has traditionally been secured, *trouthe* nevertheless remains too central a value to be relinquished without a struggle for its retrieval. This is a struggle in which Chaucer's relentlessly well-intending Franklin is not loath to engage, and he proposes a solution in his tale: *trouthe* may be preserved precisely by severing it from the outworn and unworkable restrictions of the sworn oath and by grounding it on natural and more generally available qualities of *franchise* and *gentillesse*.

The characters of the *Franklin's Tale* seek at the outset to regulate their interactions by sworn relations of a traditional character. Dorigen's and Arveragus' marriage accord is, after all, a creative extension of ideas of vassalage and lordship, with Arveragus acting both as vassal (or petitioning lover) and lord (or husband), and Dorigen acting as servant (or wife) and as lady (in both social and love relations). And theirs is a sworn understanding; he gives her his oath as a knight not to assume mastery (v.745), and she offers her *trouthe* as surety for a lifetime of true wifehood (v.759). So too will Dorigen swear a form of oath to Aurelius, when she tells him that she will grant him favors if he can do the impossible by removing the rocks that threaten her husband's safe return, "Have heer my trouthe," she says (v.998), and Aurelius later describes her *trouthe* as "sworn," though sworn in innocence (v.1601).

Yet the tale suggests that sworn promises can rigidify into constrictive legalisms. Claiming Dorigen's favors as his reward for removing the rocks, Aurelius takes care to remind her of her promise and her small accompanying nod toward *immixio manum:*

> Ye woot right wel what ye bihighten me;
> And in myn hand youre trouthe plighten ye
> To love me best . . . (v.1327–29)

As has often been observed, Dorigen's oath is less than fully binding.[40] Her promise issues from innocence (even the devil in the *Summoner's Tale* was prepared to weigh "entente"—III.1556), and Aurelius bases his own claim on the "illusioun" (v.1264) rather than the reality of the rocks' removal. Yet Chaucer's audience must now experience discomfiture as all the protagonists defy common sense and simple humanity by accepting Dorigen's word as irrevocable.

The solution proposed is to view oaths as something less than binding. For in the *Franklin's Tale* oaths are finally treated not as timeless and immutable but only (in a view the Franklin shares with most members of Chaucer's society) as finite contracts. As contracts, they are eligible for renegotiation by the parties involved[41] or for outright abandonment for good cause.[42] Aurelius seizes upon this second option of stepping out of an oath altogether when, instead of insisting that Dorigen honor her agreement, he returns to her hand "every serement and every bond / That ye han maad to me" (v. 1534–35). Within the ethos of this tale, oaths have come to appear exclusionary and out of date, and their remote and stuffy character is emphasized in Aurelius' choice of the word *serement*—a venerable and rather legalistic Anglo-Norman synonym that appears only this once in Chaucer.

Until now, every character who has sought to modify an oath has been up to no good. But the *Franklin's Tale* suggests that oaths themselves can be a part of the problem and their modification part of the solution. This modification can succeed because, at least in the world as the Franklin understands it, people are more reliable than we have assumed; within this tale, people untrammeled by sterile and restrictive covenants can be counted on to do the right thing. Even before we encounter Aurelius' and the magician's resignation of their claims in favor of the good of all, the vitality of human solidarity has been expressed at a dozen different moments. Human solidarity underlay Dorigen's promise in the first place, as she sought "in pley" (v. 988) to jest Aurelius out of his vein of piteous complaint and to illustrate the extent of her unattainability. In fact, as we might expect of a tale assigned to a teller whose whole life expresses a desire to set others at their ease, fellow feeling surfaces constantly in the narration. Dorigen's "freendes" are, for example, at constant pains to comfort her (v. 848, 895). Aurelius' brother likewise seeks to give apt "confort" (v. 1167) to him. When Aurelius and his brother meet with the magician, they talk of former "felawes" (v. 1179) and weep "many a teere" for those who have died (v. 1182). It is against this larger field of relations characterized by human friendship and concern that Aurelius decides to take into account not only his desires but "the beste on every syde" (v. 1521) and to release Dorigen from her promise. Rejecting the sterility of formalized agreements that can only bring sorrow, he chooses spontaneously to embrace the affirmative values of *franchise* (natural liberality and elevation of spirit) and *gentillesse* (the demonstrated capacity for courteous and considerate deeds)—values available not just to the particular parties to an agreement but to all persons of good will.

The Franklin's robust confidence in the accessibility of benign qualities like *franchise* and *gentillesse* has won him defenders[43] but detractors as well. Many of his critics—noting his social position as a prosperous member of the middle strata, situated as close as he can be to the *gentils* without actually being *gentil* himself—have discovered evidence of snobbery and social climbing in his hopes for his son, his lavish hospitality, and his uncritical endorsement of watered-down aristocratic values.[44] One recent scholar has sought to rescue him by arguing that he is no climber because he has already arrived; that he may be considered *gentil* already and thus has no obvious tactical objective in his endorsement of *gentillesse*.[45] The particular form of this recuperative argument is finally not tenable; whatever franklins were to become, such late fourteenth-century documents as the 1379 poll tax show that they had not yet attained gentility when the *Canterbury Tales* were composed.[46] Still, the argument that the Franklin is not a social climber makes good sense. For his views on *gentillesse* are fully and genially appropriate to the social situation he already enjoys.[47] His skepticism about sworn oaths as a basis for human agreement is quite consistent with his status as something of a "new man" in his society, a person thriving (like Chaucer himself) in a social category largely ignored in traditional descriptions of society. Furthermore, his appropriation of terms like *franchise* and *gentillesse* normally associated with the aristocratic ethos and his redefinition of those terms to render them more broadly available is precisely the enterprise that Anne Middleton has attributed to Chaucer's new men—men who " 'kidnap' terms, senses, and modes of idealization that traditionally support cultic values . . . into idealizing fictions of their own."[48]

The quality of *franchise* or natural liberality is deeply associated with the rank of franklin, in the sort of etymological tie that seemed so meaningful to medieval commentators and that may even have had something to do with Chaucer's choice of a rank for his teller: both are derived from Latin *franc* (free), referring in the former case to conduct and in the latter to nonservile birth. While the knightly Arveragus is the first exemplar of *franchise* within the tale, we are not asked to conclude that exercise of this virtue is restricted to gentlepersons. Indeed, the whole point of the tale is that such qualities are not the exclusive province of the few but are broadly available to others of varied rank. This point is made even more explicitly in the case of the companion virtue of *gentillesse*. As the magician informs us, one need not be a knight or an esquire to do a gentle deed:

> . . . God forbede, for his blisful myght,
> But if a clerk koude doon a gentil dede
> As wel as any of yow . . . (v.1610–12)

That *gentillesse* should depend less on gentle birth than on gentle deeds should not surprise us; this is the view of the old woman in the *Wife of Bath's Tale* (III.1109–16), of Chaucer's own "Gentilesse," of Scogan's closely derivative "Moral Balade." [49] Thus the Franklin reveals himself as an exponent of a view entirely appropriate to his station—in this case, the view that *trouthe* may be severed from outdated feudal practices and may inform the practices of all strata of society, gentle and nongentle alike, as they go about the business of their lives.

An earlier critical fashion encouraged us to look within literary works for "spokespersons" for their authors' views. Our own increased appreciation of Chaucer's poetry as intentional polyphony has made us properly cautious in asserting such claims today. One would be hard-pressed to prove that the Franklin's skepticism about oaths is inherently more Chaucerian than Troilus' faith in them or Pandarus' manipulation of them or Criseyde's sliding commitment to them. Nor is the Franklin's social vantage point identical to Chaucer's own. His status as a small landowner places him in a grouping with more traditional interests than those of Chaucer's fellow civil servants. The elements of traditionalism inherent in his position may have something to do with the mellow light in which he regards older genres such as the Breton *lai* (v.709–715) as well as tourneying and other venerable practices. Yet the Franklin's larger enterprise—his attempt to find a flexible and humane alternative to the feudal oath and the outworn social structure it implies—may be seen as a particularly pressing matter for those middle strata of fourteenth-century society to which Chaucer and most of Chaucer's audience and the Franklin himself all belong.

Chaucer and the members of his circle were beneficiaries of the redefinition of sworn vassalage into a variety of more supple forms. At the same time, they were in some ways burdened by their society's very success in devising a host of attractive, shorter-term arrangements, including vassalage for cash payment; sworn brotherhood; short-term retention; household service; liveries of cloth, hats, hoods, collars, signs, or badges; and a variety of other forms of alliance. One can imagine the appeal for so potentially jaded a public of the Franklin's program with its cheerful assurance that oaths can be swept away and replaced with simple good will. His program certainly is "sentimental" and would surely have been recognized as such.[50] But it remains no less urgently attractive for a fourteenth-century audience caught between an unworkable feudal ideal and a congeries of eminently workable but manifestly cynical postfeudal arrangements.

5 Time and the Social Implications of Narrative Form

CHRISTIAN ideas about time and the uses of time turn on a fundamental duality. In Augustine's words, God's *aeternitas* is immutable ("in cuius aeternitate nulla est omnino mutatio"), while *tempus* or the human time of which God is ordainer is characterized by mutability ("tempus sine aliqua mobili mutabilitate non est").[1] For God, things happen "simul," all at once; for humans, events succeed or follow one another in finite time. This is certainly the schema bequeathed to the middle ages by Boethius, who views God's simple knowing as "an eterne and presentarie estat" as opposed to the confusion of humankind, condemned to live in the "moevable and transitorie moment" (v, pr. 6). The philosophical and practical implications of these coexisting but less than fully compatible ideas of time were subject to continuing debate throughout the fourteenth century.[2]

An attitude toward time is a precondition of narrative, with different conceptions of time encouraging different narrative forms. The perspective of *aeternitas,* in which all is perceived to occur at once, encourages synchronous or extratemporal consideration of events and discourages the successive treatment of events in which narrative is usually thought to consist. The world of *tempus* or temporality, in which one moment gives way to the next ("cedit atque succedit"), supports those forms of episodic narration in which one event succeeds another in time.[3]

Among extratemporal (and hence implicitly "antinarrative") forms are certain complaints, meditations, and *visiones:* forms suited to a consideration of humanity's relation to the spiritual or transcendent, to divine order beyond apparent disorder, to the consideration of what Paul Ricoeur calls "cosmic pathos."[4] More purely temporal are episodic narratives such as early annals and those chronicles that arrange one event after another without any other evident principle of selection.[5] Also temporal are those narratives that possess an additional principle of selectivity of the sort Hayden White calls "moralization" and Ricoeur calls "configuration,"[6] permitting a narrator to choose episodes and to reject others on the basis of their contribution to a significant sequence. Among works configured by sequences of specifically human actions would be early narrative histories, romances of antiquity, and oral *contes* or *fabliaux/fablels:* forms suited to the consideration of human initiatives beginning and ending in finite time, activities subsumed under Ricoeur's "human praxis."[7]

Any such division between purely extratemporal and purely temporal narratives is obviously highly artificial. While Augustine and subsequent mystics assert the possibility of contemplating God's eternity (*Conf.* XI.xxix.39), they also know that one cannot finally stop time, that persons bound in time can finally know only *temporaliter* or temporally (*Conf.* XIII.xxix.44). So too are most forms that aspire to the extratemporal finally bound or framed temporally. Chaucer's own *Book of the Duchess,* for example, employs the resources of *visio* and complaint to engage issues of grief and consolation in ways that protract time (as in the narrator's long sufferings), idealize space (as in the "floury grene" of line 398), and suppress logical connections (as in 444–445), but it ultimately embraces episodic narrative in the Ovidian treatment of Ceyx and Alcyone and the Black Knight's account of his courtship. "Mixed" too are those narratives that are episodic and chronological in their external form, but are configured less according to human praxis than to sudden and miraculous interventions. Despite their origin in the *acta* or temporal-historical accounts of martyrdom, the saints' lives of the later middle ages were increasingly open to providential intervention and less and less concerned with causal connection among episodes.[8] Though epic and geste are ostensibly historical forms, Jacques LeGoff perceptively describes them as "negations of history by feudal society, which used historical items only to strip them of historicity in the context of an atemporal ideal."[9] The same point may be made of most medieval romance, which though episodic typically occurs in the temporal indefiniteness of what Bakhtin calls "adventure time," an indefiniteness receptive to surprising and miraculous strokes of fortune and abrupt changes of venue.[10]

Later medieval narratives thus embraced contending ideas about time. This contention may be considered on a purely aesthetic plane. Ideas about time are not, however, inherently pure but are inevitably associated with attitudes toward human action in time. We have already encountered instances in which ideas of time bear an ideological charge, as when relations of vassalage are sacralized and aligned with *aeternitas* while contractual relations are treated as a temporal and more frankly finite path to worldly advantage, or when oaths are treated as permanent while shorter-term relations of brotherhood are treated as more practical avenues to worldly benefit. Time opens narrative form—even considered objectively *as* narrative form—to socially conditioned content. Even in its most apparently aesthetic aspects, narrative cannot help being social, in the way its continuities and discontinuities speak to the purpose and meaning of human action in time.

In his constant experimentation with narrative form, Chaucer shows himself to be urgently concerned with matters of temporality in narrative. Earlier generations of Chaucer critics acknowledged this concern, but thought they detected a clear direction in his address to it: a movement from clogged and conventionalized forms of dubious narrative value, such as the vision and the complaint, to forms of freer-flowing narrativity, with episodes succeeding one another in chronological time.[11] Yet Chaucer continued throughout his career to show discomfort with the presuppositions of episodic or temporal narrative. Telltale evidence of his discomfort includes his continuing attraction to open-ended fragments, his mistrust of overly configured narratives (as revealed in his mockery of moralized conclusions), his ironic attitude toward tendentiously selective narratives (like those of the *Legend of Good Women*). Reflection on the whole of Chaucer's oeuvre suggests that he regarded temporal and highly configured narrative as only one possible form of *enditing,* and by no means the self-evidently superior form at that. Held constantly in view is the possibility of another sort of narrative that, if not wholly free of temporality, remained stubbornly open to possible extratemporal interruption by powers of fate, fortune, destiny, or providence lying beyond his human characters' reach.

Chaucer's experimentation with temporality in narrative begins as a consideration of apparently aesthetic devices. In poems like "Complaint of Mars" and "Anelida and Arcite," for example, he rather playfully and speculatively treats a single set of occurrences in both temporal and extratemporal narrative modes. Time and narrative in his more mature poems inevitably enter into more and more complex affiliation with questions of human conduct, however, and particularly with questions of human responsibility and choice. His treatment of time and narrative becomes, in a word, progressively more social.

Chaucer of the *Parliament of Fowls* and the *Canterbury Tales* foregrounds social content by advancing boldly original propositions about the preference of certain classes and vocations for certain forms of narrative—an assertion of the socially conditioned nature of apparently aesthetic endeavors.

Experiments with Narrative Form

Some of Chaucer's works that have presented formal puzzles to modern readers—such as the "Complaint of Mars" and "Anelida and Arcite"—represent his own experiments with alternative narrative possibilities, with a sense that the same situation can be treated either temporally or extratemporally and that each approach is productive in its own way.[12]

Temporality, and its bearing on human experience, is the virtual subject of the "Complaint of Mars." The introductory stanzas of the poem treat a temporal event—in this case, the awaited appearance of Venus as morning star and harbinger of the sun—as gladsome to birds and flowers and as distressing to lovers who have hidden from wicked tongues. If time can cause lovers problems, however, it can also foster cures. Just as day banishes night, so will night return: "Tyme cometh eft that cese shal your sorowe" (11). Those who have not yet chosen their *makes* should do so, and those who have already chosen should

> . . . at the leste renoveleth your servyse.
> Confermeth hyt perpetuely to dure,
> And paciently taketh your aventure. (19–21)

Patience, these stanzas suggest, will be needed if one seeks to sustain perpetual loyalty in a time-dominated existence that alternately awards favors and withholds them. The conditions of temporal existence are now explored in two extended and formally contrasting narrative passages. The first recounts Mars' and Venus' brief liaison in the form of temporal narrative (29–149), and the other expands upon Mars' reflections in the decidedly extratemporal form of the complaint (155–298).

The "story" of this liaison is temporally ordered from its beginning (in Mars' "subjeccioun"—32), through its middle (their meeting "in joy and blysse" for "a certeyn tyme"—71–80), to its end (with Phoebus' intrusion, Venus' flight and new conjunction with Mercury, and Mars' despair). Its temporality is even more pervasive than this short account might suggest, for Mars and the rest are presented not simply as pagan gods and goddesses but as planets and therefore as subject to temporal and cyclical constraints. The relentless astronomical subtext of this account creates a conjunction in Taurus between Mars with his ponderous orbit and Venus with her swifter pace ("she sped her as faste in her weye / Almost in oo day as he dyde in tweye"—69–70) and then separates them with the advent of the sun and Venus' flight. The representation of Mars and Venus in their planetary aspect is not just a clever conceit but turns this narrative account of their liaison into a testament to the inexorability of time.[13] But the problem with time in the "Complaint of Mars" is not just the certainty of its passing but the fact that one character remains unreconciled to its effects. Like the birds of the introductory stanzas who confirm their perpetual service, Mars has entered into a commitment meant to defy time and change, binding himself to "perpetuall obeisaunce" (47). Now he must accept his "aventure" (21).

Matters of temporal succession, so carefully observed in the account of the liaison, are tumbled together in Mars' complaint. Its "ordre" (155) takes us through a succession of subjects that is finally less temporal than emotional, devoted to the "ground" (163) of Mars' pain: his lady's excellence, the uncertainties lovers endure, love's mutability, lovers' possessiveness, the reasons other lovers should rue his and Venus' predicament. The complaint presumes a knowledge of what has already passed; in fact it could not proceed without such knowledge. But it takes advantage of its audience's knowledge of the temporal order of episodes to ignore that order, to engage in simultaneous consideration of its beginning and its end. Time is obliterated in the opening lines of the complaint:

> The firste tyme, alas, that I was wroght . . .
> I yaf my trewe servise and my thoght
> For evermore—how dere I have hit boght—
> To her that is of so gret excellence. (164, 167–169)

Even as these lines seem to open temporally with an announcement of Mars' early predisposition to love, he interjects an exclamation—"alas"—that presumes the audience's knowledge of the sad outcome of his affair. No sooner does he tell of his entry into love's service than he reflects ruefully on its eventual unhappy outcome—"How dere I have hit boght." These interjections are like those chastened exclamations that punctuate Guillaume's *Roman de la Rose* ("For sithen [have] I sore siked") in a general temporal collapse that finally brings

Guillaume's episodic narrative to a standstill.[14] Like Guillaume, Mars also mixes his tenses, shifting from references to the past history of his love to a temporally undifferentiated and highly subjunctive present tense in "complaint time":

> What wonder ys it then, thogh I besette
> My servise on such on that may me knette
> To wele or wo sith hit lyth in her myght? (182–184)

The obliteration of chronological distinction invites Mars—as it invites his audience—to step outside time's flow and to speculate on the meaning of temporality itself. For God, Mars complains, constrains us to love (and, by implication, to mimic God in straining for permanence in our love), even as the objects of our love turn out to be fragile and mutable in time:

> And thogh he made a lover love a thing
> And maketh hit seme stedfast and during,
> Yet putteth he in hyt such mysaventure
> That reste nys ther non in his yeving. (227–230)

Mars would surmount time's restless succession, aspiring instead to the steadfastness of God's eternal perspective. Denied the steadfastness he seeks, Mars concludes in the stalemate of unresolved complaint; a complaint rendered ironic by the audience's additional knowledge that Venus may not be as "desolat" (286) as he imagines her to be.[15]

The temporal narrative of Mars and Venus offers an experience of time's inexorable passage; the extratemporal complaint permits speculation on the vain impulse to arrest transitory objects of desire in time. The temporal narrative pauses for occasional extratemporal amplification ("O woful Mars"—106–112) and the extratemporal complaint includes several references to finite time ("I yaf my trewe servise"—167). But they differ greatly in their respective emphasis on the horizontal progress of events in time and the vertical and speculative thrust of a character who would set himself beyond time.

THE OPENING LINES of "Anelida and Arcite" suggest that Chaucer has abandoned narrative equivocation and committed himself to sequential narration according to the best classical models. Although the common subheadings of "Invocation" and "Story" are the creations of modern editors, "Anelida" does in fact begin with an extended invocation to "Mars the rede" and to Athena in her martial aspect. In the *House of Fame,* Chaucer had already become the first English poet to use the word "invocation" and the first actually to employ classical and Italianate invocations to mark a new division of the bipartite vision poem into segments based upon locus of action. Now he uses the invocation similarly, to assert an initial commitment to historical and sequential narration. He also asserts historicity when he identifies his source as an "olde storie" in Latin, his equivalent of Boccaccio's "antichissima istoria" in its insistence on the exposition of actual deeds.[16] So too does the apparently authorial epigraph from Statius' *Thebaid* emphasize the chronological order of events ("Iamque . . . Cithice post aspera gentis / Prelia").[17]

Once we enter it, though, the narrative proper will again move from a primarily temporal to a primarily extratemporal section. An anticipation of this division is embedded in the concluding line of the "Invocation": "First folowe I Stace, and after him Corynne" (21). The relevance of this line to Chaucer's aesthetic program is clarified if we recall that the *Amores* and *Heroides* were sometimes known in the middle ages as "Corinna."[18] If Statius be taken as an exemplar of historical and temporal narration and Ovid as a classical poet skilled in the extratemporal elaboration of human feelings, we have in Chaucer's statement of indebtedness an explanation for the otherwise obscure form of his poem, and even a prediction of its movement from temporal to extratemporal concerns.

The central narrative of "Anelida" begins with a series of stanzas drawn from the *Thebaid* and the *Teseida,* which treat of Theseus' homecoming (22–35) and the accession of Creon after the siege of Thebes (50–70). These passages first seem to be aimed at setting coming events in a verifiable and sequential frame. But any expectation of sequentially ordered narrative is, as every reader of the poem has noted, to be frustrated.[19] The martial invocation will issue in no combat; Theseus, left "toward Athenes in his wey rydinge" (46), will never arrive; the account of the siege of Thebes and Creon's invitation to local nobility (of whom Anelida turns out to be one) to dwell in the city are minimally relevant, but can hardly be considered essential "narremes" in the story of Anelida and Arcite. All these features have what one editor has called a "decorative" aspect.[20] But, even though they come to nothing, they still function positively as an anticipation of the *idea* of sequential narrative itself, as embodied in the *storial* segment immediately following (71–210).

This segment observes a general temporal consistency in its unfolding of Arcite's false courtship, Anelida's proofs of love, and Arcite's ultimate "newfanglenesse" (141). Even before leaving this section of his poem, however, Chaucer begins to tamper with its temporal presuppositions.[21] At the very outset of his account of Arcite's courtship, for example, he leaps ahead to reveal that Arcite "wan this lady bryght" and would prove "fals" at the end (89–98), only then returning to a description of the "mykel besynesse / Had he er that he myghte his lady wynne" (99–100). As in the *storial* portions of the *Legend of Good Women,* he offers us a temporal narrative that is both episodic and tightly woven around a predetermined theme, but offers it in a way that reveals his own uncertainty about the seriousness and reliability of any narration cast in so strait a form.

Chaucer seems more at ease with the Ovidian and extratemporal complaint in which he casts the concluding segment of his poem. The complaint is of course the natural mode for the faithful Anelida; as with Mars, the appropriate complainant rejects "newefangelnesse" and refuses to change with events, intending to set herself or himself outside the flow of time and change. Like the sworn vassal or the serious oathtaker, the one who loves "alwey" (219) believes that true service knows no temporal bounds. As Anelida complains,

> For whoso trewest is, hit shal hir rewe
> That serveth love and doth her observaunce
> Alwey til oon, and chaungeth for no newe. (217–219)

Her complaint appropriately mixes the past ("I loved oon"—221), the present ("Now is he fals"—229), and the future ("Yet come ayein"—278). She dreams of Arcite standing before her, outside of time and the flow of actual events, clad in "asure" (330) and pledging *trouthe.* She is plagued by remembraunce (350), which—like the *memoria* of devotional exercise—has the effect of reconstituting past experience within the *praesens* or the eternal contemplative present. As in the "Complaint of Mars," the location of her utterance outside any succession of real events encourages reflection on the relation of the temporal to the extratemporal. She thinks that Arcite's fickleness might have been shaped by destiny (243, 339) and wonders how God, the sovereign of all *trouthe,* could have ordained so mutable a world (311–312).

The extratemporal form of Anelida's complaint permits a fullness of consideration not available within the predominantly diachronic "storie." Rather than chafing at the "artificiality" of the complaint, Chaucer seems to rest easily within it, revealing none of the discomfort that attends his experiment with a more temporally configured form of narration. Although four manuscripts conclude with a stanza that reintroduces the idea of sequence ("sith she gan to rise"—354), it is probably a scribal addition.[22] He would seem already to have found closure in his comparison of two forms of narration (or, one might almost say, a form of narration and a form of antinarration), each with its own special characteristics and capacities.[23]

Although Chaucer's attention in each of these poems appears to have been reserved primarily for issues of narrative form, each form is at least tentatively associated with a complex of attitudes. We encounter Venus and Arcite mainly through reports of their external (and often abrupt) actions. Neither engages in extended verbalization, and neither has much reported speech except for brief and tactical utterances. Extended interludes of reflection or indecision or regret are unnecessary to either, for each adjusts easily to temporal succession. Venus "happens" to encounter Mercury shortly after leaving Mars, and Arcite has only to "see" a proud new lady to shift his allegiance and "drive" forward in her direction. The relative verbosity of Mars and Anelida, on the other hand, is a consequence of their location outside the succession of worldly events and their longing for a "stedfast and during" object of affection. Each resists temporal change, wishing that love and service might persist "for evermore." Because of its hypothetical and imaginative nature, this quest for unseen stability is conducted through verbally profuse reflections of the sort appropriate to the form of the complaint.

Personalization of Form in "Troilus"

Both the "Complaint of Mars" and "Anelida and Arcite" juxtapose two differing narrative forms. Chaucer's primary interest appears in fact to lie in form *as* form, and he connects these forms with patterns of behavior in rather schematic ways: *fals* Arcite acts false, *trewe* Anelida languishes in complaint. Chaucer's *Troilus and Criseyde* addresses a far more complex set of aesthetic objectives, and the relations it proposes between narrative forms and matters of attitude are correspondingly more subtle. *Troilus* embeds the most varied narrative structures—invocation, *proces,* epistle, song, complaint, vision—within a narrative whole that constantly shifts its own coordinates, from tragedy to history to romance and back to tragedy again.[24] We encounter characters whose attitudes toward time and change have assumed a high degree of complexity and cannot be explained as simple consequences of narrative form. Even so, the attitudes of the protagonists toward time and change remain associated with their expressed preferences and with their personal choices in matters of expressive form.

One immediately notices in Pandarus (and, to a lesser degree, in his niece Criseyde) a propensity for machination in their own interest, for bringing matters to apt and satisfying conclusion. Goal-centered as he is, Pandarus would "make an end" (I.973) of any action in which he is engaged. A virtuoso of succession and causal sequence, he revels in the invention of schemes more complex than they need to be. "God and Pandare wist al what this mente" (II.1561), jests the narrator of Pandarus' elaborate scheme to bring Criseyde briefly into Troilus' presence at Deiphebus' house, and—though the limits of Pandarus' omniscience are ultimately to be revealed (as in IV.384–385)—he seems for much of the poem to control, rather than to be controlled by, circumstance. Although Criseyde is more reflective than Pandarus (as in her inner monologue of II.694–812), her thoughts are also characteristically bent toward positive action. Even as we learn of her indecision in book II, her last reported thought is that "He which that nothing undertaketh, / Nothyng n'acheveth" (II.807–808). Despite the adverse parliamentary judgment of book IV, she remains ready to show Troilus "an heep of weyes" (IV.1281) in which reunion may be accomplished. Even her ultimate embrace of Diomede may, after all, be seen as an open-eyed adjustment to altered circumstance.

Troilus, by contrast, moves and acts at lower velocity than Pandarus or Criseyde, betraying an inertia in his actions that always tends toward stasis. His chosen mode in love is to "langwisshe" (I.569) in solitary hopelessness, and Pandarus' most avid encouragements are needed to rescue him from his tendency to enter into swoons and trances. Once enabled through Pandarus' offices to gain Criseyde's love, he can wish for nothing more than the continuance of their relations. His most energetically conducted arguments are those against taking action to abduct Criseyde (IV.547–567) and in support of his own helplessness (IV.958–1078).

Pandarus' and Criseyde's capacity, and Troilus' incapacity, for action are bound up with their attitudes toward time. The narrator of *Troilus* and all the characters are excruciatingly aware of time, of the extent to which Troilus' and Criseyde's relationship is set in the flow of time and of all that location in time implies. The audience of the poem is constantly reminded of the need to demark beginnings and endings, the *proces* or sequence of events between (II.678), the proper way to "spende" (IV.1612) time for profit, the need to see that it not be lost (III. 896), the need to "dryve" it forth when it lags (V. 389, 405). These reminders are, in turn, sharpened by the audience's awareness of Troy's imminent destruction, of its location in finite time.

The narrator is placed in a peculiarly and increasingly awkward relation to the unfolding of events, owing to the collision of his simultaneous knowledge of the entire story and his obligation to render events in temporal succession. Thus he tells us even at the height of Troilus' and Criseyde's joy, Fortune "a tyme" (III. 1714) led them on, and he reveals in a dozen ways his awareness that such joys "al to litel . . . / Lasteth" (IV. 1–2). Yet the protagonists possess their own characteristic awarenesses of temporality as well. Pandarus, for example, dictates behavior to Criseyde on the basis of her time of life ("It sit hire naught to ben celestial / As yet"—I. 983–984) and does not hesitate to enumerate the perils of delay ("So longe mote ye lyve, and alle proude, / Til crowes feet be growe under youre yë"—II. 402–403). Both Pandarus and Criseyde are constantly looking backward and forward, to the past and the present and even occasionally to the future. Time is their element and they know it well, failing only in their ability to see it all at once. Criseyde, adrift among the Greeks, realizes "to late" (V. 741) that she might have heeded Troilus' advice, charging herself in this case for knowing only past and present:

> On tyme ypassed wel remembred me,
> And present tyme ek koud ich wel ise,
> But future tyme, er I was in the snare,
> Koude I nat sen . . . (V. 746–749)

She does not know the future now, but she will know it by the end of the poem, as she laments: "O, rolled shal I ben on many a tonge!" (V. 1061). And Pandarus too comes uncomfortably close to prescience, in his "al the world upon it wolde crie" (III. 277). Time will betray them; until then, they manipulate it with confidence and style.

Troilus, on the other hand, seeks to deny time, to live outside its effects. For him, love is not a finite arrangement between changeable beings but the basis of a "bond perpetuely durynge" (III. 1754). When Pandarus, upon learning of Criseyde's imminent departure, offers the practical observation that "The newe love out chaceth ofte the olde" (IV. 415), Troilus rejects with scorn his inclination "To changen so in love ay to and fro" (IV. 485). Death would be preferable to change, a position to which Troilus moves instinctively (IV. 500ff) and to which he constantly returns as he takes to his bed, plans his sepulchre, imagines people's response to his passing (v.205, 297, 627). Troilus' longings for quiescence, for stasis, for death itself, are all finally negative and despairing expressions of an aspiration to eternal repose for which he can find no appropriate embodiment in the world of secular time. First seeking permanence in Criseyde's inherently impermanent love, then seeking philosophical accommodation to change in his misguided Boethian meditation on necessity, then seeking escape from change in death—Troilus has seemed throughout to grope blindly and incompletely toward a vantage point he will achieve only with his death and ascent to the eighth sphere. There, he condemns

> . . . al oure werk that foloweth so
> The blynde lust, the which that may nat laste,
> And sholden al oure herte on heven caste. (v.1823–25)

He condemns what changes in time, "the which that may nat laste." His own heart is directed, and he bids us direct our hearts, to "heven"—that is, to the perspective from which past and present and future become one in the stillness of time become eternal.

Pandarus' and Criseyde's acceptance of time as unavoidable succession are embodied in different uses of narrative and different attitudes toward narrative. Pandarus is, for example, a master of narratives that are both episodic and highly configured: they possess beginnings, middles, and ends, and feature incidents and observations selected to support predetermined conclusions. Other men, Pandarus observes to Criseyde, shape their tales "for som conclusioun" (II.259)—and then he proceeds to do the same, moving to "th'ende," which is the "strengthe" of his tale. Pandarus is filled with advice about how to conduct a *proces* (in the sense either of "argument" or of "linear narrative"), both to himself (as when he deliberates over the appropriate length of the *proces* he should produce for Criseyde—II.267–273) or to Troilus (as when he urges him to eschew repetition in his letter to Criseyde—II.1023–43). And we often find Pandarus taking his own advice, reeling off glib narrative inventions (such as his timely but fabricated tale of Horaste—III.796–798). He is well capable of the "paynted proces" (II.424) of Troilus' death and his own suicide, framed in order to convince Criseyde to yield, and his fluency is equally in evidence when he rings out "a proces lik a belle" (II.1615) in describing the fictitious wrongdoings of Poliphete.

To Troilus, on the other hand, the thought that the events of his unhappy lovelife might be arranged as a narrative *proces* (v.583–588) is sheer discomfort. For his preference is never, in any circumstances, for temporal narrative but rather for such forms as exclamation, invocation, letter, song, apostrophe, and—especially—complaint, which dilate and comment upon narrative significance. Even as Troilus mistrusts temporal succession and dreams that things in his life might go on forever, so does he regularly step outside of the flow of time to comment, reflect, philosophize. This tendency is often humorously portrayed, as when—learning that consummation of his love is near—he pauses to invoke Venus, Jove, Mars, Apollo, Mercury, and Diana. ("Artow agast?" quizzes Pandarus, incapable of comprehending Troilus' penchant for delay—III.737). But it is also more wrenchingly portrayed in Troilus' formal, but still painful, spoken and written apostrophe (V.547), song (V.638), letter (V.1317), and numerous complaints, all in the closing book of the poem.

Even as Pandarus and Troilus respectively prefer temporal and extratemporal narration, so is the poem as a whole poised between these modes. Despite pauses for narrative invocations, for Troilus' histrionics, and for Criseyde's inner reflections, the narrative action of the first three books moves forward apace. Although the narrator veils the rapidity of Troilus' and Criseyde's courtship in order to foster a sense that Criseyde is won only "by proces and by good servyse" (II.678), the events of the courtship actually accelerate through a tightly sequenced pattern that allows only three days for Pandarus' machinations and that implies consummation in an additional week.[25] The fourth and fifth books, on the other hand, seem deliberately to jumble time. Book IV begins in indeterminate time (though we later learn that three years have elapsed—V.8–14). The pace of the poem is undercut by Troilus' choice of inaction and the extratemporality of complaint-time. The chronologies of Troilus' and Criseyde's first ten days apart are intertwined for ironic effect in book V, and our time sense is further confused by static portraits and undated letters. The narrator will ultimately disavow any attempt to keep track of narrated time (V.1086–88).[26]

The attempts of Pandarus and Criseyde to use time, and the attempt of Troilus to arrest its flow, are all submerged at least temporarily in the poem's closing revelation of the chaos and negativity of time-bound and pagan experience. Yet this critique of temporality may also be seen as essential for the assertion of another view of time, in which temporal restlessness and self-seeking are replaced by the certitude of God's eternally present gaze. Troilus' strange reticences and withdrawals and fits of inertia and protracted complainings turn out to have been mutely prophetic, after the fashion of those figures of

Old Testament antetype who unknowingly enact patterns of an ultimate revelation still veiled in temporality. The poem moves toward a vantage point from which Troilus' discomfort with temporality makes sense. Looking down from the eighth sphere, he realizes an ideal of extratemporality that has thus far found only partial and deflected expression. It is an ideal that the narrator, in the heat of his endorsement of Troilus' rejection of the world (v. 1828–69), seems at least temporarily to share.[27]

The Social Basis of Attitudes toward Time and Narrative

Time is the medium that links certain narrative forms and ensembles of attitudes about human activity. Temporal narratives are hospitable to characters who seek to control their own fates, who would put time to effective use, who would improve their worldly positions without reference to a world beyond. Extratemporal narratives are hospitable to characters who anticipate providential intervention in mundane affairs, who seek commitments and affiliations that survive the passage of time, who mistrust worldly prosperity. Although the external forms of narrative provide an appropriate setting for these respective attitudes (and may even, in "Complaint of Mars" and "Anelida and Arcite," play a part in summoning them into being), it would be an exaggeration to suggest that forms of narrative actually produce them, that these attitudes are simply epiphenomena of the narrative process. Although these attitudes are an important element of characterization (as observed in *Troilus and Criseyde*), it would also be an exaggeration to say that they are simply functions of personality, of individual traits or foibles. They transcend the narrative forms they inhabit and the particular characters who embrace them, having instead the more general character of socially created and ideologically charged structures of thought, sustained by the principal political and economic institutions of the age.

Jacques LeGoff boldly relates the temporal and extratemporal views of time to human activities and institutions, in his "Merchant's Time and Church's Time in the Middle Ages."[28] Merchant's time, as he describes it, is the secularized basis of productive effort, providing the terms in which use and productivity can be measured. Church's time is experienced in relation to eternity, from which it is provisionally borrowed, and its sole possession by God renders it unavailable for measurement, mortgage, or profitable use.

Merchant's time embodies an impulse toward secularization of human activity, consistent not only with economic impulses toward material gain through investment or trade but with all aspects of existence that involve finite striving toward worldly goals. It is consistent with the emergence of the "natural" state as a creation of humankind for human objectives; with the idea of cooperative or fraternal alignments among those wishing to attain temporary goals; with the temporary and unsworn contract as a way of defining and limiting the extent of personal indebtedness.[29] Church's time belongs not only to the church but to all those who would insist on the continued involvement of God in human affairs, and the elevation of earthly activity to permanent significance in its relation to an eternal hierarchy. It is consistent not only with the hierarchy of the church but with theocratic kingship and the concept of the ruler as God's vicar on earth; with the idea that the social hierarchy is divinely ordained; with sworn relations of vassalage transcending considerations of temporary self-interest.[30]

As suggestive labels that connect two views of time with human activities and institutions, the phrases "merchant's time" and "church's time" are more than justified. The merchant is a perfect exemplar of the new attitude toward time as desacralized (in its detachment from the round of ecclesiastical observance), measurable (by that device first prevalent in the fourteenth century, the publicly displayed twenty-four-hour clock), and available for practical use.[31] Also, though the church certainly made its compromises with the increasingly secularized sense of time in the thirteenth and fourteenth centuries, it continued to insist on the possible sanctification of earthly activity through its connection with the timeless, heavenly order of God.[32]

This being said, we must nevertheless note the obvious fact that merchant's time was not the sole possession of merchants, or even of the slightly more inclusive group comprised by "the bourgeoisie," and that church's time did not belong to the church alone. Sylvia Thrupp has persuasively shown that the "commercial" determination to turn time to economically productive use was hardly confined to merchants, and that the fourteenth and fifteenth centuries saw considerable interpenetration of the economical, cultural, and social lives of London merchants and gentry.[33] Patricia Eberle has supplemented those findings, showing that the commercial outlook and the language of commerce were the possession of all social groups, not just the merchants, in Chaucer's day.[34] We know that the aristocracy was in no way averse to trade, monopolization, investment, usury, or any other activity that we can imagine as manifestations of a "commercial attitude" and a determination to make productive use of time. By the same token, we know that the merchants of Chaucer's day were, for all their secularity in economic outlook, also the most fervently pious segment of late fourteenth-century English society. Although sparse, evidence of book ownership suggests that the reading of fourteenth-century urban merchants was most often devotional in character.[35] LeGoff has elsewhere described the medieval merchant as "totally infused with the spirit and practice of religion,"[36] and Sapori has argued for the "deep religious feeling" of the Italian merchant of the same period.[37]

Most members of the upper and middle strata habitually juggled *both* ideas about time. LeGoff observes that, for the Christian merchant, church's time "was essentially a second horizon of his existence," and he cites to the same effect Poulet's observation that "For the man of the Middle Ages, then, there was not one duration only. There were *durations,* ranked one above another."[38] Different domains of activity were saturated by different conceptions of time, and we need not insist that the merchant held a single attitude whether on the quays or at prayer, the aristocrat whether planning a pilgrimage or investing in the wine trade. The likelihood that an individual might entertain different ideas of time on different occasions does not, however, refute the social connectedness of thinking about time. Rather, it affirms the connection by linking time with different areas of socially defined activity.

CHAUCER asserts a social basis for ideas about time and narrative—first, rudimentarily, in the *Parliament of Fowls* and then, far more complexly, in and between certain of his *Canterbury Tales.* So ready is he, in fact, to assert the determining force of the social that he engages in a deliberate strategy of exaggeration. He renders the connection between time, narrative, and social experience unmistakable by advancing the bold claim that particular ideas of time and narrative rest in the sole possession of particular social groups. To be sure, his own equation of class and temporal/narrative preference emerges as a frank simplification, an enabling idea that carries him toward a somewhat different goal. But this goal remains fully social: it is the assertion of a layer of extraliterary implication in what might otherwise seem the entirely self-contained issues of temporality and form.

The *Parliament of Fowls* weighs different varieties of love for their contribution to social good ("commune profit") or social disruption ("likerous"-ness). Despite the interpretative questions left open by the narrator's noncommittal stance, the poem appears to present certain of the socially productive varieties of love more favorably than less productive alternatives. Nature's part of the garden, with its broadly expressed movement toward the practical goal of procreation, seems preferable from almost any perspective to Venus' statically arrested precincts, with their antihistorical jumble of love's victims painted on the walls.[39] Less definitively settled, however, is the more particular issue addressed in the avian debate, that of the duration of service to be expected from one who loves. Chaucer rather pointedly suggests that this is an issue on which different social groups will hold different and possibly irreconcilable positions.

The narrator of the poem has already revealed what might be considered a socially defined attitude toward duration in love. He declares at the outset that he fears the long apprenticeship that Love requires, within so short a life ("The lyf so short, the craft so long to lerne"). He goes on to explain that he has neither experienced love himself nor knows how Love pays people's wages: "how that he quiteth folk here hyre" (9). In one sense he is simply expressing his continuing inability to comprehend the rewards of love, but his mundane metaphor, in which Love pays out *hyre* or wages to his servants, is unexpected and revealing. For it displays the narrator's relation to Love less as that of vassal to lord than as that of hireling or temporary worker to employer. Should this narrator enter Love's service at all, he will enter it not as a sworn and permanent retainer but as a temporary and conditional adherent—as a "day laborer" or contract worker in the vineyard of love. His humdrum imagery sends us back, in fact, to the mention of love's "craft" in line 1. Here, as elsewhere, "craft" refers to love's "art." But, when filtered through this narrative sensibility, it also gains a retrospective second-level sense as a mere occupation or trade. Interested in serving love on the one hand but totally unable to comprehend conceptions of timeless or unrestricted service on the other, the narrator as usual presents himself as a party of one, adrift somewhere between the two poles of the coming debate on duration and love's service.

Standing in strong contrast to the narrator's hedged attitude toward the service of love are the tercel eagles with their rejection of finite bonds in favor of the extratemporal responsibilities of traditional vassalage. Choosing the formel eagle, the first tercel declares that he "evere wol hire serve" (419), and emphatically insists in quadruple negative that, rewarded or not, his service will never end: "ne nevere for no wo ne shal I lette / To serven hire" (439–440). Duration of service remains the crucial issue among these would-be vassals of love, and the somewhat more literal-minded second tercel states his case accordingly, claiming to "lenger have served hire in my degre" (453). The third, evidently defeated in respect of long service, reveals his lesser gentility by staking his claim on intensity, as being as ready for death in combat "as he that hath ben languysshyng / This twenty wynter" (472–473). Whether associating their service with infinite duration (like the first eagle) or infinite intensity (like the third), all show equal disdain for temporality, for successive developments in time, and for the choices necessitated by time. Like that elite handful admitted to the garden of Sir Mirth in the *Roman de la Rose* and unlike ordinary citizens with more urgent commitments, these aristocrats do have time to love. Not only are they serene about time in the honored fashion of the gentle lover, but they see beyond, or through, time to a more transcendent and permanent ideal. Good service, requited or not, seems to them its own reward.

That the eagles, most worthy of nature's creations, embody an aristocratic stance toward love seems apparent from contextual references to their degree, supported by medieval works of natural science and heraldry.[40] No less socially defined appear to be the attitudes of the lesser birds who interrupt them in noisy debate. The invitation to propose particular social identifications for their four groupings ("foules of ravyne," "sed-foul;" "water-foul," and "worm-foul") has been irresistible to many, although efforts have sometimes been marked by the temptation to adopt schemata of greater specificity than the text will bear.[41] The "foules of ravyne" seem obviously enough to be of the same general class as the eagles, though presumably of lesser rank within it: they might be considered the barons of the avian parliament, first to speak in formal debate and most jealous of parliamentary prerogative (545–546). The seed-fowl, revealed in their opinions as ideologically allied with the former group, may plausibly be associated with the nonaristocratic gentry. Identifications of the water- and worm-fowl have been more varied, but common sense points in the direction proposed by Brewer, that their affiliations should be found among those groups actually involved in Parliament: "The national parliament was composed of representatives of the knightly class and representatives of what we would now call the middle class—burghers, rich tradesmen, and so on. It is not unlikely that the lower birds are in certain ways representative of these classes . . . (the peasants . . . hardly enter the question)."[42] A reasonable balance is struck by Robinson, who imagines the worm-fowl as "bourgeoisie" (as presumably citizens and burgesses in craft and trade) and the water-fowl as the "great merchants." [43]

As already mentioned, the *gentil* birds, including the birds of prey and apparently the seed-fowl, affirm the views of the eagles on longevity of service ("Though that his lady everemore be straunge, / Yit lat hym serve hire ever"—584–585) and other matters. But, essentially uninterested in the eagles' static and extratemporal stances, the worm- and water-fowl are unrestrained in their demand for a "swythe verdit" (503) that will bring closure to their open-ended pleading. In contrast to the *gentils,* with their rejection of the possibility of "chaunge" within the vassalage of love (582), the lower fowl favor a more time-bound and opportunistic approach, in which a rebuffed lover may seek a more satisfactory arrangement elsewhere: "but she wol love hym, lat hym love another!" (567). The poem ends appropriately, with the tercel eagles getting what they want (continued service) and the remaining fowl getting what they want (their *makes*).

Provoking the avian debate is not simply the tercels' attitude toward duration in service, but the form in which they express it: that of the protracted *ple* or parliamentary/legal plea or appeal (485). These legal appeals in turn have much in common with that other form of appeal, the complaint. Common ground with the complaint includes their versification, their emphasis on the speaker's need or lack, and their full exploitation of an extratemporal mode. This extratemporality is expressed through their ideal of fixed service to a transcendent and "sovereyne" figure. They admire her, as it were, "from below"—seeking to reach her through intensity of feeling rather than to win her through succession or passage of time (rejecting any thought that they might, in the disdainful words of the royal tercel, "in proces love a newe"—430). And their rejection of temporality is expressed through the simple duration of their speeches. The narrator implies that they said *much* more than he has reported, that their speeches lasted "from the morwe . . . Tyl dounward went the sonne wonder faste" (489–490).

The lower birds' interruption is at once an objection to what the tercels have said and to the form in which they have said it. In demanding that the tercels "Have don, and lat us wende!" (492), the lower fowl express their frustration with commitments that disregard the pressure of temporality on ordinary citizens and also with the unduly protracted form in which those commitments are embodied. "Comune spede" (507) will be served not only by the substitution of a set of attitudes favorable to the productive use of time, but also by the return to a "blow-by-blow" form of episodic narration that moves beyond stalemate to resolution. The practical advice of the lower fowl—that the eagles find more compliant mates or that the other fowl be permitted to choose their mates and go—is presented, as the goose says, with a minimum of "taryinge" (565). Wishing to effect a move from the "cosmic pathos" of the eagles' extratemporal complaint to their own more urgent "praxis," they also shift into faster-paced exchange with more explicit goals in time.

By assigning transcendent views to his aristocratic fowl and their allies and mundane ones to the worm- and water-fowl, Chaucer engages in a deliberate simplification, akin to those he will embrace within the *Canterbury Tales*; the laughter that his "gentil foules" direct at his goose (575) implies a division similar to that within the pilgrimage between *gentils* who want moral content and *cherls* who want harlotry. That this division is exaggerated was undoubtedly evident to Chaucer, writing from a vantage point situated somewhere between the aristocratic and bourgeois segments of his own society, and well prepared to appreciate in his own terms the truth of a proposition of which even Bédier, with all his determination to show that the fabliaux were bourgeois in origin, was aware: that "Ni les bourgeois n'etaient si prosaïques que nous l'avions supposé ni les chevaliers si idéalistes." [44] Why, though, would Chaucer have chosen to restate with such exaggeration an aspect of cultural incompatibility that, though it probably did exist, existed only in a muffled and diffused way?

By drawing a bold relation between cultural and social conflict, and by enriching his chosen form of avian debate or "judgment" with the specifically social idea of the deliberative forum or parliament,[45] Chaucer shifts from the amatory to the civic arena.[46] Further, his poem embodies an ultimate civic reassurance: socially based disagreements can be aired in forums that are adequate to containing difference and even in some cases to resolving it. All but the tercel eagles are given their appropriate mates, and representatives chosen from the total community join voices in celebratory song. Nor are the tercels, for all their apparent adherence to transcendent ideals, prevented from reentering the stream of history and productive choice later in time. Chaucer has, after all, situated them in Nature's part of the garden rather than in Venus' static, ahistorical, and unproductive domain.[47] By infusing the apparently socially innocuous form of the love debate with socially charged views, Chaucer suggests that, even when ardently held by representatives of different classes, social differences can be reconciled with legitimate civic aims. His exaggerated equation of attitudes and styles has enabled him to address and allay fears of socially based division within a realm of apparent aesthetic fancy.

CHAUCER is certainly no less aware of the social implications of his different Canterbury narratives, and his allocation of narratives among socially diverse tellers gives him an additional means of underscoring these implications. As continuing and unresolved critical debate would suggest, however, the issue of the social basis of his assignments is exceedingly complex.[48] Any given instance requires attention to the social assumptions borne by the narrative form, the apparent social perspective of its teller, and the ways in which the assignment heightens the audience's sense of social implication. These formidable tasks are often complicated by a further, characteristic maneuver, in which Chaucer introduces his own tacit criticisms, both of the social assumptions of his narrative and the social perspective of his teller. My response to these procedural difficulties will be to concentrate on a single instance (or, more accurately, on two instances so intricately intertwined that they must be considered one): the social implications of Chaucer's assignments to his Knight and to his Miller.

The Canterbury pilgrims describe the *Knight's Tale* as a *storie* (I. 3110–11), presumably meaning to compliment its dignity, its venerability, its value as instruction.[49] They have, at the same time, hit upon a more appropriate designation than "romance" (popular with modern critics because of its incorporation of certain amorous and chivalric materials[50]) or epic (a form from which it is derived and many of whose materials it adapts[51]). Its external form is that of *storial* narrative, manifesting the same *series narrationis* or "organized succession" of events first apparent in twelfth- and thirteenth-century historiography.[52] If historical, though, the Knight's narrative remains conservatively fixed in a distinctively medieval approach to history writing that devalues strict temporality, preferring instead (in the words of Pocock) "to pass by the succession of particulars itself as revealing nothing of importance" and "to view each particular in its relation to eternity."[53] Though, to be sure, historical in the sense that it deals with a succession of episodes in time, the *Knight's Tale* is ultimately configured less in relation to human choices than to providential interventions. Thus in its formal dimension the *Knight's Tale* represents a fusion of the temporal with the extratemporal, of essentially horizontal narrative (that moves—albeit haltingly—through a series of events in the lives of its protagonists) and vertically interrupted narrative (punctuated by fissures through which the audience gains glimpses of a consequentially involved heavenly hierarchy).[54] The Knight's narrative finally rejects a conception of history as a record of human accomplishments and embraces a conception of providential history subject to intervention from above.

Those who approach the *Knight's Tale* as temporal narrative, find their expectations repeatedly frustrated. The poem does indeed possess a sequential ordering of events in time, but they unfold at a ponderous pace. Palamon and Arcite are confined by Theseus "perpetuelly" (I. 1024), in a state that passes "yeer by yeer and day by day" (I. 1033) until they are returned to eventful temporality by their first glimpse of Emelye. Arcite, out of prison and returned to Athens in disguise, bides his time as an esquire of Theseus' chamber for "thre yeer" (I. 1446). Palamon escapes in the "seventhe yer" of his confinement (I. 1462). Once mandated by Theseus, the tournament between Palamon and Arcite is to occur in "fifty wykes" (I. 1850). Mourning for Arcite's death ceases "By processe and by lengthe of certeyn yeres" (I. 2967). At times, narrative progress seems to halt altogether, as in Arcite's and Palamon's parallel complaints, the one finding himself free but deprived of the sight of Emelye, the other remaining in Athens but unfree (I. 1219–1333); or the description of the temples of Venus, Mars, and Diana (I. 1918–2088); or that of Arcite's funeral obsequies (I. 2853–2966). Even those critical moments at which characters seek to act in their own behalf, as when Palamon, Arcite, and Emelye supplicate their respective gods, have a static quality. The stateliness and formality of these actions finally becomes, as Charles Muscatine pointed out, an element of meaning within the poem, an attempt on the part of its characters to oppose ordered ceremony and stable meaning to the chaotic forces that threaten to overwhelm them.[55] In another sense, though, the slow and erratic succession of episodes in story-time suggests that narrative meaning finally resides beyond the boundaries of human actions or of the events portrayed. Meaning is finally revealed precisely in those moments at which narrative disruptions direct our attention away from human choice in time and toward a source of miraculous intervention.

The narrative continuity of the *Knight's Tale* lies open to constant disruption, in forms that originate outside the scope of human action.[56] The narrative, in fact, begins with such a disruption, as Theseus' triumphal procession is halted by the sorrowing Greek women, just at his point of "mooste pride" (I. 895). Then unwinds a series of narrative coincidences that, the narrator hints to us, may be more than coincidental. Emelye's initial appearance to Palamon just happened, "fil ones" (I. 1034), and Palamon looked out his window "by aventure or cas" (I. 1074). Palamon finally escapes prison "by aventure or destynee" (I. 1465) and happens "by aventure" (I. 1516) to be hidden in a bush when Arcite rides into the woods for his May observance. Of the subsequent convergence of all the principals in that very place, the narrator once again notes its strangeness ("somtyme it shal fallen on a day / That falleth nat eft withinne a thousand yeer"), but takes a further step, attributing it definitely to "destinee," which executes God's "purveiaunce" and the rule of "the sighte above" (I. 1663–72).

The principals are uncertain of the interest of the gods, attributing events within the poem to the less formal operations of Fortune (I. 1861, 2659). But we learn that the gods are interested in the events of the poem—as far as their nature as detached astrological influences permits them to be.[57] These are, the audience learns, gods who cannot be influenced by supplication; the effect of the visits of Palamon, Arcite, and Emelye to the temples of their deities is not to alter events but merely to receive enigmatic indications of what has been foreordained. And the ultimate dispensation lies with Chaucer's creation Saturn, who rules by the power of his wide "cours" (I. 2454–55). He is responsible for that most startling of interventions, the "furie infernal" that starts from the ground to precipitate Arcite's fatal fall just when he has won victory by his own exertions. Revealed at such moments, and particularly at this one, is the inability of these characters to determine their own fates. The locus of significance is displaced, from the horizontal relation of one event to another (from, for instance, the inference that Arcite, having won the tournament, will receive Emelye's hand in marriage) to the anomalous occurrence that signals the vertical intervention of a vastly, though erratically, more powerful heavenly hierarchy. The repeated interventions of the gods in human events encourage that displacement of attention we ordinarily associate with allegory, suggesting a locus of meaning in another sphere. Revelation of further confusion within the sphere of the gods must, however, frustrate any attempt by the audience of the poem to impose an orderly pattern on these divine interventions.

This displacement is, of course, more apparent to the audience of the poem than to its characters, who are left to puzzle out the significance of the dislocations that deprive them of control over their own destinies. The most impressive response to prevailing uncertainty is that of Theseus, who adopts a stance consisting of several interrelated elements, all responsive to revealed limitations in his own control. One is his humane flexibility, his willingness to reconsider his own pronouncements in relation to new conditions or changing awareness; we see this in his switch from an angry to a compassionate response to the Greek women, his initial severity and eventual clemency when he comes upon Palamon and Arcite fighting in the woods, his decision to "modifye" (I.2542) his tournament rules in order to protect life, and his ultimate encouragement of Palamon and Emelye to "maken vertu of necessitee" (I.3042). Another is his quest for a reaffirmation of authority—both earthly and divine—in his projected faith in a benign heavenly hierarchy, ruled not by the malign and arbitrary Saturn but by a more even-keeled "Juppiter, the kyng" (I.3035).

Chaucer takes care that his audience understands Theseus to be wrong, emphasizing that the malign Saturn (his own creation and addition to his source) is in control. Mediating between Theseus' hopeful projections and his audience's certain knowledge of the worst is the Knight-narrator, whose uncomfortable task is to reconcile his characters' aspirations with his audience's knowledge of the harsh actualities in the world of the tale. (The very hopelessness of this task may help to explain the narrator's often-discussed flippancies on the occasion of Arcite's death—I.2759–60, 2811–15.) The particular irony of the narrator's task is that the form of his narrative (including its punctuation by divine interventions in human affairs) and Theseus' philosophizing (including his yearning for theodicy) seem ripe for Christian revelation, a revelation denied to the characters of the poem and acknowledged to its audience only in its closing lines (I.3099–3100).[58] The poem is, one might say, incipiently Christian in its configuration, which directs the characters' attention toward a heavenly hierarchy and encourages the hope that this hierarchy might be benign.[59] That it denies its own implied promises is part of its continuing challenge and appeal.

Opposed in every way to the *Knight's Tale* with its heightened sensitivity to the supramundane is the *Miller's Tale* with its unfettered attack on all forms of transcendence. Much attention has been paid to the *Miller's Tale* as a parodic requital of the *Knight's Tale,* emphatically announced in the Miller's statement of intentions (I.3125–27), confirmed in derisive echoes, and borne out in his creation of a love triangle parallel to that of the *Knight's Tale* at a different level of social existence.[60] Of more direct interest here, however, is the sense in which the *Miller's Tale* is a requital or "reply" to that of the Knight not simply in respect of different components of narrative, but *as* narrative—as a different form of narrative with entirely different presuppositions about the nature of human action in time.

If the *Knight's Tale* is traversed by openings through which the audience glimpses the eternal, the *Miller's Tale* is relentlessly temporal. One episode succeeds another in time, from Nicholas' and Alisoun's first compact to the Saturday when John the Carpenter leaves town and the would-be lovers hatch their plot to the Sunday when Nicholas informs John of the impending flood to the Monday night denouement.[61] Moreover, as opposed to the *Knight's Tale* with its action always at the edge of entropy, the characters in this tale make *use* of time. Nicholas, surely the most "sodeyn" character since Diomede (v. 1024), first seeks Alisoun's love "al atones" (I. 3280) and, when convinced that he must wait, consoles himself with the reflection that his clerkly guile will enable him to spend his time or "whyle" more productively than any carpenter (I. 3299–300). Because events in this tale are bent to practical use, their rationale is to be sought within the world of the tale. These events do not simply succeed one another in time, but are configured according to materials at hand, choices made, and actions taken within the tale itself, without recourse to providential or other external intervention.[62]

The narrative form of the *Miller's Tale* offers us causality completely different from that of the *Knight's Tale,* a causality purged of the extratemporal and ideal and situated within the world of practical affairs. The tale abounds in concrete details (tubs, axes, ladders, *kultours*) and definitive actions (hard embraces, kisses rightly and wrongly directed, stealthy ascents and precipitous descents), but what sets it so decisively apart from the *Knight's Tale* is the close arrangement of these details in larger patterns, in which even surprises are then seen to derive coherently and perhaps even inescapably from all that has gone before.[63] This aspect of the narrative is evident in Chaucer's care to provide every detail of the contrivance by which Nicholas persuades John to mount into the roofbeams and hang there in his kneading tub, ax in hand to cut the cord when the water comes, and thus establishes all the preliminaries to John's eventual reintroduction to the scene. Similarly, when Absolon decides to strike back with a puissant instrument, it is produced not from thin air but from within the milieu of the tale; we learn the location of the smithy from which he gets his kultour, the approximate time of night (or day) at which he gets it, the name of the smith, and even how he grasps it ("by the colde stele"—I. 3785) to carry it back to John's house.

Chaucer's motive in providing circumstantial detail is of course literary rather than ethnographic; however offhandedly they are first introduced, an extraordinary number of the material objects mentioned in the narrative turn out to be involved in its cause-and-effect relations.[64] The same general point may be made of the tale's setting in physical space. In contrast with the *Knight's Tale,* in which the characters (when not specifically confined or located within such purposefully constructed space as prison, temple, or tournament ground) spend much of their time in undefined areas, the characters of the *Miller's Tale* move in and about a house so carefully described that one scholar has deduced its plan.[65] The setting of the tale is three-dimensional and "real," in the same sense in which time is real in this particular time/space configuration: time is progressive and space is three-dimensional, not to persuade us of their actuality but to sustain a narrative in which all the causes of its main actions are evident and in view. Knowing the arrangement of the house, we need not wonder where John has gone while the bedroom antics ensue; up in the roof-beams he remains very much within the physical space designated as consequential for the action of this tale. His sudden reappearance is not an intrusion from a realm unknown and uncharted, but a surprising refocusing of the audience's attention on someone who has never left the physical setting of the tale but has remained within its circumference all along.

So too is the denouement of the tale prepared at the level of character. While not exactly rounded in the sense of characters in nineteenth-century fiction, about whom we learn all kinds of things that tempt us into assumptions about how they might behave outside the works in which they appear, the characters of the *Miller's Tale* are fully arrayed in traits that determine the choices they make. The "comic justice" of the tale has been explored by a number of critics, all of whom have observed the congruence of the traits of the characters, their choices, and their fates.[66] The dreamy Absolon, the most orally fastidious character in literature, confronts stark reality in the form of Alisoun's "naked ers." The arch-contriver Nicholas characteristically tries to "amend" or improve upon an already-good joke, and thus opens himself to Absolon's rebuke. Although John the Carpenter never really manifests the jealousy of which the Miller and Alisoun accuse him, he certainly renders himself vulnerable to Nicholas' contrivance by his own smug piety ("Ye," he says of himself, "blessed be alwey a lewed man"—I.3455). And, as most readers have agreed, what could be more fitting than Alisoun's escape? For, in her naturalness and lack of pretension (the Miller compares her to an early pear tree, a swallow sitting on a barn, a kid or calf following his mother, a jolly colt, and a dozen other natural things), she is already a completely comfortable inhabitant of the wholly mundane world of this tale.

The audience has at its command all the detail it needs—and is distracted by very little it does not need—to enjoy the delightful sequence of events that constitutes the denouement of the tale: motivated by his need to elaborate every contrivance, Nicholas lets fly a fart; earlier idealism now dispelled, Absolon launches his stroke; scorched, Nicholas cries for water; awaiting notice of Noe's flood, John seizes his ax and cuts the cord; tumbling down is not just John's physical person, but an entire weight of contrivance. John's reintroduction is a surprise, but a surprise grounded in Aristotelian cause-and-effect.

The self-sufficient narrative world of the *Miller's Tale* frustrates any inclination to look for norms or causes beyond its chronological and spatial bounds. Intimations of transcendence, to be sure, flicker through the tale, in the incongruous idealism of Absolon's small-town love language,[67] in the ironic echoing of language from the Song of Songs and other biblical details,[68] in John the Carpenter's readiness to believe in a new providential intervention in human affairs. Yet such allusions are no great challenge to the sufficiency of this world. In this sense, the exegetical critics who have usefully traced the biblical echoes within the tale have gotten their effect exactly wrong. These references to *trouthe* in love service, to pure spousal, and to God's providence make no dent in the materiality of the tale. Mocked, rather, is the very possibility of transcendence. The idealistic Absolon learns fast after his confrontation with Alisoun's hairy ass ("For fro that tyme that he hadde kist hir ers, / Of paramours he sette nat a kers"—I. 3755–56). The tale's intermittent scriptural echoes are subsumed into the wild farcicality of an "exquisitely orchestrated climatic chaos" that even the grimmest exegetical readings have finally acknowledged to be "funny."[69] Poor John's expectation of Noe's second flood is revealed as "fantasie" and "vanytee" (I. 3835), and is considered nothing short of madness by the residents of this town and this tale.

Illusions are shown to be excess baggage in a world whose valorization of the immediate and tangible is embodied in the narrator's proverb: "Alwey the nye slye / Maketh the ferre leeve to be looth" (I. 3392–93). This tale is a virtual paean to calculation: to the right of characters to get on with it without outside interference, to exploit opportunities, to get into scrapes resulting from their own quirks, foibles, and obsessions. The *Knight's Tale* seeks a public morality, encouraging the assumption of public stances in relation to the dictates of an unseen absolute; the private, self-willed passions of the two lover-knights are treated as problematic and threatening to social stability. Fulfillment here in the *Miller's Tale* is more likely to be private and to involve frankly personal aims; though John's house and bedroom are finally transformed into semipublic space, they remain infinitely more private than the crowded theater or the hushed parliament of the *Knight's Tale*. Undistracted by sources of revelation or standards of conduct set beyond their own desires, the characters of the *Miller's Tale* seek to fulfill their desires in a world of present possibility.

Both the narrative form and the particular content of each tale assert a socially conditioned view of human experience. The one neglects orderly chronology, disdains causal relations between events, and views human fortunes as dependent on the sporadic intervention of an unseen hierarchy. Its form bears traditional assumptions about the replication of the feudal hierarchy in heaven—assumptions with some residual currency in most segments of society even in Chaucer's essentially postfeudal age. The other treats this world as the arena of consequential action and relates events successively or horizontally within a time-bound and above all causal scheme. Its form bears assumptions about the deployment of human action for personal advantage—assumptions that were more and more prominent in the increasingly urban and commercial world of the later fourteenth century.

These views coexisted within the social strata comprising Chaucer's possible audience, and so do they coexist within the *Canterbury Tales*. In one aspect of their coexistence, they are distributed between individual tales, such as those of the Knight and the Miller. In another and more subtle aspect of their coexistence, they vie within individual tales. For, unwilling even briefly to allow either view to appear unproblematic, Chaucer takes the further step of challenging each tale's assumptions from within its boundaries. Separately considered, the tale of the Knight and the tale of the Miller may each be seen to embody a view of human experience in time and a criticism of that view.

Although the form of the *Knight's Tale* repeatedly directs our attention to the extratemporal and the eternal, its perspective on the involvement of the heavenly hierarchy in earthly affairs is anything but reassuring. Despite Theseus' professed faith in the ultimate wisdom of a divine plan directed by the well-intending Jupiter, the audience is insistently made aware of the impersonality and destructive malignity of these gods. The imagery with which Chaucer arrays the oratories of Venus, Mars, and Diana is cause enough for concern, but most disturbing of all is the self-characterization of Chaucer's Saturn, that force of chaos beyond apparent order, evident to the audience even as he is concealed from Theseus' gaze:

> . . . myne be the maladyes colde,
> The derke tresons, and the castes olde;
> My lookyng is the fader of pestilence. (I. 2467–69)

Rather than an avenue of relief from the uncertainties of temporal existence, these deities are at best a doubling of the prevalence of selfish conduct in the earthly sphere, at worst a source of further disorder. When Jupiter is unable to end the strife between Venus and Mars on behalf of their respective suitors, it is Saturn, the very personification of disorder, who fills the vacuum. His solution depends not on the "wise purveiaunce" contemplated by Theseus (I. 3011), but on the repayment of atavistic loyalties. Mars will help his knight but Venus will prevail, since (as he tells her) "I am thyn aiel, redy at thy wille" (I. 2477). The "furie infernal" that causes Arcite's horse to bolt (I. 2684) is hardly the result of a providential arrangement in mankind's interest; it is a result of cronyism and sharp dealing among the gods.

The narrative form of the *Knight's Tale* is, in this sense, employed ironically. Providential-seeming interruptions in the scheme of narrative causation have the effect of turning the audience's attention heavenward, in search of an explanation for the truncation and apparent arbitrariness of earthly events. These disruptions in temporal sequence reveal, however, a scheme that is anything but providential. Rather than a confirmation of earthly hierarchy, these unruly celestials call hierarchy itself into question, mocking even the idea of an escape from temporality.

Even as the *Knight's Tale* incorporates a critique of its own impulse toward the eternal, so does the *Miller's Tale* question its own temporal presuppositions. Despite its prevailing tendency to celebrate the values of persons who shape their own destinies in a world of fast-moving and potentially productive time, the *Miller's Tale* also seizes a unique and surprising moment to upend its own assumptions. This is the moment when John has tumbled from the rafters, to lie "aswowne" on the floor:

> The neighebores, bothe smale and grete,
> In ronnen for to gauren on this man,
> That yet aswowne lay, bothe pale and wan,
> For with the fal he brosten hadde his arm.
> But stonde he moste unto his owene harm . . .
> The folk gan laughen at his fantasye;
> Into the roof they kiken and they cape,
> And turned al his harm unto a jape.
> For what so that this carpenter answerde,
> It was for noght; no man his reson herde.
> With othes grete he was so sworn adoun
> That he was holde wood in al the toun;
> For every clerk anonright heeld with oother.
> They seyde, "The man is wood, my leeve brother";
> And every wight gan laughen at this stryf. (I. 3826–30, 3840–49)

Nicholas earlier felt momentary pain upon losing a "hand's breadth" of skin to Absolon's poker but was instantly restored. John, in contrast, lies in a faint, pale with the pain of a broken arm from which he will not soon recover. Arrayed against him is a body of clerks, united by the immediate and opportunistic bonds of group interest. John has been isolated by his cranky and inappropriate adherence to a body of beliefs inconsistent with the self-interested ethic of this tale: by his superstitious faith in divine intervention and providential design, and by his spontaneous concern for Alisoun and even for Nicholas.

Even though the *Miller's Tale* is essentially a celebration of the mercantile or commercial attitude of calculation in one's own interest, its concluding festivity is tempered by a recognition that this attitude entails significant costs. Most evident is a loss in human solidarity. In the *Knight's Tale* the dictates of the gods afflicted an entire human community and Arcite was communally mourned. Here the only solidarity is that of the jeering clerks who close ranks upon the exclusionary grounds of shared interest. John is left to "stonde . . . unto his owene harm," to suffer alone.[70] Acknowledged in his fate is the extent to which the opportunistic conduct of the *Miller's Tale* has its own limitations, its own capacity to create victims.

THE KNIGHT'S and the Miller's tales introduce and interrogate two differing constructions of reality: one hierarchical in its imagined structure, vertical in its impulses, and extratemporal in its aspirations; the other antihierarchical in its imagined structure, horizontal in its impulses, and temporal in its aspirations. That these constructions are also social is beyond doubt, for they activate understandings of human ties and obligations current within Chaucer's society. The Knight's unswerving faith in an hierarchical order (however qualified by our insight into the actual character of the pagan gods) and the Miller's paean to the pursuit of temporary self-advantage (however qualified by John's undeserved pain) gain force from their appeal to contradictory social impulses. They draw upon two contending ideological ensembles that can be traced within and beyond the boundaries of literary works, the one attached to the transcendent and sworn, and the other to the mundane and contractual.

As in the *Parliament of Fowls,* Chaucer has taken an ambitious step by suggesting that these ensembles rest in the unique possession of particular social classes or groups. By his assignment to the Knight he suggests that certain forms of chivalric narrative, and their presuppositions about the permanent and extratemporal basis of loyal belief, are the special possession of the aristocracy and the higher echelon of gentry. By his assignment to the Miller he suggests that certain kinds of comic tales, and their presuppositions about opportunistic self-aggrandizement, are the special possession of small entrepreneurs situated at the margin between the bourgeoisie and the rural peasantry.

To be sure, the Knight's *storie* draws upon elements of romance and, in a more shadowy way, late classical epic and Italian *cantare,* all of which have in common an attachment to broadly "chivalric" ideals.[71] And the Miller's comic tale draws upon the oral tradition that informed the French fabliaux,[72] with its repeated representation of lesser townspeople very much of the Miller's own stripe.[73] But neither these literary forms nor the ideological ensembles to which they are hospitable can be assigned to particular class groupings with anything like the certainty with which Chaucer goes about his task. Recent research has established that knights were not themselves likely to tell romances or even necessarily to prefer them. Fourteenth-century audiences for English romance were extremely diverse and certainly embraced the middle strata as well as the aristocracy.[74] Nor were peasants, small entrepreneurs, and lesser tradespeople the principal tellers or hearers of comic tales like the Miller's, however often they might populate them as literary characters. Nykrog has argued that the intended and implied audiences of the fabliaux were predominantly aristocratic, and—while subsequent commentators have pointed out that fabliaux like other genres might be adapted for various social levels—his formulation stands as an important corrective to the impressions that Chaucer's influential assignments urge upon us.[75]

Even though not finally persuasive as social data, the assignment of these two tales to representatives of different social groups reminds the audience that their narrative genres, and the different assumptions about human action in time they bear, are the creations of persons in their social existence. The effect of assigning the one narrative to the foremost of the *gentils* and the other to an egregious *cherl* is to intensify their social messages. By simplifying and heightening the social relatedness of the two narratives, Chaucer renders that relatedness inescapable.

One might expend considerable ingenuity defending the "roadside drama" argument that each tale remains a plausible expression of its assigned teller's world view. One could argue that the traditional view of the vertical relations between the earthly and heavenly hierarchies within the *Knight's Tale* is appropriate to a devout gentleperson in the service of his earthly and heavenly lords, and that the elements of disillusionment in the tale express the modifications of earthly loyalty and hierarchy experienced by fourteenth-century knights of retinue. One could also argue that the celebration of horizontal and self-interested relations in the *Miller's Tale* is appropriate to a lesser tradesman, and that any reservations express its teller's own insecure location between the prosperous urban *gens de meistre* on the one hand and the rural *agricole* on the other. Each line of analysis has its share of truth, but each is sustained only by rather considerable effort and by a willful obliviousness of the fact that, once the two narratives are launched, the voices of their nominal tellers virtually disappear.[76]

Like a sign on the road warning the driver that certain forms of work lie ahead, the assignment of each tale to a highly socially differentiated teller functions as a signal of historicizing intention. For each tale does embody a historical consciousness of considerably more subtlety than its teller might be expected to possess. The Knight as nominal teller of his tale appears to discover no limitation in Theseus' closing speech, and his closing effusions over Palamon's and Emelye's happiness strain the credulity of any audience. Yet Chaucer as poet has pressed beyond the presumed consciousness of the Knight to provide his audience with matter for somber and specifically historical reflection. Choosing a narrative form constituted of genres hospitable to hierarchical and extratemporal ideals, he has mounted a critique of hierarchy decidedly expressive of a postfeudal century in which antihierarchical currents were at large. The ostensible teller of the *Miller's Tale* seems wholly satisfied with his own closing tribute to his narrative's symmetry and justice. Yet Chaucer's concluding look at John, fainted in pain, again offers his audience a telling and historically specific insight. Choosing a narrative committed to individualism and self-exertion in finite time, he cuts back across the grain to criticize such assumptions about human activity, to show the damage inflicted by these assumptions upon the commonality of persons at all points on the social scale.

The historical consciousness embodied in these two tales draws on contending formations widely available to members of the upper *and* middle strata in Chaucer's day—formations themselves saturated with ideologically based assumptions about hierarchy and community, the sacred and the mundane. To some extent, as I have suggested, both ways of seeing the world were more or less simultaneously available to most of these persons. The greatest fourteenth-century aristocrats were not unacquainted with commerce, and the merchant class was probably the most hectically devout of its day. But the social grouping most extensively traversed by these conflicting versions of social reality was Chaucer's own. His was a group whose *gentil* rank and position within the court opened it to imaginative participation in Richard II's fitful dreams of theocratic kingship,[77] and a group whose unlanded status compelled involvement in the commerce of service or goods. Chaucer preeminently occupied what Eagleton calls a "dissentient conflictual position" within his own society, a position that throws the ideological faultlines of his literary production into high relief.[78] In this case, however, rather than tracing the faultlines in the repressions and distortions entailed by Chaucer's commitment to a unitary, hegemonic formation, I would locate them *between* the two ideological ensembles I have sought to describe; two ensembles that vied for the loyalty of late fourteenth-century *gentils* and non*gentils* alike, in uneasy and ultimately contradictory counterassertion.[79]

From the vantage point of today, the first of these ensembles may be viewed as decidedly on the wane, as a failing survival of an earlier state of feudalism and obsolete social arrangements: hieratic, sworn, eternal. We may also view the second as dynamic in its expression of a new commercial outlook that touched all social groups with its promise of a redeployment of human energies: fraternal, contractual, opportunistic. We have, in short, some basis for viewing the conflict between these ensembles as a clash between a fading, feudal hegemony and a rising, commercial counterhegemony. This would certainly be the view, if not the chosen terminology, of those scholars who have chronicled the achievements of the "rising bourgeoisie." But the evidence of Chaucer's poetry would suggest that he found each of these ensembles very much alive and in contention within the structures that defined his aesthetic and social worlds. From the special vantage of his inherently "dissentient" position, Chaucer was situated to respond to the countercurrents of a historically and ideologically charged moment, without necessarily concerning himself with issues of rise and decline.[80]

The historicizing consciousness of these two tales is located in Chaucer's own experience and authorial activity, in his discovery of the artistic means to inscribe a heightened ideological conflict within literary texts. Available to him were narrative genres—including those represented by the Knight's and Miller's tales—that not only offered apt "sites" for the inscription of crucial ideological formations, but whose social forms actively encouraged their definition and production. The inclusive formats of the dream vision and the tale collection offered Chaucer a means of juxtaposing narrative genres and the ideologies they expressed in ways that encouraged consideration of their inherent contradictions. This is, of course, an aspect of the achievement of the *Canterbury Tales* as a whole, with its rejection of the uniformity common to previous collections in favor of a mixture of genres and styles.[81] This mixture, in turn, permits consideration not only of aesthetic variety but also of the contending social assumptions inherent in its component narratives.

6 A Mixed Commonwealth of Style

IN THE course of Chaucer's General Prologue, the company of pilgrims first falls by chance into "felaweshipe" and then, prompted by Harry Bailly, constitutes itself more formally by choosing the innkeeper as its "governour" or figurative prince. Harry initiates the process of choice, asking that the pilgrims show their hands as a sign of "assent" to his "juggement." The pilgrims agree, swearing that they "wol reuled been at his devys" (I.816).

Charged with political implication as this moment may be, I am not suggesting that it be read as political allegory; the common endeavor over which Harry will preside will be a tale telling rather than any more explicitly political arrangement, and it is to his supervision of this contest that the pilgrims swear their "othes" of submission (I.810). Yet the investiture of Harry Bailly (like the contest of style over which he will preside) bears a social encoding that extends its meaning. For the *Canterbury Tales* here begins with that peculiarly medieval amplification of the Aristotelian theory of the natural state, a social contract.[1] The *pactum* between ruler and ruled, a staple of medieval thought, was bound up in an act of voluntary choice or election. It is in relation to this deeply held idea, for example, that Henry IV sought the consent of the estates to his rule ("Status cum toto Populo . . . ut Dux prefatus super eos regnaret unanimiter consenserunt"—*RP*, 3, 423), and subjects including Chaucer were not slow to connect this acclamation with the principle of "free eleccion" ("Purse," 23). Harry's election and the oath sworn to him as "governour" also have the effect of constituting the pilgrims as something more than a random fellowship; they are bound within the special circumstances of the pilgrimage into a temporary *res publica* or polity, for the duration of their ride to Canterbury and back again.[2]

Like other commonwealths, this one is composed of various social levels—it would be described as socially "mixed" or "heterogeneous" in the terms of medieval political discourse—and its participants exhibit a considerable diversity of social impulse. The pilgrimage thus necessarily confronts an issue that besets any heterogeneous social body: the quest for *coherentia* or the coherent relationship of parts, for *concordia* or agreement among them. Socially based insurrections like that of the Miller, vocational feuds like that of the Friar and Summoner, abuses of good faith like that of the Pardoner or of community like that of the Manciple, will all be encountered within the life of this particular body politic and must be repressed, contained, or surmounted if the body is to survive. Later medieval political discourse frequently concerns itself with the necessity for such accommodations and the means by which they might be effected. John of Salisbury, for example, suggests that social coherence may be maintained either hierarchically (by subjection of inferiors to superiors), on the one hand, or communally (by the sense of interdependence that regards a harm done to one as a harm done to all) on the other.[3] Just as we have found both principles at work elsewhere in medieval social description—in vertical versus horizontal descriptions of social ties, for example—so are they at work within theories of the natural state. My interest in this chapter is not to reduce the *Canterbury Tales* to one more such social theory. Yet, in one of its aspects, Chaucer's work may be seen as informed by ideas of the state and as a figurative reconception of the state in the terms of a discursive community. By situating Chaucer's narratives in a field of speculation about the nature of Christian polity, we open additional senses in which—even when most apparently aesthetic—they are the bearers of social implications.

Social Heterogeneity and the Natural State

Available in the later fourteenth century were several competing descriptions of the state, which offered ideologically charged characterizations of the relations between diverse social groups and the larger state in which they are situated. Of these competing descriptions, one in particular seems richly suggestive in its explicit embodiment of ideas implicitly realized in the stylistic and generic relations of Chaucer's text. This is the ideology of the "natural state," with its recognition of social diversity and its emphasis on the reconciliation of diversity according to a standard of the common good.

The natural state of the thirteenth and fourteenth centuries may, however, be seen not as a wholly consistent formation, but as a theoretical attempt to reconcile two existing emphases. One of these is the hierarchical or "descending" view, in which the polity is ordained by God, sacralized, modeled upon pseudo-Dionysian concepts of hierarchy, and expressive of principles of subjection between higher and lower orders. The other is the communal or corporate view, in which the polity is seen as contractual, created voluntarily by humankind for its own well-being, and modeled upon the body or organism with its interdependent parts.

The first of these models held nearly complete sway before the enthusiastic embrace of Aristotle's *Politics* in the late thirteenth and fourteenth centuries, and continued through the fourteenth and fifteenth centuries as the dominant model for ecclesiastical organization and as an influential alternative model of the secular state. It is exemplified by the influential theories of Giles of Rome (Aegidius Romanus), especially in his traditionally motivated defense of papal authority, *De ecclesiastica potestate*. There, having specified in detail the orders of the heavenly hierarchy, he asserts the applicability of this model not only to the ecclesiastical hierarchy (an assertion no contemporary theorist would have denied) but also to the social organization of the laity and the imperial state, descending from the emperor through kings, princes, dukes, and others.[4] This principle of descent or subordination is itself natural or observable "in rebus naturalis"—with, as he declares, the bridlemaker serving the soldier, the stonecutter serving the builder, and so on through the ranks of society.[5]

Also observable prior to the resurgence of Aristotle is the nonhierarchical or corporate tradition of the state as an organic whole composed of interdependent parts (although in the twelfth and earlier thirteenth centuries its realization is often obscured by the more dominant hierarchical model). Representative of such early formulations is John of Salisbury's twelfth-century image of the *res publica* as a kind of body ("corpus quoddam") subject to a prince in whose election the people may concur ("ad eum praeficiendum totius populi uota concurrunt"—V.6). The subjection of the members of the body to the head is conclusively asserted ("uniuersa membra se subiciant capiti"—VI.25). Nevertheless, the prince does not simply preside over a descending scale but over a complex interdependency, with a wound to one member affecting all and with a standard of coherence ("coherentia capitis et membrorum rei publicae"—VI.25) uniting all.

The availability of Aristotle's *Politics* after 1260 provided a theoretical site within which the hierarchical and corporate theories of the state could be reconciled, but with a wholly unprecedented degree of deference to corporate theories. The theoretical opening for this elaboration was Aristotle's assertion that the polity is natural (rather than ordained) and that man is by nature a political animal ("quoniam natura civitas est et quoniam homo natura civile animal"—I. 2).[6] Aristotle's assertion was promptly and extensively embraced,[7] an embrace not to be viewed simply as an event in the history of ideas, but as a response to the emergence of multiple and influential social groups on the medieval social scene. (Documentation of this emergence lies in the province of social history and cannot be attempted in this study, but the influence of this emergence can be felt as a form of pressure on the content of a number of late medieval texts.)

The first influential commentator to seize on the *Politics* was Thomas Aquinas, whose *De regno* was composed before the end of the 1260s, obtaining circulation in its own right and even more broadly throughout the fourteenth century in the composite *De regimine principum*.[8] Aquinas forthrightly applies Aristotle's premises, asserting that it is natural for man, as a social animal, to live in a group ("Naturale autem est homini ut sit animal sociale et politicum, in multitudine vivens, magis etiam quam omnia alia animalia, quod quidem naturalis necessitas declarat"—I. 1).[9] This impulse to live "in societate multorum" presupposes a coordination of functions, so that people engaged in diverse activities might assist each other ("ut . . . diversi diversis inveniendis per rationem occuparentur"—I. 1). The diversity of the regnum requires an agency to direct it toward the common good ("ad bonum commune") and—just as divine providence rules the universe and the heart or head rules the human body—so does the king rule the body politic. This rule is not, however, ordained but is based on the consent of the people, acting according to their natural instincts. As Aquinas says in relation to the deposition of the tyrant, who acts in relation to his own well-being rather than that of the commonwealth, a people that acts in the first place to provide itself with a king ("providere de rege") has the right to remove him by the same process if he abuses his power (I. 6).

The Aristotelian/Thomistic view of the natural state, in which the ruler enjoyed a consensual or contractual relation with his subjects, was to dominate fourteenth-century English thought. Even the conservative Giles of Rome adopted many of its premises in his early *De regimine,* and progressive theorists such as Jean de Paris and Marsilius of Padua elaborated his propositions about the naturalness of the state and the interdependence of its parts for the good of the whole. This elaboration occurred in two areas of particular interest here: in a heightened attention to the variety of the social and civil impulses the ruler is expected to resolve; and in the degree of their insistence on the contractual nature of rule, as expressed through popular consent and through representative and consultative mechanisms.

With respect to diverse impulse, Jean imagines that, just as the soul unites the heterogeneous human body or "humanis corporis etherogeneum," so does the ruler lead a mixed ("mixtum") polity (ch. 1).[10] Dispersal of persons seeking their own interests is to be prevented by the leadership of one person seeking the common good ("multitudo . . . in diversa dispergitur nisi ad bonum commune ordinetur per aliquem unum cui sit cura de bono communi"). But the inner diversity of resulting communities militates against a single kind of ruler; the people choose different kinds of rulers to accord with their diverse communities ("secundum diversitatem communitatum"—ch. 3). In a similar vein but with characteristic argumentative zest, Marsilius views humankind as composed of contrary elements ("compositus ex contrariis elementis"—1.4.iii[11]) that are potentially destructive but are channeled through inclination toward different offices or vocations (distinguished after Aristotle as the agricultural, that of the artisan, the military, the financial, the priestly, and the judicial—1.5.i). These offices or vocations may be resolved into two social groups or classes—the honorable class *(honorabilitas)* and the common mass *(vulgus)*. Nature prompted people toward these different occupational groups and classes, and the state or polity is the site within which they are constituted as socially useful activities (1.8.i). So conceived, the state is less an embodiment of God's hierarchical plan than it is an arena for the active resolution or conciliation of competing social interests here on earth.

This natural state is not exempt from hierarchical principles, including its direction by a ruler who exercises a function analogous to that of God in heaven or the soul in the body. This principle of rule is, however, less ordained than it is instituted by consent, through election or popular choice. Thus Jean asserts that "kingly power . . . is from God and the people electing" ("potestas regia . . . est . . . a Deo et a populo regem eligente"—ch. 10), and he argues that the power of the first emperor derived from the acclaim and action of the people, to whom it belongs to subject themselves to whomever they wish—(ch. 15). Jean appears to treat this notion of consent as a constitutive fiction, a theory of origins, rather than as a matter of practical possibility. But Marsilius' formulation of the same issue, developed within a context of early Italian civic humanism, is at once more practical and more extreme. The well-tempered government, he tells us, is based on the will or consent ("voluntas" or "consensus") of voluntary subjects (I. 8.iii). Legislative authority in the state rests with the whole body of citizens or the "weightier part" ("valentior pars"—I. 12.iii), and he forthrightly asserts that the power to elect the ruler belongs to the legislator or the citizens ("ad legislatorem seu civium universitatem"—I. 15.ii).

Such a state may be viewed not as a hierarchy of parts subordinated one to another, but as a community constituted of different orders or vocations; not as an inferior manifestation of an unseen and atemporal order, but as a natural entity defined by human choice in finite time; not as sacred and ordained, but as secular and founded upon human consent. By no means devoid of hierarchical tendency, in such matters as Marsilius' emphasis on the *valentior pars,* the state is yet opened to the active involvement of all orders and parts. Still seen as a body, this state has received a new soul; priestly no longer, the soul is now the citizenry, and they invent the *civitas* or state.

These elaborations of the natural state occurred within polemical and rather specialized discussions of the relation of the empire to the papacy and were confined to a finite readership. Yet the ideas with which they dealt reached a wider fourteenth-century public in a variety of forms. John Wyclif, for example, seems not to have known Marsilius and regarded Marsilius' ally Ockham as a realist adversary, but he nevertheless reaches parallel conclusions about the separation of the temporal and ecclesiastical hierarchies by characteristically novel means. Arguing, for example, that possession of material goods depends on a state of grace, he concludes that a corrupt church is subject to temporal lordship.[12] This autonomous temporal lordship is headed by a king, but the king is not divinely appointed; his government is collective, involving "al his counseillores, as lords and prelatis, and alle men of the Parlement counceilinge therto."[13] An argument similar in its claims for temporal authority, and for collective rule, is that of Walter Burley, who suggests in his mid-fourteenth-century commentary on Aristotle that a multitude consisting of the king and nobility and wise men rules the kingdom ("in regno multitudo constitut [sic] ex rege et proceribus et sapientibus regni quodammodo principatur").[14] Interestingly, he like Wyclif cites the English *parliamentum* or parliament as an illustration of the power of the multitude.

Also circulating in fourteenth-century England were several works entitled *De regimine principum,* including those of Aquinas and his continuator and—especially—that of the young Giles of Rome. However traditional the arguments Giles would later adopt as papal apologist, the main line of thought in his *De regimine* is definitely Aristotelian, with its stress on natural inclination toward community ("Natuyre a donne a homme naturel enclinance a fere et a establir communete"—p. 268),[15] its invocation of the metaphorical body politic (with people assembled under the prince "comme plusors membres sont assemble en I cors et ont divers offices pro le cors mieuz vivre"—p. 271), and on the precedence of natural law (establishd "par le consentement de le gent"—p. 346).[16]

These texts variously embody an idea of the natural state, drawing upon a cluster of ideas that are associated with sufficient regularity to render their interconnection clear. Central among them are the following: The state is natural rather than ordained (and hence more a product of human choice than providential ordinance). It is secular rather than sacred (and hence operates more by its own laws than those of a divine superstructure, and more by contract than by sacred oath). It is temporal rather than atemporal (and hence subject more to mutation than to stasis). Its separate parts are more likely to be regarded as interdependent or communal than as hierarchical or stratified, and they are defined more by function than by their approximation of perfection. Above all—and here I would locate the immense appeal of this complex of ideas to thinkers of all persuasions in the late thirteenth and fourteenth centuries—the state is regarded as a site for the active reconciliation of diverse social interests, rather than as a static framework designed to perpetuate inequalities.

This complex of ideas may be considered an "ideology," in its function of reworking disparate social information in forms that can guide individual conduct and that permit its textual embodiment. Thus we have encountered ideas of the natural state in a variety of different genres and forms: in Aquinas' *liber* or book of advice to princes, in Jean de Paris' *treatise* or series of linked treatises,[17] in Marsilius' *liber* joining several political *dictiones* or discourses; in Wyclif's parliamentary *bill* or *petition;* in Burley's *commentarius* on the works of Aristotle. If these varied works have been produced by the ideology of the natural state, they are also its producers, redeploying various of its tenets in support of a spectrum of imperial and national causes too complicated to trace at this time. Even these relatively expository *libri* and treatises are, in other words, socially energetic—not simply reflective of an ideology but transformative of it, bending it to use, whether to uphold the claims of an emperor against a pope (Jean, Marsilius), a king against an ecclesiastical establishment (Wyclif), a king against extremes of tyranny and democracy (Aquinas, Burley).

This ensemble of ideas about the natural state as a product of diverse social impulses was available to Chaucer when he created his temporary polity of Canterbury pilgrims. The ideological presuppositions of the natural state function as a suggestive "middle term" between his own experiences of social conflict and a literary text that refigures social conflict as a conflict of genres and styles. His realization of certain conceptions consistent with the natural state is, however, far from a passive reflection of the familiar. Instead he offers us a wholly fresh reconstitution of the natural state, with its own distinctive contours, suppressions, and imaginative connections. The large and diffuse ensemble of social texts, attitudes, and practices that constituted the ideology of the natural state need not, in this respect, be seen as a source for Chaucer. Rather, it offered him a body of interrelated significations and metaphors, flourishing in a historically defined set of circumstances, that was useful in constructing an artifice that recognizes diversity and conflict among ranks, interests, and styles as inherent in the nature of ordinary social existence.

Chaucer's Commonwealth

Chaucer's own commonwealth of Canterbury pilgrims may easily enough be aligned with the model of the natural state, with its varied or "sondry" persons figuring the mixed or heterogeneous populace of Jean de Paris and its *gentils* and *cherls* standing in for the *honorabilitati* and *vulgi* of Marsilian theory. Chaucer's pilgrims are also cast, like the citizens of the natural state, into a condition of temporality, in which their form of self-rule is determined not by imitation of permanent categories but by choices made among available alternatives. Here, though, the specifically narrative dimension of the *Canterbury Tales* opens a set of possibilities different from those of the relatively expository and nonnarrative treatises with which we have just been concerned. For, despite their incipiently dynamic conception of the commonwealth as a site for the reconciliation of diverse interests, these treatises depict a social model in relative arrest; aside from occasional references to good counsel and parliamentary participation, they are essentially unable to reveal the processes by which a commonwealth resolves differences over time. Chaucer's pilgrimage, by contrast, moves through time, and the temporal basis of its narration introduces a powerful engine of conciliation unavailable to expository writers on statecraft.[18]

The great resource of narration, fully exploited in the *Canterbury Tales,* is its capacity to reveal the self-maintaining processes by which a social body may act in time to accommodate new social groups, reconcile disputes, and chastise antisocial impulses. The pilgrimage—as Victor Turner reminds us, speaking generally but with particular relevance to the case at hand—offers a "processual" form, with challenges to the social order enacted in a series of dramas set in linear time.[19] In his pilgrimage Chaucer draws on the power of literary language to enstate or even exaggerate conflict in contexts that need not lead to violent schism. To the extent that rupture does occur, he draws on the power of narrative to represent conciliation as a temporal process, to offer his audience a privileged space within which otherwise intractable problems may be invoked and—hypothetically if not actually—resolved.[20]

A case in point is the Miller's violent disruption of the intended order of pilgrim-tellers and his assertion (at once social and stylistic) of his right to inclusion. This incident affords a particularly vivid instance of a drama constantly enacted in Chaucer's poetry, a drama in which a hierarchy is established, challenged, and finally modified as a result of the challenge, with the incorporation of the challenger into the resultant new order.

A prototype of this drama occurred in the *Parliament of Fowls,* when Nature established a hierarchy by inviting the most "worthi" (392) tercels to speak according to their degree, with the other birds following "by ordre" (400). This order was no sooner established than abused by the lengthy speeches of the tercels, and was challenged ("Have don!"—492ff) and ultimately penetrated by the lower fowl. The result of this penetration was the establishment of a temporary institution—a "parlement"—hospitable to diverse social levels (from *gentils* to *cherls*) and a polyphony of socially defined voices (from the gentle and atemporal pleading of the avian aristocrats to the more loamy and less patient speech of the worm- and water-fowl). This provisional resolution situated varied voices within an institutional framework, without denying their social difference. The point was reinforced as chosen representatives then joined in a roundel, presumably rendered polyphonically, with each voice distinct but contributing to a final effect.

As with the hierarchical description of the birds in Nature's garden, the General Prologue itself begins with an essentially hierarchical presentation of the pilgrims (clustered with their companions and retinues) in roughly the order of social rank: starting with the Knight, then persons of some social pretension within the ranks of the regular religious, then the middle strata, then members of the lower classes, beginning with those who fulfill their roles and ending with those who abuse them.[21] The tales themselves begin in a similarly hierarchical vein, with the rather obviously rigged lottery falling to the Knight, and with Harry Bailly's intention of tale telling "bi ordre" revealed in his subsequent invitation to the Monk. The eruption of the Miller into this order of tellers is no less abrupt than that of the lower fowl; echoing their "loude noyse" in his "Pilates voys," he offers us a social and stylistic equivalent of a form of breaching behavior previously disclosed in the General Prologue, that of breaking down doors with his head.

Harry Bailly recognizes the socially insurrectionary element of the Miller's behavior, speaking familiarly and condescendingly to him as "my leeve brother" and suggesting that a "bettre man" first tell a tale. In an attractive underscoring of the social dimension of the Miller's self-insertion, Alfred David has characterized his tale as "a literary Peasants' Rebellion."[22] (The Miller is of course no peasant, but this fact need not concern us, in the light of research suggesting that participants in the Peasants' Revolt included many yeomen, artisans, and craftsmen.[23]) David's compact phrase is true to the social dynamism of the Miller's intervention, and—in its emphasis on the self-consciously literary nature of his revolt—additionally alert to the rapidity with which the Miller's social revolt is transmuted into a matter of style (with his requital transferred from the Knight himself to the Knight's *tale*). Despite the ominous terms in which the Miller's upheaval is couched—including blasphemous and highly aggressive profanity, sarcasms directed toward the generic elevation of the Knight's *storie,* assiduous disclaimers on the part of the narrator, and scornful parody of somber moments in the *Knight's Tale*—the tale he tells would have been a good deal more congenial to the tastes of Chaucer's predominantly gentle audience than its rather fraught manner of presentation would imply (more welcome, certainly, than the Miller himself at one of their social gatherings). The transmutation of a social revolt into a stylistic revolt may with some legitimacy be seen as a way of smothering or defusing a legitimate recognition of irreconcilable differences within the *Tales.*[24] But, in another sense to be discussed later, the expression of socially based disagreement in the arena of style rather than social action opens a variety of strategies for carrying forward social debate in other terms. Restated in terms of style, the Miller's rebellion is subject to a process of conciliation and integration far more rapid and less painful than that experienced by the rebellious peasants in 1381.

Relevant to the Miller's interruption and ultimate social integration is Turner's description of the several stages of social conflict, beginning with a breach of a norm regulating social intercourse, passing through crisis and redressive action, resulting either in reintegration or in irreparable schism. Here, as in most such instances in the *Canterbury Tales,* the consequence of the Miller's intervention is obviously reintegration. Most crucially, the Miller's penetration of the intended hierarchy is successfully accomplished, not only in the sense that he completes his own tale but that tale telling "bi ordre" will be supplanted by an entirely new and nonhierarchical set of criteria, with tellers either self-nominated or chosen according to the new perspectives or departures promised by their vocation or demeanor. Further, the Miller's tale is itself legitimated by the body of pilgrims; while diverse judgments are registered, "for the moore part they loughe and pleyde" (I.3858). In fact, the only seriously aggrieved person is not a *gentil* at all, but Oswald the Reeve, and his complaint is neither social nor stylistic but vocational in nature. His own tale told in "cherles termes" (I.3917) may be regarded as the next stage in a descent to petty wrangling among the lesser vocations, a descent that the *gentils* might be imagined to applaud.[25] Yet, viewed in relation to its style, it may be seen as solidifying the impetus behind the Miller's stylistic rebellion, which is to open the tale telling to varied, socially based discourse.

Personal animosities will continue to surface, but social difference will not again play so crucial a role in explaining conflict. Social considerations do surface faintly from time to time. The Clerk's ironic engagement of the Wife of Bath in his envoy would seem to spring not so much from personal animosity (though one might imagine the horror of so conservative a social satirist at the Wife's unregulated behavior) as from a distaste for her theories of governance. Harry Bailly's impatient rejection of the Franklin's concern with "gentillesse" has been read in its immediate context as a rebuke to his ambition for upward mobility[26] (though his tale develops a definition of the concept in better keeping with his social station). The collective skittishness of the *gentils* at the Pardoner's impending performance has a social inflection (though it is immediately transmuted into a socially encoded theory of genre, with their expressed preference of "som moral thyng" rather than the Pardoner's apparent commitment to *ribaudye*). For the most part, though, other motivations, faithful to certain aspects of fourteenth-century experience but a good deal less dangerous, are advanced instead. Most prominent are the vocational quarrels of the Miller and the Reeve, the Friar and the Summoner, and between Harry Bailly and several different pilgrims. Other motivations involve the moral shortcomings of particular pilgrims, as when the Manciple cannot refrain (even in the perverse form of his apology) from malice in chivvying the drunken Cook. Even when not obviously socially motivated, however, all these instances retain an aura of social implication, in their bearing on the maintenance of temporary polity, in the sense in which they tend either toward reintegration or toward schism.

The condition of membership in the pilgrim community is of course participation in the tale telling, and the relation of individual pilgrims to their fellow tellers is ultimately judged in large part by the "use" to which their tales may be put. Whether the standard of judgment by *myrthe* or *solaas* on the one hand or *sentence, moralitee,* or *doctryne* on the other, the criteria by which a tale may be found useful are flexible and generous. But transgression remains a possibility.

The Pardoner, for example, seriously threatens presuppositions upon which the community of tellers was founded. His marginality within the community has initially been suggested by such indicators as his placement last in the order of pilgrims. His reluctance to contribute positively to the narratively defined economy of the tales is more pointedly indicated at such moments as his interruption of the Wife of Bath in order to stage his personal pretensions (III. 163–168) and by his hostile and self-important insistence that his fellow pilgrims receive his tale only on his own terms (VI. 320–328). His animosity is suggested in the way he responds to the *gentils'* request for "som moral thyng" (VI. 325): with a barrage of exempla saturated with mockery of his fellow pilgrims' hope of moral or spiritual profit. This is, after all, a community formed for the express purpose of exchanging edifying discourse, and the Pardoner places his fellows in a double bind by offering them discourse at once artful and false, in such a way that anyone responding positively to his admonitions becomes his dupe. Other pilgrims have failed to further profitable aims—the narrator's tale of *Sir Thopas* lacked "murthe" *or* "doctryne" and thus wasted potentially gainful time (VII. 931–935); the "sentence" of the Monk's tragedies was so debatable as to lose him his audience

(VII.2767–2802). But only the Pardoner is guilty of the particular bad faith of presenting a tale that mocks any auditor gullible enough to respond to its invitations.

The Pardoner himself seems to seek amends at the conclusion of his tale, offering his auditors a moment of candor (VI.916–918) and engaging in what I read as conciliatory buffoonery when he attempts to sell pardons after all (VI.919–945). Yet his habitual contempt invades the very process of jesting conciliation. Whatever its tone, his invitation to Harry Bailly to kiss his relics (VI.943–944) is properly interpreted as a submerged invitation to abasement ("Thou woldest make me kisse thyn olde breech"—VI.948), and the laughter of "al the peple" (VI.961) suggests that Harry's response represents that of the community as a whole. At hand here is a schism-threatening conflict serious enough to require the mediatory talents of the ultimate "governour" of the pilgrimage, the Knight, who sponsors a ritual of reintegration (VI.962–967). The sincerity of this reconciliation cannot be assessed. But only the Knight's intervention would seem to have prevented a schism between the community and its most precariously situated member (VI.968).

The importance of preparedness to share discourse as a precondition for membership in the pilgrim community is made yet more explicit in the *Canon's Yeoman's Prologue*. The Canon shows no lack of desire to join the pilgrims, having—as he says—ridden hard for three miles "for youre sake, / By cause that I wolde yow atake, / To riden in this myrie compaignye" (VIII.584–586). At first he seems a promising recruit, in his display of zeal, in his yeoman's assertion that he loves "daliaunce" (VIII.592), and in an appearance of jocundity that prompts Harry Bailly to ask, "Can he oght telle a myrie tale or tweye?" (VIII.597). An indication of larger problems to come is Harry's slightly dubious "oght" ("at all"); the yeoman is indeed doing most of his talking for him. And we are to learn that the Canon is dubious about discourse and what it might reveal. We learn that he invariably had "suspecioun / Of mennes speche" (VIII.686–687), that he is among those guilty people who suspect (not unrightly, in this case) that others are talking about them (VIII.688–691). He seeks to forbid speech, telling his yeoman to "spek no wordes mo" and accompanying his admonition with threats (VIII.693–694). When Harry Bailly assures the yeoman that his speech will be protected—a condition of a community literally founded on discourse—the Canon flees, in an act of voluntary separation (VIII.702). To the other faults partially disguised by "pryvetee" may be added a fault prohibitive of membership in this community: fearing what it might reveal, he will not share his discourse for the good of all. His yeoman, by contrast, is won away and joins the community of willing tale tellers.

The commonwealth of Canterbury pilgrims thus maintains itself over time, as a body of people prepared to share discourse according to rules to which all have submitted themselves. It maintains itself not by ignoring social and vocational difference, but by demonstrating its capacity to resolve social dramas and flareups as they arise, in favor of continued *coherentia* among its diverse parts. The maintenance of this discursive commonwealth does not, by the way, depend upon eradication of social or vocational difference. The *gentils* are still gentle and the *cherls* are still churlish, and nothing suggests that the Friar and Summoner hate each other the less or that the enmity between Harry Bailly and the Pardoner has really gone away. But the pilgrimage continues, dealing with socially based dissensions as they arise, finding a way to submerge disputes in that realistic form of *coherentia* that seeks a common ground among otherwise incompatible interests.

Even this limited assertion of *coherentia* must of course be seen as a considerable distortion of factional and schismatic actuality. Viewed as an ideologically constructed bridge between Chaucer and his predominantly *gentil* public, it must be acknowledged a self-interested distortion as well, presenting a solution congenial to their own aims (maintenance of social order, but on terms receptive to previously excluded or underacknowledged ranks and groups) as a general solution for the good of all. Self-interested or not, it remains a bold and socially energetic solution, finding its own point of entry to the contemporary discussion of the mixed commonwealth, in order to muster fresh images of inclusion, accommodation, and reconciliation against the most threatening social divisions of the day.

Issues of Hierarchy and Community

If social energies are tacitly expressed in the representation of the pilgrim body as a mixed and self-sustaining commonwealth, social issues are also raised for explicit consideration in the content of the tales the pilgrims tell. That the content of the Canterbury narratives should embrace both hierarchical and communal models of society, and should negotiate various compromises between them, is no surprise. We have already observed the coexistence of both conceptions within theories of the natural state and within Chaucer's pilgrim band.

Hierarchical formulations are amply represented in the tales they tell, but are never presented unequivocally or permitted to stand without contest. Whether embodied in representations of the heavenly order in relation to the earthly order, the civil ruler in relation to his subjects, or even the Christian in relation to his own faculties and impulses, the authority of hierarchical models is repeatedly qualified or undermined by the circumstances of their presentation.

The ultimate authorization of earthly hierarchy lies in the relation of the heavenly to the earthly order, and Chaucer tends to explore this relation in the relatively neutralized regions of classical mythology, reconceived as a system of astrological relations. Thus removed from considerations of Christian necessity, the relevance of the celestial hierarchy as a precedent for the secular political order is opened to question within an area imaginatively related to, but still insulated from, essential Christian belief. Such an interrogation of the power of a celestial order to impress itself constructively upon earthly disorder is extensively developed within the *Knight's Tale*. We have already had occasion to consider how little benignity the astrologically defined gods of that tale offer their human counterparts. Their legitimacy is traceable mainly to the respective breadths of their arcs (as in I.2454)—a celestial equivalent to the definition of earthly power by the extent of domains—but this legitimation suggests the dispassionate nature of their relations to earthly affairs. Such autonomy as they possess, as when Saturn acts to stop the quarrel between Venus and Mars, is exercised not in relation to human well-being but to favoritism and old family ties. What remains to be noted is that the "strif" among the gods—with Venus and Mars each claiming favor for her or his adherent and with Jupiter unable to halt the quarrel—is less a model for redress of earthly disorder than a magnification of that disorder within the heavenly sphere. Palamon's "all-for-love" attitude, Arcite's pragmatism, and Emily's wish to escape possessive male love are in fact *projected* into the heavenly sphere, where they are coupled with the wholly damning agency of Chaucer's malign creation, Saturn.[27]

The failure of these gods to offer a constructive "descending" model as an object of emulation is exemplified even more clearly in the *Merchant's Tale*. There the movement of the tale to another narrative level and the introduction of an intervention-minded Pluto and Proserpine promote no solutions. Pluto's gift of sight to January leads not to knowing but to additional confusion and dotage, and Proserpine's gift of "suffisant answere" (IV.2266) guarantees May's continued resistance to her spouse. The introduction of these gods may be seen as an expansion, rather than a resolution, of January's and May's problems: Pluto replicates January's capacity for self-deception when he finds the latter an "honurable knyght" (IV. 2254), and Proserpine affirms May's brazen self-regard by adding a new weapon to her arsenal of deceptions. The relationship drawn between the celestial and earthly levels of this tale is less one of descent than of perverse ascent, with an earthly quarrel perpetuated in the realm of the gods.

Even as heavenly hierarchies are stripped of much of their authority as models for earthly conduct, so are earthly magistrates called repeatedly into question for their failure to practice good lordship. The lord of the manor, asked at the end of the *Summoner's Tale* to judge the sleight practiced by the "cherl" of his village, weighs the churl's action (III. 2217), rather offhandedly dismisses it (III. 2242), and finally warms to the churl's wit only because of its potential to embarrass the friars (III. 2292). But, as Lee Patterson has argued, this response involves no redress for the churl's grievances, but rather disarms them with laughter and dehistoricized aesthetic appreciation.[28] Portrayed in a darker register are the lustful connivances of the "governour" and false justice Appius against the virtuous Virginia in the *Physician's Tale*. Chaucer has, as Sheila Delany points out, partially de-historicized this tale, suppressing discussion of struggle between unlawful authority and the plebs.[29] Yet the abuse of hierarchical authority is still underscored by the account of Appius' "conspiracie" (VI. 149), in which a "cherl" is suborned to claim Virginia as his "thral" (VI . 183), with this heightened social terminology serving to remind the audience that Appius is actually an agent of social dislocation, setting a "cherl" against a worthy "knyght." Chaucer's most searching examination of the abuse of the hierarchical ideal is, however, to be found in his *Clerk's Tale*.

Much like its sources in Petrarch and Old French,[30] and to an even greater extent than either, the Clerk's account of Griselda's travail may be read as a virtual paean to "obseisaunce," to the subordination an inferior owes to a superior in a hierarchical situation. This tale, like all of Chaucer's tales, embraces many voices, including those of predecessor texts, of Chaucer the poet-narrator, of the Clerk himself. But if one may generalize in so complex a matter, the predominant voice of the tale is that of the Clerk, and he is presented to the audience as conservative satirist, elaborately deferential to authority in his own conduct and in his literary imagination.[31] This is the theme he sets in his exchange with Harry Bailly, just when we hear his voice in something closest to its distinctive form:

> "Hooste," quod he, "I am under youre yerde;
> Ye han of us as now the governance,
> And therfore wol I do yow obeisance . . ." (IV.22–24)

This theme of subordination "as now" to temporal authority is insisted upon throughout: in protagonist Walter's "obeisant" lieges, in his people's imagining of marriage as "that blisful yok / Of soveraynetee," in the obedience of his knights and squires, in Griselda's "obeisaunce" to her elderly father, in the portrayal of Janicula as "feithful lige" to Walter and Walter's respect for Janicula's paternal rights, in Janicula's wish that Walter "govern" as he wishes, in Walter's demand of obedience from Griselda, in Griselda's own "obeisaunce" to Walter's wishes, and elsewhere. The tale concludes with a reaffirmation of these apparent convictions in the Clerk's scathing poem in praise of the Wife of Bath and her "secte" for their attempted seizure of "maistrie" (IV.1172) in the marital relation.

Yet, even as the *Clerk's Tale* extends the Petrarchan ideal of obedience to one's ruler—whether husband or marquis—its boundaries also contain a critique of this very notion. This surfaces in varied forms, including an undertow of discomfort over Walter's excesses, a covert introduction of alternative norms, and overt criticisms of his motivations. Whether we view this critique as issuing from Chaucer or from his Clerk, it calls into question many features of the hierarchical ideology that the tale seems to advance. One element of this critique, as David Wallace points out,[32] is the introduction of a sense of civic responsibility, embodied in the "peple" who communicate with Walter through a chosen representative. Although they are ultimately to be seduced by Walter's gift for civic display (IV.983–1005), the terms in which they are first introduced stand as an argument for Walter's abuse of his responsibility for good governance. This standard is further enforced by Griselda's own attention to "commune profit" and to relief of civil discord (IV.431–434)—a standard against which Walter, with such tactics as his lying misrepresentation of his subjects' views (IV.624—637), is obviously found wanting.[33] Another element is Walter's own transgression against the very system of subordination to which he so often appeals and which the narrative so warmly endorses. This transgression is most evident in his rejection of his subjects' interpretation of marriage as a "blisful yok / Of soveraynetee, noght of servyse" (IV.113–114). Despite the benignity of this view and its consistency with the ideology of the tale, Walter rejects it to treat marriage as unwelcome "servage" (IV.147), resisting entry into the temporal and generative cycle his subjects propose to him (IV. 121–126) and choosing instead a restless consultation of his own desires more appropriate to tyranny than to good lordship. Yet another element is the irrational and obsessive nature of Walter's actions, prompting attempts at explanation by the clerk/narrator that fall so short of their purpose that they raise more questions than they put to rest. The Clerk's comment on obsessiveness, for example, serves more to underscore this trait than to relieve Walter of responsibility for it:

> But ther been folk of swich condicion
> That whan they have a certein purpos take,
> They kan nat stynte of hire entencion,
> But, right as they were bounden to that stake,
> They wol nat of that firste purpos slake. (IV. 701–705)

Such doubts about Walter lead to a strengthened denial of the link between Walter and Griselda, on the one hand, and God and the patient Christian on the other. Chaucer's sources think it scarcely possible that a contemporary woman could imitate Griselda ("que michi vix imitabilis videtur" . . . "que a paine me semble ensuivable et possible"), while the idea is "inportable" or not to be borne in Chaucer's Middle English (IV. 1144).[34] As a result of all these adjustments, the narrative both evokes the ideology of hierarchical and descending governance and calls that ideology into question. If the members of Chaucer's audience were as stirred by this tale as were Petrarch's friends (and especially the one who, thinking it a true story, burst into tears), they must have been stirred more by Griselda's plight than by her particular adherence to the descending structure of assumptions about governance responsible for putting her there.[35]

References to hierarchy are not always cautionary. Yet, even when most positively invoked, hierarchy is offered less as a self-evident part of God's plan for the cosmos, and more as a potentially flawed system that can only be maintained by human vigilance and good will. Hierarchy may, for example, be viewed as the ultimate subject of the *Tale of Melibee,* but the narrative reveals its flawed nature and the necessity for its restoration by good counsel. The failure of hierarchy is revealed at each level at which the tale operates: literally the tale describes a man who has sustained attack by his enemies and who, learning to accept good counsel, earns their rightful submission; allegorically (or, more specifically, anagogically[36]) it describes a Christian who has left himself open to temptation and who must regain control of his impulses and desires by the exercise of his prudence or better judgment. At either of its principal levels of meaning, the climax of the tale is prepared by Melibee's reconciliation with God, a reconciliation that will—Prudence promises—cause his enemies to "fallen at youre feet" (VII.1717–18). Melibee's proper domination of his errant enemies (allegorically his unruly impulses) is in fact restored, as he receives "hire obligaciouns and hir boondes by hire othes" (VII.1827) and their "obeisance" (VII.1855).

Whether Melibee be taken as a person of prominence in a civil commonwealth or as the head of his own microcosmic "body," his movement through good counsel to resumption of proper lordship is the motive force of this narrative. His reinstatement is not only conveyed through incident (the acceptance of Prudence's counsel, the surrender of his enemies) but is supported by imagery. As in other versions of the narrative, Melibee enters as a prosperous householder, presumably of the upper bourgeoisie: "A yong man . . . myghty and riche" (VII.967). Once he is restored to proper lordship, however, his position is enhanced, and his enemies submit to him as to a great feudal lord: "we submytten us to the excellence and benignitee of youre gracious lordshipe" (VII.1821). The ultimate restoration of hierarchy is in fact signaled not only by Melibee's advancement to the status of "greet lord" (VII.1860), but by the reinstatement of a powerful system of analogy that Walter's irrational cruelty had forced tellers of the Griselda story to disavow. Melibee, showing leniency to his enemies, treats them as he hopes in turn to be treated by a merciful God. The end of the narrative finds Melibee, restored and enhanced, enacting the earthly role of *imago dei,* an image or vicar of God.

Melibee's accession to the role of *imago dei* is not simply ordained, but the result of necessary exertions. He must learn to modify his impulses by attention to good counsel, discreetly sought from appropriate counselors. He must, conversely, learn to reject bad counsel inappropriately delivered, and especially that of an unruly multitude. He has erred at the outset by calling together an unruly rout of strangers, flatterers, and ex-enemies, who have drowned out wise voices and given rash advice. He should, according to Prudence, have gathered a small body of those "approved in conseillynges" (VII.1162), rejecting the less valuable advice of "a greet multitude of peple, ful chargeant and ful anoyous for to heere" (VII.1243). Prudence's political advice is of course unexceptionable. It is "pre-Aristotelian," for Albertanus' mid-thirteenth-century *Liber,* the ultimate source of the French version adopted by Chaucer, is an informal collection of maxims gathered from such common sources as Jesus Syrach, Seneca, Petrus Alphonsus, and Publius Syrius.[37] Despite its informality, though, it adopts a modified position on hierarchy that would be found generally acceptable in most traditions of medieval political analysis, in which the head of the civic body rules in consultation with Marsilius' *valentior pars,* stopping short of the more chaotic elements of democracy.

Chaucer's ultimate source in Albertanus and his actual source in Reynaud were originally employed to assert what Olson describes as "the consultative as opposed to the absolutist view of the prerogative of the King,"[38] and we may assume this to be among Chaucer's purposes as well.[39] But it also fulfills a general thematic purpose, that of restating traditional presuppositions about hierarchy in a form compatible with the generally antihierarchical and communal thrust of the *Canterbury Tales* as a whole. Among the diverse themes of Chaucer's work, the ideology of the descending state ruled by a lord in the image of God still finds a place, though in a relatively unsevere form, in which the head of the polity tempers his rule according to the collective advice of those best situated to offer counsel.

A Literary Model of Social Diversity

Always receptive to forms that permitted juxtaposition of genres and styles, Chaucer moved in the course of his career toward framing fictions (parliamentary debate, processual tale telling) that provided additional justification for generic and stylistic variety by encouraging the introduction of multiple, independent, and unresolved voices. Critics have been responsive to these emphases but have normally explained them in aesthetic terms: a recent and keen study of Chaucer's "drama of style" finds it to be "artistic" rather than personal or social in nature;[40] a fine discussion of generic variety in the *Canterbury Tales* concludes with the rather feeble explanation that "Chaucer wishes to demonstrate his poetic mastery."[41] A more complete explanation must move beyond a presumption of purely aesthetic motivation, to recognize the social conditioning of certain categories of aesthetic choice.

Chaucer's generic and stylistic variation, and his multiplication of the different vocalities by which this variation is sustained, may be viewed as a mediated response to factionalism and contradiction within his own social experience. In this sense, the aesthetic project of the *Canterbury Tales* may be linked to a social project of importance for

Chaucer's time, and of particular urgency for the social and literary circle within which he lived and composed his poetry. The clamor of new social groupings for admittance to public awareness and public process was a salient fact of late fourteenth-century social life, and it posed a crucial challenge to the contemporaneous social imagination. Viewed in relation to this challenge, Chaucer's *aesthetic* enterprise of defining a literary space that permits free interaction of different forms and styles may be placed in reciprocal relation with the *social* enterprise of defining a public space hospitable to different social classes with diverse social impulses.

The nature of this reciprocal relation must be more carefully considered. In a stimulating article on the *Parliament of Fowls,* A. C. Spearing has taken to task recent historically oriented critics who have declared that poem "political" and who have invoked political treatises from outside the poem in order to establish its essential unity.[42] I would argue that the shortcoming of the critics he attacks is not in finding the poem political, but in finding it unified in relation to a single principle of thought and in their appeal to texts not necessarily known to Chaucer in order to establish that unity. The *Parliament of Fowls* and the *Canterbury Tales* are eminently social and political in their implications, but are not so specifically *determined* by particular political theories or events that we can adduce texts or events from outside the poem to supply interpretative omissions. Although I believe society and history to be "absent causes" of Chaucer's aesthetic choices, they are absent in ways that frustrate our attempts at recovery and that hardly authorize their confident use as mortar to fill gaps in Chaucer's text.[43] Chaucer's usual tendency is deliberately to efface any demonstrable connections between contemporary politics and the meaning of his text. The success of this effacement may be measured in the extent to which the social implications present in his text are not simply "reflections" either of history or of theory, but are newly produced by a process that deliberately minimizes contemporary topical reference.

A vivid instance of Chaucer's ability to deal with the most charged political materials in ways that forbid us to draw solid conclusions about his intentions is the apparent reference in the *Nun's Priest's Tale* to the rising of 1381. The *Nun's Priest's Tale* is itself the most consciously aesthetic of Chaucer's productions, constituting itself in an ultraliterary register that no longer even purports to reflect social reality but that revels in its dependence on established voices, themes, modes, and genres, many of which have been (or will be) encountered on the Canterbury pilgrimage. Numerous critics have commented on the extent of its impartial attraction to other voices.[44] Its recycling of voices ranges from a reprise of the Prioress' "Mordre wol out" (VII. 3052) to a startling and possibly inadvertent anticipation of Chaucer's own "Al that is writen is writen for oure doctrine" (X. 1083). It embraces themes ranging from authority, textual citation, false counsel, woman's counsel, the qualities of husbands, necessity and free will, rhetoric, and interpretation itself, to Chauntecleer's and Pertelote's own debate between his reliance on hierarchy and transcendent meaning and her more humdrum causality based on the humors of the body. Its reliance on established modes and genres ranges from exempla, scientific treatises, miracles, romance, bestiaries, through—most crucially—tragedy as defined by the Monk and redefined by the Knight, and "epical" beast fable.

The literary supersaturation of this tale in turn creates an environment of expectations within which even historically charged references like that to "Jakke Straw and his meynee" (VII. 3394) may be detached from their troubling social implications. Introduced in a decidedly minor key, as a *comparatio* designed to convey the racket in the widow's farmyard upon the abduction of Chauntecleer, the reference to Jack Straw's incitement to kill Flemings is placed on the same plane of reference as the songs of mermaids in the sea, Boethius' love of music, the deeds of Lancelot, the Pharaoh's baker, the sorrowing ladies of Troy. Flemings were brutally killed as a result of such incitements, not far from Chaucer's own door and in the decade in which he began the *Canterbury Tales*. This comparison is nevertheless stripped of blood and terror, no less than the Prioress' "Mordre wol out" is stripped of venom and Chaucer's own concern about the relation of writing to doctrine is stripped of spiritual anxiety, by the assertively literary stylization of the context in which they now appear. Even though it does not ignore the fate of the Flemings, Chaucer's reference evokes the rising reassuringly, in a way that lessens its risk. Rather than a historicization of the barnyard squabble, we actually have here a dehistoricization of the 1381 rising with its presumably unsettling effects on most of the London populace and on Chaucer's stratum in particular. Its volatility substantially defused, Chaucer's reference is assimilated to the literary register of allusion and imagery in which the tale is arrayed.

Yet to say that Chaucer excludes political references from the *Canterbury Tales,* and that he insulates his audience against the most startling aspects of those references he does include, is not to declare his work unhistorical. For history, suppressed at the level of allusion, is reintroduced at the level of form. The contribution of the *Nun's Priest's Tale* to history lies not so much in its allusions as in its socially charged assumption that diverse levels of argumentative style, socially conditioned genres and forms, and kinds of utterance can inhabit the same literary space, cooperating for the profit (here defined as literary *solaas*) of all. The *Nun's Priest's Tale,* together with the *Canterbury Tales* as a whole, conveys the reassuring message that competing voices can colonize a literary space and can proliferate within it without provoking chaos or ultimate rupture. We have already encountered a similar proposition at a different cultural level, in those treatises on statecraft that argue for the accommodation of heterogeneity in the form of the natural state. Here the argument is made in the relatively more tractable form of literary discourse, but it is no less social in its implications.

The assertion that history is an absent cause of aesthetic form would seem to be safe indeed, if no acts of interpretation are to be based upon it and if the assertion itself is unsusceptible to proof. Yet the texts of the *Parliament of Fowls* and the *Canterbury Tales* do contain indications of the sense in which mixed style is proposed as an aesthetic figure for social heterogeneity. Chaucer's proposal of stylistic variety as a figure for social difference relies on a rhetorical and literary connection between social levels and levels of style already well established, and in fact regarded as self-evident, within medieval tradition.[45] Conceived within this supportive tradition, the texts of the *Parliament of Fowls* and the *Canterbury Tales* bear manifest indications of their own social encoding, with Chaucer himself insisting on the social basis of generic and stylistic choice. The respective styles of the higher and lower fowl in the *Parliament* are connected with the speakers' status as *gentils* and *cherls*. Even the often-obtuse narrator has no difficulty in identifying the tercels' plea as "gentil" (485), and the tercelet does not hesitate to label the duck's words as those of a "cherl," seasoned with the socially defined "donghil" from which they came (596–597). The narrator of the *Canterbury Tales* makes the same connection at the outset, when he asks that his plain speech not be taken as evidence of "vileynye" (I.726)—a word that, though sometimes used figuratively to attribute base behavior to the better born, retained most of its literal sense of peasant origins (of association through villeinage to the feudal agricultural unit or *vil*). This same connection is of course made in the "cherles . . . manere" in which the Miller tells his tale (I.3169). Social perspective is, the narrator goes on to suggest, embodied not only in matters of style but in generic choice; he contrasts the "cherles tale" of the Miller with other, more dignified forms that embrace "gentillesse" (I. 3179).

The social basis of generic preference is amply borne out in the pilgrims' own responses. Provoking the Miller's eruption in the first place was the special admiration of the "gentils everichon" (I. 3113) for the Knight's storial narration, and the Miller in turn wins the broader approbation of diverse "folk" (I. 3855). Chaucer likewise connects different genres to particular strata: a historical narrative with subthemes of conquest, tourney, and dynastic succession is assigned to the militaristic Knight; a comic tale with its celebration of the lower body to the carnivalesque Miller; a work of pseudo-hagiographical derring-do to the complacently pious Man of Law; and so on. Similarly, he assigns different forms of narrative with different presuppositions about human action in time to different sorts of pilgrims. Whatever their own ethical or spiritual character, more traditionally situated characters like the Knight, the Squire, the Monk, and the Prioress tend toward narrative punctuated by assertion of the atemporal and the transcendent. Representatives of lower or more recently emerged strata tend on the other hand to embrace temporality and causality, as in tales by the Miller, the Reeve, and the Shipman. These associations between social levels of tellers and the styles, genres, and forms of narrative are imaginary in nature. Fabliaux were really read by knights and esquires, popular romances were addressed to every level of society, love lyrics were preserved in monasteries, and miracles circulated in popular collections. Chaucer offers his conventionalized points of attachment not as serious assertions about the social basis of production and reception, but as fanciful recastings that playfully flaunt the social basis of taste even as they evade the task of specifying it in a detailed way. Playful or not, however, these recastings serve to alert their audience to an area of social implication, in which different textual features suggest differences in the social sphere. Even though the relations that Chaucer draws between the genres and styles of his tales and the social situations of his tellers are offered as frank stylizations, they still invite deeper questions about the social messages that aesthetic features may bear.

Chaucer's frequent allusions to the social basis of literary production and taste alert his audience to a project of representation and conciliation, in which style- and discourse-conflict are associated with class conflict in the environment of lessened risk provided by a literary work. The form of the *Canterbury Tales* permits the elaboration of vocal and stylistic difference, in an ultimately reassuring arena. Whatever the frictions among Chaucer's pilgrims, no blood is shed; although temporary alliances are formed, the pilgrim polity is not riven by self-interested faction; however overweening Harry Bailly's sway, tyrannicide need not occur. Such *quiting* as occurs is more likely within and between tales than between their tellers, as we observed in the case of the Miller, whose revolt was directed at the tale rather than the person of the Knight. The special property of literary language as the vehicle for socially based disagreement is that it permits highly contrastive voices to co-exist, while reassuring its audience that extreme stylistic discrepancies need not fracture the enterprise. The hospitality of Chaucer's "framing fiction" to the varied styles and genres and forms in which his tellers express themselves, and to the ultimate irreconcilability of their voices, thus enables the perpetuation of a commonwealth of "mixed style," with ultimately reassuring implications for the idea of the natural state as a socially heterogeneous body that recognizes the diverse interests and serves the collective good of all.

A SPECIAL property of the *Canterbury Tales* is the extent to which its generic and stylistic variety is couched in polyvocality, in its embrace of separate and distinctive voices as a means of asserting social difference. Chaucer's poetry was always polyphonic, permitting the juxtaposition of separate themes and generic structures within the external form of a given work, but it becomes increasingly polyvocalic in its capacity to contain unreconciled voices as we move from the avian disputants of the *Parliament* to the distinctive and ultimately incompatible voices of Troilus and Pandarus and Criseyde to the yet fuller degree of autonomy assigned to the diverse Canterbury speakers. The Canterbury tales are richly polyphonic *and* polyvocalic, in the sense that, like medieval music, they pursue autonomous lines of development, and in the twentieth-century sense that they remain independent and unmerged. The principal theorist of this latter sense is of course Bakhtin, who argues that the precondition for true polyphony is that its voices are never subject to dialectical resolution, but remain unmerged in "unceasing and irreconcilable quarrel." [46] Chaucer critics have long appreciated the senses in which his commitment to autonomous voices inspires debate, though critics of an earlier day regarded the principal debates of the *Canterbury Tales* as subject to dialectical resolution.[47] In recent years critics have moved to embrace more fully the concept of Chaucer's polyphony, as defined both by medieval practice and modern theory, and his poetry is now characterized by such terms as "contrastive," "exploratory," a repository of "partial truths," "pluralistic," "inconclusive," "plurivalent," and "disjunctive." [48]

Rather than repeating the work of the many critics who have set out to demonstrate the polyphonic presuppositions of the *Canterbury Tales,*[49] I wish instead to pose a related question: in what sense is Chaucer's commitment to polyvocality *itself* a socially significant gesture? I have asserted that the stylistic and generic variety sustained by Chaucer's varied speakers is a figure for social variety, within the more conciliatory sphere of literary language, and Bakhtin's own description of polyphony in Dostoevsky's novels specifies the dynamics of this process. Bakhtin argues that Dostoevsky's polyphony is a refraction, through available literary possibilities, of the "contradictory multi-leveledness" of his own society. He argues that, had Dostoevsky perceived multi-leveledness as residing only in the human spirit, he could have created an ultimately monologic novel that took as its subject the contradictory evolution of the human spirit; instead, since he found multi-leveledness in the objective social world, he brought it into his novels as an equivalent for irreducible social contradiction.[50] Bakhtin here points to the possibility of an ultimately monologic portrayal of diversity, as opposed to a portrayal of diversity that is polyphonic through and through and could not have been otherwise because of divisions in the author's experience of society. The *Canterbury Tales* is, I believe, polyphonic in this latter sense, and the polyphony is bound up in its identity as a social text.

One need not search far for instances of Bakhtin's monologic portrayal of diversity, in works by Chaucer's contemporaries and (though far less often) in his own works as well. Gower's *Confessio,* for example, gives us a series of narratives that reveal a new and upside-down world of discord in which each estate of society shirks its responsibilities and places its selfish interests before the common good. Yet the task of the poet, according to Gower, is to assert ultimate "acord." And Gower sets out authorially to achieve a hypothetical state of accord through a number of devices intended to constrain interpretation, including direct authorial commentary, narration by the single-voiced Genius, Genius' own extensive commentary, persuasive Latin headnotes to the books of the poem, and authorially composed Latin glosses, all intended to line up these vices "arewe," to place them in their "degrees," and to show their relation to an ideal standard of selfless love.[51]

Diversity is described in similarly monological fashion at various moments in Chaucer's own work, especially when he adopts the voices of limited tellers. Such a moment is that of Cambyuskan's feast in the *Squire's Tale*, where the "prees" of folk swarm in to "gauren" or gape at the magical gifts (v. 189–190). Their conclusions are varied: "Diverse folk diversely they demed; / As many heddes, as manye wittes ther been" (v. 202–203). Some derive their views from "old geestes" or the recitations of "jogelours," others spout pseudo-science, others suppose the presence of magical art, and no opinion is clearly to be preferred to any other: "thus jangle they, and demen, and devyse / Til that the kyng gan fro the bord aryse" (v. 261–262). Still, as much as diversity is insisted upon, this discourse remains monologic. Its perspective is consistently controlled by the Squire, who conveys his scorn for the people and his disregard for their views by a variety of strategies, including their portrayal as an undifferentiated swarm of "folk," aspersions about the authoritativeness of their knowledge (v. 235), and their ignorance in seeking to judge "thynges that been maad moore subtilly / Than they kan in hir lewednesse comprehende" (v. 222–223). The Squire, knowing the tradition within which such marvels occur (romance, rather than "gestes" or old science), knows how they are to be taken. The seeming diversity of the views he describes is thus undermined by the singlemindedness with which he dismisses them as objects of interest.

Such instances are rare in Chaucer's poetry, however, and his more ambitious attempts to recount illustrative narratives with a single voice show signs of authorial dissatisfaction with such limitation. Those *tragedies* told by the Monk in a spirit of "diligence" (VII. 1966) in order to illustrate his "honestee" (VII. 1967) constitute such a single-voiced collection within the boundaries of the *Canterbury Tales*. While the inner tone of the tragedies yields no irrefutable evidence of parody, Chaucer must be suspected of some irony in turning a currently fashionable international form over to the relentlessly monologic Monk.[52] Its own unvarying explanatory frame (that Fortune's wheel will "out of joye brynge men to sorwe"—VII. 2398), its stultifying reiteration of its own intentions ("Of Sampson now wol I namoore sayn"—VII. 2090), and its ponderous admonitions ("Beth war . . ."—VII. 2140) disclose the perils of monologicality. That Chaucer intended such a disclosure is confirmed by his textualization of a critique of the Monk's unvarying "hevyness" and monotony in the responses of the Knight and the Host (VII. 2767–2805). The Monk "clappeth lowde" (VII. 2781)—rants on repetitively and without variation—and

Harry Bailly's suggested solution lies in diversification: "sey somwhat of huntyng, I yow preye" (VII.2805). The Monk of course refuses this invitation to variation, and it remains to the Nun's Priest with his mock-tragic disclosure of Fortune's reversal and rereversal to inaugurate that multiple disclosure in which, for Chaucer, ample treatment of a subject consists.

A more complex experiment with single-voiced narration occurs in the *Legend of Good Women,* where one narrator again sets out to recount a series of instances illustrative of established criteria. Here, however, Chaucer varies his inner tone, playfully experimenting at revealing the shortcomings of temporal narration ("wel coude I, if that me leste so, / Tellen al his doynge to and fro"—2470–71) and at times stepping entirely outside his own narrative stance to address his audience directly ("Be war, ye wemen . . . / And trusteth, as in love, no man but me"—2559–61). Sensitive critics have revealed the extent to which Chaucer in the *Legend* varies his narrative voice by deliberate textual play.[53] Yet were those early critics really so wrong when they took literally Chaucer's narrator's protestations that he is "agroted herebyforn / To wryte of hem that ben in love forsworn" (2454–55)?[54] Whatever the inner play of the *Legend's* text, it remains less representative of Chaucer's mature practice than the *Canterbury Tales,* in which a proliferation of narrators opens the possibility of independent centers of narrative authority, each with its own distinctive personal or social or generic identity.

Helen Cooper describes Chaucer's "house of fiction" as one that offers vantages through various windows, each presenting a perspective peculiar to a particular genre and each with its own partial truth,[55] and her metaphor is apt in its emphasis on Chaucer's rejection of a single, univalent "truth" and preference for truths embodied in multiple voices. This is not to say that the claims of different Canterbury narratives to validity go unchallenged. The Wife of Bath's inversion of traditional authority is promptly challenged by the Clerk's reassertion of the necessity for submissiveness, the Merchant's disenchanted account of an abuse of human trust is promptly challenged by the Franklin's assertion of human trustworthiness to do the right thing once freed of sterile agreements. But, just as no claims are permitted to stand unchallenged, so is no claim—however overidealized on the one hand or jaundiced on the other—presented to us as devoid of any truth at all. The polyphonic work is, as Bakhtin has reminded us, "dialogic through and through,"[56] and it is grounded not simply in a perverse human nature that refuses to recognize transcendent truth, but in an experience of a society constituted by various groups, each with its own version of reality.

Like Bakhtin's Dostoevsky, Chaucer may be viewed as having "participated in the contradictory multi-leveledness of his own time,"[57] and the form of his work as the expression of a socially determined view that presupposes irreconcilable difference. The form of the *Canterbury Tales* is not, of course, to be regarded as a direct reflection of a society riven by faction and socially based disagreement, but rather as a mediation of that view. "Mediation" is here taken not in its most traditional Marxist sense, in which the contradictions inherent in a given situation are restated at different cultural levels with added concealment but without any progress toward resolution. Mediation is, rather, conceived in an alternative—though, I would argue, still Marxist—sense, as a positive social process, which does not simply restate intractable situations but restates them *in terms more amenable to resolution.*[58] The potential of this restatement for socially constructive resolution lies in the receptivity of Chaucer's chosen form to the language of conflict. The socially creative form of the *Canterbury Tales* permits a relatively untroubled contemplation of extreme difference, a degree of difference that could not be acknowledged in the social sphere without danger to the participants. The literary language of the *Canterbury Tales* is thus "conciliatory" in the sense proposed by Macherey, in its ability to restate and to accommodate extremes of opinion as great as those of Chaucer's social reality, but to accommodate them "avec moins de risque," undangerously.[59] This accommodation is, as Macherey would be quick to point out, imaginary, since it has no necessary effect on social reality. Yet, in its literary reproduction of a social reality that embraces varied social tendencies for the good of all, Chaucer's work itself becomes a social agent in the constructive possibilities it imagines and poses.

The Silent Plowman and the Talkative Parson

Chaucer has used the vehicle of a temporally and socially defined pilgrimage to inscribe a community of mixed discourse that models the possible harmony of a mixed state. The space within which he imagines his discursive community has, however, been precariously maintained. It has, on the one hand, required an extreme stylization of actual social conditions in late fourteenth-century English society, including near erasure of the numerical preponderance (and the sometimes threatening claims) of those agricultural workers who comprised over nine tenths of the English populace. It has, on the other hand, required deferral of the claims of an authoritative spiritual system that minimizes the importance of secular society even as it somewhat paradoxically insists on the organization of secular society according to divinely ordained hierarchy. The complicated exclusions that render Chaucer's mixed commonwealth possible are epitomized in the silence of the Plowman, the single peasant participating in the pilgrimage. The deferral of a system of spiritual transcendence inimical to the natural and mixed temporal state is brought to an end by his suddenly loquacious brother, the Parson, with his rejection of the "draf" of fabulation in favor of the "whete" of unmediated doctrine (x. 35–36).

The Plowman is admitted to the *compaignye* of pilgrims, but without a tale. In this regard, Chaucer's practice is consistent with that of most commentators on the natural state, among whom even the relative democrats emphasize the participation of a *gravior pars,* noting the importance of the peasantry but assigning it no consequential role. John of Salisbury is typical in his praise of the *agricolae* he calls the *pedes* or feet of the commonwealth, classing them among those who are useful or profitable to the commonwealth but who have nothing to do with its governance ("quae nec ad praesidendi pertinent auctoritatem et uniuersitati rei publicae usquequaque proficiunt"—vi. 20). And even the democratic Marsilius classes agricultural workers among the *officia* rather than the *partes* of the state—with the former exercising necessary functions and belonging to the *vulgi* and the latter participating in civic rule and belonging to the *honorabilitates* (i. 5). Hierarchical theory tended to demand a single thing of these workers—obedient service or *obsequium*—while suggesting that this service would be repaid with other kinds of benign assistance ("Debent autem obsequium inferiora superioribus quae omnia eisdem uicissim debent necessarium subsidium prouidere"—*Polycraticus,* vi. 20). Organic theory tended to conceal this demand within broader assertions of reciprocity ("singula sint quasi aliorum ad inuicem membra"—*Polycraticus,* vi. 20). Often commingled, each justified major exactions from agricultural producers, while simultaneously expecting servitude and denying a consequential civic role. In this regard Chaucer's silent servitor is fully assimilated to an ideology that asks much of him in the way of willing work (he is a "trewe swynkere"—i. 531), cheerful relinquishment of the surplus value of his toil ("His tithes payde he ful faire and wel"—i. 539), and acceptance of broad communal obligation ("He wolde thresshe . . . for every povre wight"—i. 536–537).

All preliminary indications suggest that the voice of the Plowman, when Chaucer came to give him one, would not have been a voice of complaint, as was the Plowman of the Chaucer apocrypha who decries clerical theories of agricultural labor ("They make us thralles at hir lust" [60]). But we are not finally to know. For, as Patterson has argued, the voice of peasant protest is effectively erased within the *Canterbury Tales*.[61] He finds that this voice is given limited articulation in the Miller's prologue and tale, and even more limited articulation in the case of the Wife of Bath, but that it is progressively suppressed in favor of a depoliticized and transhistorical subjectivity. Patterson's argument is plainly essentially correct, although one wonders if the exclusion of the peasantry might not be even more thoroughgoing than he supposes; the Miller and the Wife of Bath are rural small producers, but hardly peasants or *agricolae* in any meaningful sense of the word.[62]

But I agree that, certain traces notwithstanding, Chaucer has virtually excluded the peasantry and rural small production from the *Canterbury Tales*. Just as the peasantry is slighted both descriptively and functionally in medieval political theory, so does Chaucer suppress its numerical and economic importance in the process of establishing his commonwealth of mixed literary discourse. Briefly to venture an absurd reduction: just as Chaucer would have been unlikely to imagine a commonwealth that admitted to full participation the 90 or so percent of the populace in various states of peasantry or villeinage, so could he hardly have created a literary counterpart to his own civic experience while drawing some two dozen of his speakers from the ranks of peasants and villeins. A price has certainly been paid, in regard to accurate representation of the peasantry and to direct articulation of the voice of peasant protest.[63] Yet this devaluation of peasant concerns is an act of exclusion that, paradoxically, opens a narrative space within which the mixed middle strata produce a literary model of social diversity.

CHAUCER'S literary model of social diversity is itself increasingly threatened by forces hostile to those practices of fabulation and artificial use of language on which his discursive community is founded. The reliability of fabulation as a means of embodying the truth is questioned as early as the Pardoner's prologue and tale. The dilemma is posed in the Pardoner's contention that a "vicious man" can nevertheless tell a "moral tale" (VI.459–460)—a dilemma that, as we have seen, creates discomfort for the pilgrim audience and for subsequent audiences as well. This mistrust of what might be called the uses of fabulation is extended in the *Manciple's Tale* to the act of tale telling itself (cautionarily represented in the silencing of the song of the crow as punishment for indiscriminate conversation or "false tale"—IX.293) and to the narrator's mistrust of language in relation to its referent (in his acknowledgment of the "loaded" judgment implied in his choice of the word "lemman" to describe Apollo's wife's lover—IX.205–222). That the *Manciple's Tale* is about "the failure of words" has been mentioned on several occasions.[64] What remains to be added here is that the failure in question is not only a general failure of reference but a failure of *socially charged* reference, of language in its capacity justly to represent the social implications of human action. *Lemman* is one of those courtly terms that, as Donaldson reminded us, slipped a good deal between the thirteenth and fourteenth centuries.[65] The narrator accordingly pauses to note its harsh, or at least drab and ordinary, connotations, informing us that nothing separates the misconduct of a "wyf" of "heigh degree" and a "povre wenche" except the words by which we describe their behavior:

> . . . the gentile, in estaat above,
> She shal be cleped his lady, as in love;
> And for that oother is a povre womman,
> She shal be cleped his wenche or his lemman. (IX.217–220)

Then follows a crude and assertively male observation, driving home the point that beneath the words the behavior is the same:

> And, God it woot, myn owene deere brother,
> Men leyn that oon as lowe as lith that oother. (IX.221–222)

Called into question here is the meaningfulness of social specification in language: "lady" (in the sense of "beloved") versus "lemman," and by implication the broader categories of "wyf" and "lady" versus "wenche" and "womman." The *swyving* is all the same, regardless of social category, and the categories have begun to blur a bit too. But the idea that different discourses are appropriate to different social levels, that certain genres and even certain styles may be assigned to persons of certain social levels, has been one of the crucial enabling ideas of the *Canterbury Tales.* Once this equation of social level and discourse is called seriously into question, Chaucer's creation of a community of discourse as a figure for a mixed commonwealth loses a crucial underpinning. That this wound to Chaucer's narrative enterprise is essentially self-inflicted suggests a crucial shift in the status of narrative itself, and this shift is shortly to be confirmed in the words with which the Parson prefaces the penitential treatise that will be his "tale."

All the Canterbury tales that preceded the Parson's are *narrationes* and possessed of plots (even if, as in the case of *Melibee,* thinly so). But it is specifically plotted narrative (that is, fabulation itself and not just Aesopic fable) that the Parson rejects when he refuses to tell "fables and swich wrecchednesse" (X.34).[66] He will instead dispense the pure "whete" of doctrine directly, offering "moralitee and vertuous mateere" in the form of an unplotted *tretys* (X.35–38). And, even before he commences his tale, several conditions that have promoted the rampant narrativity and the stylistic variousness of this discursive community are decisively altered.

Immediately altered is the pilgrims' attitude toward temporality. Until now the pilgrimage itself has—along with the tales the pilgrims tell—unfolded in the temporal realm, in the space of Bakhtin's "historically productive horizontal."[67] An atmosphere congenial to the resolution of narrative conflict in time has, despite occasional openings to the eternal, prevailed. Now we are reminded—rather urgently—that time is at a premium; late afternoon has come and Harry Bailly tells us that his plan is complete for all tales but one and that haste is essential if the Pilgrims are to be fruitful before the setting of the sun. No longer invited to participate in a leisurely temporal unfolding of narrative events, the pilgrims are requested to give "space" (X.64) to the Parson, whose tale will in fact be a spatial rather than a temporal dilatation of various penitential themes. This is not to say that the Parson's tale is brief, which it is most assuredly not, but that its shape will follow the extratemporal demands of the project he sets for himself. The "haste" enjoined by Harry Bailly is a haste to begin his undertaking; once begun, its exposition of a timeless sacrament proceeds without the pressures or interruptions that would signify the passage of worldly time. Its ending in fact is not in temporality at all, but in a timeless vision of a realm of permanent "sikernesse" (X.1077) and in Chaucer's contemplation of Christ reigning in eternity, "per omnia secula."

Also signaled by the Parson's prologue is the end of the *compaignye* of Canterbury pilgrims as a socially varied body of speakers oriented toward pluralistic discourse. Until now the pilgrims have rarely agreed on anything (unless we are to take the sobriety that settles on "every man" at the end of the *Prioress' Tale* as a form of agreement). More often, responses lapse into discord or blatant partiality of understanding, or else apparent unanimity turns out to mask varied response, as at the end of the *Knight's Tale* ("nas ther yong ne oold / That he ne seyde it was a noble storie / . . . And namely the gentils everichon"—I.3110–13). Now, however, we find the audience united in its assent to the Parson's austere intention of telling a moral tale, in prose, emphasizing unmediated doctrine, and redirecting this temporal pilgrimage to an atemporal home in "Jerusalem celestial" (X.51):

> Upon this word we han assented soone,
> For, as it seemed, it was for to doone—
> To enden in som vertuous sentence. (X.61–63)

Harry Bailly has "the wordes for us alle" (X.67) when he gives the Parson free rein and promises audience. For the implication is that the Parson's "sentence" will transcend division and social difference, addressing itself to all Christians without regard to condition, in its awareness of their bondage and need for spiritual repair. The pilgrims are unlikely to slip from this new vantage back into temporality and social dissension. For the *Parson's Tale* would subsume the world of varied temporality into its timeless categories.[68]

The Parson's analytical frame is thoroughly traditional in ways that suggest how far afield Harry Bailly was in judging him a "Lollere" in the canceled endlink to the *Man of Law's Tale.*[69] In marked contrast even to "The Two Ways" by Chaucer's friend Clanvowe, with its reliance on self-regulation, the *Parson's Tale* seeks full submission to church authority as embodied in its injunctions and sacraments. The existence of sin in the world is traced not to erroneous human choice but to failure of full obedience to God (X.338) and to a withdrawal from contemplation of God's timeless blessings into a world of temporal reward. As Chaucer notes, in free adaptation of Augustine: "Deedly synne . . . is whan a man turneth his herte fro God, which that is verray sovereyn bountee, that may nat chaunge, and yeveth his herte to thyng that may chaunge and flitte" (X.367). Chaucer's apparent addition here is the concept of the "sovereyn" nature of God's bounty—an addition that refers mainly to its universal excellence but that also arrays God in the attributes of a supreme ruler from whom beneficence flows and to whom obeisance is due.[70] Running through the *Parson's Tale* is an argumentative and imagistic strain suggesting that the errant Christian has failed to accept God's good lordship, has sought to be a free subject of history and choice who can pursue a variety of temporal options instead of submitting freely to God's singular and permanent sovereignty. This imagery solidifies around the most visible and traditional manifestation of God's eternal order, in the suggestion that the Christian become a vassal of God: the Christian must "yeven his body and al his herte to the service of Jhesu Crist, and therof doon hym hommage" (X.314). The *Parson's Tale* recommends, in effect, a refeudalization of relations, within that sphere of hierarchical transcendence that afforded the original pattern for the descending ideology of high medieval feudalism.

Proponents of the natural state never questioned the hierarchization of the spiritual realm; their project was to drive a wedge between that influential model and the more mundane and less sacral operations of the world of natural law. Jean de Paris could cite pseudo-Dionysius to the effect that the subordination of divine ministers to one leader is a matter of divine statute, even as he argued that the laity may choose different sorts of rulers according to natural inclination (ch. 3). Curialists like the later Giles of Rome and James of Viterbo were, however, unwilling to concede the autonomy of a natural sphere, insisting instead that the world of temporal reality order itself according to the more authoritative ecclesiastical model. Just as, Giles says, we have distinguished three hierarchies and nine ranks among the clergy, so should we be able to find these gradations among the laity (II, ch. 13).[71] So says Chaucer's Parson. Viewing the Christian as a faithful vassal within the spiritual hierarchy, he presses for a sacralization of the temporal sphere. Posed in his tale is a social model quite inhospitable to the array of new social relations and impulses emergent in the thirteenth and fourteenth centuries.

Within the hierarchizing formations of the *Parson's Tale* the horizontal world of new social arrangements exists only as a deviation to be condemned, and condemn it the Parson does—both in response to his sources and in his own elaborations. We need not be surprised that the Parson casts a cold eye on the new forms of retaining, with their encouragement of large households and retinues. Pride, he tells us, is manifested "in holdynge of greet meynee"—or at least in those retinues formed for motives other than the common good, in which case "they be of litel profit or of right no profit" (X.436). Now, departing from his source, he elaborates on those contemporary abuses of lordship that detract from its inherent worth: "and namely whan that meynee is felonous and damageous to the peple by hardynesse of heigh lordshipe or by wey of offices" (X.437).[72] Outright criminality on the part of retinues was of course decried throughout the second half of the century; in condemning the use of "offices" to further the claims and careers of associates, the Parson additionally condemns those new forms of practice by which Chaucer and many members of his circle flourished.

The Parson attacks improper lordship and constructs a model of lordship compatible with the public good in his description of avarice. He elaborates his source in criticizing lords for imposing improper duties and taxes (x. 68), but goes on in a lengthy digression apparently composed entirely by Chaucer (x. 753–774) to explain that his complaint against abuse of degree is not to be construed as an attack on degree as such:

> I woot wel ther is degree above degree, as reson is, and skile is that men do hir devoir ther as it is due, but certes, extorcions and despit of youre underlynges is dampnable. (x. 763)

That degree is inherent in the universe seems apparent to the Parson, and he supports his perception with the argumentative resources at his command ("as reson is" . . . "skile is"). The system that subjects one person to another is, by extension, divinely ordained:

> certes, sith the time of grace cam, God ordeyned that som folk sholde be moore heigh in estaat and in degree, and som folk moore lough, and that everich sholde be served in his estaat and in his degree. (x. 770)

The justification for this system lies in service, in the assertion that

> if God hadde ordeyned that som men hadde hyer degree and som men lower, / therfore was sovereyntee ordeyned, to kepe and mayntene and deffenden hire underlynges. (x. 772–773)

This lengthy passage protects hierarchical claims by a number of argumentative means—not only by a concept of reciprocal service but by quasi-egalitarian hints that "of swich seed as cherles spryngen, of swich seed spryngen lordes" (x. 761) and that even a lord may be "a cherl to synne" (x. 763). But this reassertion of hierarchy ignores such later fourteenth-century developments as the admission of new social groups, broadened participation in the affairs of the realm, and the creation of new institutions designed to assure the availability of good counsel. The principle of hierarchy is firmly reinstated, with each person situated within a vertical *ordo* or scheme of subjection, and its success depends on the willingness of each person to accept the responsibilities attending his or her place within that scheme.

If the polyphony of the *Canterbury Tales* is a figuration of the variety of the natural state, the monovocality of the Parson's closing treatise is appropriate to the announcement of a more rigid, descending order. The finality of the Parson's utterance is enhanced by its appeal to divine ordinance. Its finality is further enhanced by its status as the last of the tales, told by common consent and followed by the closely associated Retraction, in which Chaucer responds *in propria persona* to the Parson's admonition to repent. And, beyond any of these considerations, the practice of monovocality *itself* aspires to finality. As Bakhtin has observed, "Monologue pretends to be the *ultimate word*. It closes down the represented world and represented persons."[73] In a sense this monologue does close down the *Canterbury Tales,* by denying the autonomy of that natural and varied world of temporality to which the Canterbury pilgrimage offers a literary and stylistic counterpart.

In other important senses, however, the *Canterbury Tales* resists closure, denying to any one pilgrim the finality of utterance to which the voice of the Parson would aspire. One aspect of this denial resides in the manifestly unfinished and fragmentary nature of the *Tales* itself. For an element of the Parson's authority has been our acceptance of his tale's status as the "last word," the concluding utterance of a finished literary work.

His tale does, to be sure, enjoy undoubted status as the last of Chaucer's intended narratives, whether the "thropes ende" (x. 12) that the pilgrims are entering as he begins to speak refers to the outskirts of Canterbury (on a "one-way" journey) or London/Southwark (on a "round trip"). But six centuries of scribes, editors, and critics have moved beyond this indisputable fact to a presumption of near-completion that lacks ultimate support in internal evidence. Starting with the activities of the earliest fifteenth-century scribes and editors,[74] this unifying enterprise reached a climax in the middle decades of this century, through a convergence of conclusions derived within two apparently incompatible critical tendencies. Ralph W. Baldwin, accepting the assumptions about organic unity inherent in the "new criticism," launched his argument for the conversion of the *Tales* from a literal to a symbolic journey to "Jerusalem celestial" (x. 51).[75] Concurrently, D. W. Robertson and his associates launched their argument for the exegetical unity of the *Tales,* including the rather willful misreading of Chaucer's "this litel tretys or rede" (x. 1081) as an application of his Retraction not only to the completed *Parson's Tale* but to the entire work.[76]

Against such claims for Chaucer's final intent must be weighed his own insistence on his work as open, provisional, and unfinished. Our tendency to imagine Chaucer's tales as a "Canterbury book" must, in the first instance, minimize the provisional nature of any arrangement of its inner fragments.[77] Beyond this fact lie other indications of Chaucer's refusal to fix his tales in a definite scheme: his distribution of narratives among many voices, his refusal to invest authority in his often-befuddled narrator or to create a Gowerian genius figure as authoritative interpreter, his minimal interest in devices such as glosses by which Gower and other contemporary authors promoted ultimate monovocality.[78]

Just as Chaucer's text announces its own unfinished nature, so does the evidence of early reception argue for random and piecemeal dissemination. Chaucer's immediate audience would have encountered his work not in presentation volumes, or any volumes at all, or even necessarily in manuscript form.[79] Rather, Chaucer's most immediate and most prized audience must have known his poetry in a discontinuous and segmented way, largely through oral rendition and occasionally, at best, through fragmentary manuscripts. To the extent that we can reconstruct a contemporary response to Chaucer, we must imagine that response less as contemplation of a finished order and more as an awareness of local juxtaposition, of ideas placed side by side, in unresolved contention.

The Parson therefore presents us with a paradox: with a voice that would transcend worldly fragmentation and division, situated in a work that treats fragmentation and division as inevitable aspects of life in the world. Chaucer's own Retraction may offer a partial resolution of this paradox, in its suggestion that the proper response to the Parson's admonitions lies beyond the temporal sphere and beyond works that imitate that sphere—in sacramental time, in "omnia secula." To the limited extent that the Parson's views about hierarchy and transcendence refer back to that temporal and mutivoiced site of personal and ideological contention offered by the *Canterbury Tales,* they must take their chances, among a multitude of contending conceptions.

IN SITUATING the Parson's voice at the end of his pilgrimage, Chaucer has shown respect for its special claims. But, at the same time, in *deferring* the Parson's voice to the end of the pilgrimage, Chaucer has opened a discursive space within which various conceptions of social reality can coexist. The impetus behind the Parson's voice is assertively utopian, in the sense that it would deny division and faction by transcending it. But another, more modestly directed but no less utopian, impulse infuses Chaucer's later poetry as well, in his exploitation of the conciliatory possibilities of literary language to offer his audience a mixed commonwealth of discourse.

Chaucer's commonwealth is implicitly utopian in its accommodation of varied socially and vocationally defined voices and points of view, its opening of existing hierarchies to infiltration by new classes of people and categories of discourse, its treatment of heterogeneity as a normal condition of civic life.[80] A commonwealth so conceived obviously had much to offer Chaucer himself and that new group of fellow gentlepersons "en service" so prominent in his immediate audience. Yet, however densely implicated in its own historical situation and however charged its significance for its original audience, Chaucer's work continues to command the attention of succeeding readers. Its appeal is not that it exists on an aesthetic plane beyond the social fray. Rather, its appeal owes much to its rich situation between contending social models, its subtle poise at the boundaries of rank and class awareness. The comprehensiveness and argumentative energy with which Chaucer's work opens itself to its historical moment allow readers in posterity a continuing opportunity to refresh their own belief in social possibility.

Notes

Index

Notes

Abbreviations

Unless otherwise indicated, all Chaucer references are to *The Riverside Chaucer,* 3rd ed., ed. Larry D. Benson (Boston: Houghton Mifflin, 1987).

Bird, *Turbulent London*	Ruth Bird, *The Turbulent London of Richard II* (London: Longmans, Green, 1949)
Chaucer, *Works*	*The Complete Works of Geoffrey Chaucer,* ed. W. W. Skeat. Vol. 7: *Chaucerian and Other Pieces* (Oxford: Clarendon Press, 1897)
Chroniques	*Oeuvres de Froissart,* ed. Kervyn de Lettenhove, 25 vols. (Brussels, 1870–1872)
CPR	*Calendar of the Patent Rolls Preserved in the Public Record Office,* 1377–1389 (London: Stationery Office, 1895–1900)
Gower, *Works*	*The Complete Works of John Gower,* ed. G. C. Macaulay, 4 vols. (Oxford: Clarendon Press, 1899–1902)
Hulbert, *Official Life*	James Root Hulbert, *Chaucer's Official Life* (1912; rpt. New York: Phaeton Press, 1970)
Knighton	Henry Knighton, *Chronicon,* ed. J. R. Lumby, 2 vols. *Rerum Britannicarum Medii Aevi Scriptores,* no. 92 (London, 1889–1895)
Langland	*Piers Plowman: The B Version,* ed. George Kane and E. Talbot Donaldson (London: Athlone Press, 1975)
Letter-Book H	*Calendar of Letter-Books . . . of the City of London: Letter-Book H,* ed. Reginald R. Sharpe (London, 1907)

Life-Records	*Chaucer Life-Records,* ed. Martin M. Crow and Clair C. Olson (Oxford: Clarendon Press, 1966)
Minor Poems	Chaucer, *The Minor Poems,* ed. George B. Pace and Alfred David. Vol. V. 1: *The Chaucer Variorum* (Norman: University of Oklahoma Press, 1982)
RP	*Rotuli Parliamentorum,* ed. J. Strachey (London, 1783)
Sources and Analogues	*Sources and Analogues of Chaucer's Canterbury Tales,* ed. W. F. Bryan and Germane Dempster (1941; rpt. New York: Humanities Press, 1958)
Thrupp, *Merchant Class*	Sylvia Thrupp, *The Merchant Class of Medieval London* (1948; rpt. Ann Arbor Paperback, 1962)
Tout, *Chapters*	T. F. Tout, *Chapters in the Administrative History of Mediaeval England,* 6 vols. (Manchester: Manchester University Press, 1920–1933)
Walsingham	Thomas Walsingham, *Historia Anglicana,* ed. H. T. Riley, 2 vols. *Rerum Britannicarum Medii Aevi Scriptores,* no. 28, pt. 1 (London, 1863–1864)
West. Chron.	*The Westminster Chronicle, 1381–1394,* ed. L. C. Hector and Barbara F. Harvey (Oxford: Clarendon Press, 1982)

Preface

1. The idea of history as "absent cause" is borrowed from Fredric Jameson, *The Political Unconscious* (Ithaca: Cornell University Press, 1981), p. 101.

2. Paraphrasing Marx, *A Contribution to the Critique of Political Economy* (New York: International Publishers, 1970), p. 21.

3. The traditional model, in which urban and early capitalist economies challenged static and feudal ones (as advanced by Pirenne, Sweezy, and Cipolla), has been broadly challenged and largely supplanted by a new model, in which medieval cities were internal to feudalism and both were challenged by emergent rural production (Dobb, Hilton). The complexity of this continuing debate is suggested by the papers collected as *The Transition from Feudalism to Capitalism,* ed. Rodney Hilton (London: New Left Books, 1976).

4. Its uneven character is suggested by Eric Hobsbawm: "The transition from feudalism to capitalism is not a simple process by which the capitalist elements within feudalism are strengthened until they are strong enough to burst out of the feudal shell. What we see time and again . . . is that a crisis of feudalism *also* involves the most advanced sections of bourgeois development within it, and therefore produces an apparent setback." *Transition,* p. 163.

5. Holton, *Cities, Capitalism and Civilization,* Controversies in Sociology, vol. 20 (London: Allen and Unwin, 1986), p. 84.

6. For this term I am indebted to Jean-Charles Payen, "Les Eléments idéologiques dans le *Jeu de Saint Nicholas,*" *Romania,* 94 (1973), 484–504.

7. Etienne Balibar and Pierre Macherey, "On Literature as an Ideological Form," in *Untying the Text: A Post-Structuralist Reader,* ed. Robert Young (London: Routledge and Kegan Paul, n.d.); original and fuller version published as "Présentation," Renée Balibar, *Les Français fictifs* (Paris: Hachette, 1974).

8. On the availability of alternative social formations as a support to authorial choice, see Raymond Williams, *Politics and Letters* (London: New Left Books, 1979), p. 357. On the terms of individual social "knowledgeability," available for discursive expression and interrogation, see Anthony Giddens, *Central Problems in Social Theory* (Berkeley: University of California Press, 1979), esp. pp. 72–73.

9. As argued, for instance, by Louis Althusser, "Ideology and Ideological State Apparatuses," *Essays on Ideoiogy* (1971; rpt. London: Verso, 1984), pp. 1–60, esp. 49–50.

10. This view is succinctly stated in Balibar and Macherey, "On Literature as an Ideological Form." Terry Eagleton frequently seems to advance the same point, though he also cautions against the assumption that a work is *always* about what it seems to exclude, in *Criticism and Ideology* (1976; rpt. London: Verso, 1978), pp. 92–93.

11. I remain particularly indebted to Raymond Williams, *Marxism and Literature* (Oxford: Oxford University Press, 1977), pp. 108–114. A more recent study congenial to my approach is Alan Sinfield, "Power and Ideology: An Outline Theory and Sidney's *Arcadia,*" *ELH,* 52 (1985), 259–277. Also in harmony with my closing observations are the remarks of Jean E. Howard, "The New Historicism in Renaissance Studies," *EHR,* 16 (1986), 30.

1. Chaucer and the Structure of Social Relations

1. For the origins of the idea of social hierarchy in the writings of Pseudo-Dionysius on celestial and ecclesiastical hierarchies, see Walter Ullmann, *Principles and Politics in the Middle Ages* (New York: Barnes and Noble, 1961), pp. 46–56, 117–149.

2. For this convenient phrase—with its evocation of a social grouping which includes such diverse and partially stratified ranks as knights, esquires, gentlepersons, merchants, citizens, burgesses, clerks, lawyers, and prosperous guildsmen—I am indebted to Thrupp, *Merchant Class.*

3. Henry de Bracton, *De Legibus et Consuetudinibus Angliae,* ed. George Woodbine and Samuel E. Thorne, vol. 2 (Cambridge: Harvard University Press, 1968), p. 32.

4. Georges Duby observes that social descriptions based on the three estates routinely suppress any serious examination of mutual obligation, in favor of an assertion of the necessity and value of hierarchy. See *The Three Orders: Feudal Society Imagined,* trans. Arthur Goldhammer (Chicago: University of Chicago Press, 1980), pp. 34, 59, 117.

5. In thirteenth-century England, counts were equivalent to earls and would have been ranked above barons; prior to emergence of baronets and the intermittent treatment of knights-bachelor as aristocratic, the barons were the lowest of the English lords; "magnates" and "vavasours" had no legally recognized status, although the terms are sometimes encountered as synonyms of recognized estates.

6. I am here using "ideology" not simply as a perjorative synonym of "deformation" or "concealment," but in the more general sense of a broad complex of variously motivated cultural and political structures that sustain a given social formation. On the distinction between these two senses, see Raymond Williams, *Keywords* (1976; rev. ed. London: Oxford University Press, 1983), pp. 153–157.

7. For the idea that ideology consists both of "allusion" to actual social conditions and "illusion" in the production of imaginary social relations, I am indebted to Louis Althusser, "Ideology and Ideological State Apparatuses," *Essays on Ideology* (1971; rpt. London: Verso, 1984), p. 36.

8. *The Sermons of Thomas Brinton, Bishop of Rochester,* vol. 2 ed. M. A. Devlin, Camden Society, ser. 3, vol. 86 (London, 1954), p. 259.

9. Abdel Hamid Hamdy, "Philippe de Mézières and the New Order of the Passion," *Bulletin of the Faculty of Arts* (Alexandria University, Egypt), 18 (1964), 1–105; reference from Anne Middleton, "War by Other Means: Marriage and Chivalry in Chaucer," *SAC, Proceedings,* 1 (1984), 125.

10. John of Salisbury describes the commonwealth ("res publica") as a body ("corpus") of which the head is the prince, the heart is the senate, the eyes, ears, and tongue are judges and governors of provinces, the hands are officials and soldiers, the stomach and intestines are financial officers and

lawyers, and the feet are peasants or husbandmen ("agricolae"). While his description, like most in its subsequent tradition, remains partially hierarchized, it is notable both for its willingness to include estates between the prince and the peasantry and for its emphasis upon their interdependence. With regard to particulars, however, his *praesides* (governors) and *quaestors* (financial officials) retain a pronounced Roman flavor and do not advance our understanding of medieval society as much as one might wish. See *Polycraticus,* v.ii, ed. Clemens Webb, vol. 1 (Oxford: Clarendon Press, 1909), pp. 539–540.

11. *Sermons,* vol. 1, ed. Devlin, vol. 85 (London, 1954), p. 111.

12. On the status of knights in the thirteenth century, see S. Harvey, "The Knight and the Knight's Fee in England," *Past and Present,* 49 (1970), 3–43.

13. On the separation of the barony from the knights, see K. B. McFarlane, *The Nobility of Later Medieval England* (Oxford: Clarendon Press, 1973), p. 274.

14. Parliaments of the fourteenth century had not yet specifically divided themselves into two houses, but their secular representation was nevertheless stratified by the distinction between the lords or barony with their hereditary right to parliamentary summons and those who were elected from the shires, cities, and boroughs of the realm. On the eventual division into two houses, see S. B. Chrimes, *English Constitutional Ideas in the Fifteenth Century* (Cambridge: Cambridge University Press, 1936), pp. 126–130. On the specific summons of the barony to Parliament, see F. W. Maitland, *The Constitutional History of England* (Cambridge: Cambridge University Press, 1955), pp. 82–89. Of particular interest here is the classification of the knights with "les autres." The sense that the knights are the commons, or are to be considered as among the commons, developed gradually in the course of the century. At the 1326–1327 Parliament, for example, petitions were advanced by "les Chivalers & la Comune," implying that the knights and commons were acting in concert but were not strictly to be identified (*RP,* vol. 2, p. 5). In 1339, Parliament consisted of the "Grantz" and the "Communes," and a stratified list of those present implies but does not specifically state that the knights are among the latter group (those present include "les Prelatz, Countes, Barouns, & autres Grauntz, et Chivalers des Counteez, Citeyns & Burgeys de Citez & Burghs"—*RP,* vol. 2, p. 107). By mid-century, however, the identification of the knights with the commons was explicit and secure. In 1348, Parliament as a whole is defined as consisting of "Prelatez, Countes, Barons, & Communes du Roialme," and the latter group was described as consisting of "Chivalers des Countees, & autres des Communes" (*RP,* vol. 2, p. 200). In 1351–1352, petitions of commons were described as launched by "les Chivalers, Citezeins, & Burgeis, qi sont venuz a cel parlement pur les Countess" (*RP,* vol. 2, p. 240).

15. This treatment of the middle groups is conditioned in several respects

by contemporary social developments. The increased emphasis on craft guilds is appropriate to the early 1380s, when John Northampton was mounting his most strenuous challenge to the prevalence of the merchant-dominated victualing guilds (see Bird, *Turbulent London,* pp. 17–27). After mid-century the middle groups had been gaining steadily in civil importance, as exemplified by the centrality of the citizens and burgesses to parliamentary discussions of finance and war subsidy.

16. Even the most pragmatically couched documents, as Robert Darnton has trenchantly reminded us, serve less as repositories of fact or as "miniature replicas" of social structure than as records of how observers observed their social reality ("A Bourgeois Puts His World in Order," *The Great Cat Massacre and Other Episodes in French Cultural History* [1984; rpt. New York: Vintage Books, 1985], pp. 107–143; for a similar view see Clifford Geertz, "Thick Description," *The Interpretation of Cultures* [New York: Basic Books, 1973], p. 9). The emphasis of my study lies more on contemporary self-understanding than on material change. Yet, while seeking to avoid naive suppositions about the accessibility of a "hard and fast reality" beyond these texts, I remain interested in those points at which social developments of the late fourteenth century influenced textual representation, and have sought to indicate some of them in the course of this chapter.

17. *RP,* vol. 2, p. 278. This was to be a short-lived ordinance, withdrawn in response to a petition of the very next Parliament that all persons be able to dress as they see fit. (One can imagine that the very parliamentary representatives who first sponsored the ordinance in order to consolidate their own social positions might have become disaffected upon finding themselves inhibited from further aggrandizement.) See Frances E. Baldwin, *Sumptuary Legislation and Personal Regulation in England,* Johns Hopkins Studies in Historical and Political Science, ser. 44, no. 1 (Baltimore, 1926), p. 55.

18. The rise of esquires in the fourteenth century as revealed in rolls of arms has been described by N. Denholm-Young in *The Country Gentry in the Fourteenth Century* (Oxford: Clarendon Press, 1969), esp. pp. 4–5; the same phenomenon has been approached through military and civil demands for esquires' services by Nigel Saul, *Knights and Esquires: The Gloucestershire Gentry in the Fourteenth Century* (Oxford: Clarendon Press, 1981), pp. 20–29. "The class of squires," according to Denholm-Young, "had by the fourteenth century for all practical purposes attained equality with that of knights" (p. 22). On the same phenomenon in thirteenth-century France, see Duby, *The Three Orders,* pp. 294–295.

19. *Country Gentry,* p. 4. The notion of gentlepersons without other, explicit rank became quite common in England in the fifteenth century, but the French *gentil homme* or *gentils home* is reserved for lords, knights, and esquires in most fourteenth-century uses. See Saul, *Knights and Esquires,* pp. 26–28.

20. Two documents that suggest the complexity of these stratification

issues might be mentioned briefly. One is a 1384 ordinance in which the Guild of St. Christopher, Norwich, opened its meetings with a prayer for all the estates of society. This ordinance imagines an aristocratic group, consisting of "oure lorde the kyng, oure lady the qwen, Duckes, Erles, Barouns, and Bachelers," and a nonaristocratic group divided into two tiers, the first consisting of "alle knyghtes, squyers, citizeins and Burgeys, fraunkeleyns" and the second of "alle trewe tyliers and men of craft" (*English Guilds,* ed. Toulmin Smith, EETS, OS, 40 [London, 1870], p. 23). A slightly anachronistic reminder of the previously higher station of knights is the inclusion of a category of knights-bachelor among the lords. Here, as in parliamentary summons and elsewhere, the higher of the two middle groups appears to be divided into gentle ranks (knights and esquires) and nongentle ranks (citizens, burgesses, and franklins). Of subsequent interest for the case of Chaucer's Franklin is the inclusion of franklins among the nongentle (see Chapter 4, below). The borderline status of knights is suggested in the somewhat optimistically conceived pairings into which the early fifteenth-century *Dux Moraud* divides its audience: emperors/kings, earls/barons, bachelors/knights, squires/yeomen, and knaves/pages (*Non-Cycle Plays and Fragments,* ed. N. Davis, EETS, supp. text 1 [Oxford, 1970], p. 106).

21. Tout, *Chapters,* vol. 3, pp. 347–349.

22. *Anonimalle Chronicle,* ed. V. H. Galbraith (Manchester: Manchester University Press, 1970), pp. 127–129.

23. *RP,* vol. 3, pp. 57–58.

24. "Class, Status, Party," in *From Max Weber* (New York: Oxford Galaxy, 1958), p. 181.

25. Ibid., p. 187. On the historical function of status consciousness in obscuring class consciousness, see Georg Lukács, *History and Class Consciousness* (1968; rpt. MIT Press, 1971), pp. 58, 172. But see also his caution about applying historical materialism to precapitalist social formations (p. 238).

26. *Life-Records,* p. 5.

27. Chaucer's royal service may have commenced as early as 1366. A cryptic record places a "Geffroy de Chauserre" identified as "escuier englois" and three companions in Navarre in the spring of that year. See *Life-Records,* p. 64.

28. Chesterton, *Chaucer* (London: Faber and Faber, 1932), p. 39.

29. See R. W. Southern, "The Place of Henry I in English History," *Proceedings of the British Academy,* 48 (1962), 127–170.

30. Denholm-Young, *The Country Gentry,* pp. 4–5; Saul, *Knights and Esquires,* pp. 20–29.

31. Tout has shown that Richard II made considerable use of knights and esquires of the chamber as "convenient instruments" for his work, but that even during his reign a downgrading of the chamber's role in governance began; with Henry IV and the introduction of significant numbers of non-

gentle Lancastrian civil servants into the business of government, its decline continued. See Tout, *Chapters,* vol. 4, pp. 341–343; E. F. Jacob, *The Fifteenth Century, 1399–1485* (Oxford: Clarendon Press, 1961), pp. 30–31. Further corroboration of the decline of the chamber at the end of Richard's reign is offered by Chris Given-Wilson, *The Royal Household and the King's Affinity: Service, Politics and Finance in England, 1360–1413* (New Haven: Yale University Press, 1986), p. 166.

32. As well documented in Hulbert, *Official Life.*

33. Given-Wilson's estimate of £25 as a typical income for a king's esquire would place Chaucer's earnings (leaving aside those of his wife) near the middle of this group (p. 263).

34. *Life-Records,* pp. 269–270, 294–299.

35. Ibid., p. 99. Hulbert argues, however, that mixed criteria of function and duration of service determine the two categories, and that Chaucer was listed in the second because of his short service in the court (pp. 25–30). Additional evidence that Chaucer was reasonably well positioned occurs in a document of 1371–1373 which lists him among 62 esquires of the chamber ("scutiferis camere regis")—though the "inner circle" construed by this particular document is so enlarged as to lack much significance (*Life-Records,* p. 100). Richard F. Green makes the point that "whenever the lists draw the distinction between squires (or valets) of the chamber and those of the household he is invariably included under the latter category." See his *Poets and Princepleasers: Literature and the English Court in the Late Middle Ages* (Toronto: University of Toronto Press, 1980), p. 68.

36. Virginia Leland has kindly confirmed, in correspondence, that Chaucer's reference to having "borne arms" more likely refers to military service than to having been "armed" in the heraldic sense.

37. *Life-Records,* pp. 340–374.

38. Ibid., p. 26.

39. Thrupp, *Merchant Class,* p. 245.

40. Chenu, *Nature, Man, and Society in the Twelfth Century,* ed. J. Taylor and L. Little (Chicago: University of Chicago Press, 1957), p. 65.

41. Ganshof, *Qu'est ce que la Féodalité?* 3rd ed. (Brussels: Office de Publicité, 1957), p. 103; also pp. 98–105.

42. Ibid., pp. 139–147, 195.

43. Medieval commentators do of course temper their comments on hierarchy by stressing the reciprocity of obligations. Bracton, for example, emphasizes the lord's obligation to defend the tenant as well as the tenant's obligation to serve his lord, and in fact so warms to his point that he declares the connection of lord and tenant to be of such magnitude that the lord owes as much to the tenant as the tenant to the lord, excepting only reverence ("Est itaque tanta et talis connexio per homagium inter dominum et tenentem suum, quod tantum debet dominus tenenti quantum tenens domino praeter solam reverentiam"—*De Legibus,* p. 228).

44. Duby, "La Féodalité? Une Mentalité médiévale," *Annales,* 13 (1958).

45. Ganshof, *Féodalité,* pp. 193–196.

46. Bryce D. Lyon, *From Fief to Indenture: The Transition from Feudal to Non-Feudal Contract in Western Europe* (Cambridge: Harvard University Press, 1957), pp. 5–40.

47. Ganshof, *Féodalité,* p. 149.

48. Lyon's earlier conclusion—argued in "The Feudal Antecedent of the Indenture System," *Speculum,* 29 (1954), 511—was that all performance of feudal obligations for fief-rent had ceased in the fourteenth century. *From Fief to Indenture* extends to the beginning of the fifteenth century the survival of feudal relations based on fief-rent, thus enlarging the period in which the practices of feudal retaining by fief-rent and nonfeudal retaining by indenture coexisted; see esp. pp. 272–273.

49. McFarlane, "Bastard Feudalism," *Bull. Inst. Hist. Research,* 20 (1943–1945), 161–180.

50. "Porce que nostre bien ame William Wallerant . . . nous ad fait son homage pur certeins terres et tenementz queux il tient de nous . . . vous mandons que, maintenant vieues cestes et prise du dit William suffisante seurtee de nous faire bien et loialment les services et custumes a nous duz pur les terres et tenementz susditz, et de nous paier prestement le relief si aucun a nous ent appartientent, cessez a destreindre le dit William pur son dit homage, et si aucune destresse eiez du lui pris par celle cause la facez liverer et relesser en manere come appent." *John of Gaunt's Register,* ed. E. Lodge and R. Somerville, 2 vols., Camden Society, 3rd ser., vols. 56–57 (London: Royal Historical Society, 1937), vol. 2, p. 367.

51. J. M. W. Bean, *The Decline of English Feudalism,* (Manchester: Manchester University Press, 1968), esp. pp. 1–6.

52. "Le dit Thomas serra tenuz . . . a servir le dit roy et duc tant en temps de pees come de guerre a terme de sa vie, et de travailler ovesque lui as queles parties que plerra au dit roy et duc, bien et covenablement arraiez pur la guerre. Et prendra le dit Thomas du dit roy et duc a terme de sa vie pur son fee tant en temps de pees come de guerre vynt marcs par an des issues de la receite del seignurie de Highamferrers . . . Et serra le dit Thomas en temps de pees a bouche et gages de courte a ses diverses venues illeoques en manere come autres esquiers de son estat et condicion sont, et en temps de guerre le dit Thomas serra a bouche ou gages de courte come autres esquiers da sa condicion serront" (*Register,* vol. 1, p. 16).

53. *Knights and Esquires,* p. 83.

54. Lifetime indentures may be slanted even more explicitly toward peacetime service than the one in question. On 13 April 1383, the Duke concluded an indenture with William Barewelle, esquire, for lifetime service and work in business matters for his honor and profit at all reasonable times ("pur lui servir et travailler en ses busoignes pur son honour et profit en Engleterre a terme de sa vie, a touz les foiz qil serra resonablement requis

ou garniz par le dit roy et duc ou son conseil"—*Register,* vol. 1, p. 25).

55. "Bastard Feudalism," pp. 169, 173–177.

56. According to G. L. Harriss, McFarlane adopted a more favorable view of retaining by indenture in his 1959 lectures on livery and maintenance: "While McFarlane originally saw the change to a fiscal and contractual obligation as betokening the emergence of a 'loosely knit and shamelessly competitive society,' he and others subsequently interpreted the new forms as attempts to strengthen the bonds of lordship and the ideals for fidelity threatened by the multiplication of tenures." See Introduction to K. B. McFarlane, *England in the Fifteenth Century* (London: Hambledon Press, 1981), pp. ix–xi.

57. Ibid., pp. ix–x. Additional emphasis on the coherent evolution of contract retaining from the feudal system, especially at the end of the thirteenth century, is offered in a richly suggestive article by Scott L. Waugh, "Tenure to Contract: Lordship and Clientage in Thirteenth-Century England," *EHR,* 401 (1986), 812–839.

58. *Knights and Esquires,* p. 98. See also Christine Carpenter, "The Beauchamp Affinity, a Study of Bastard Feudalism at Work," *EHR,* 95 (1980), 514–532, with its conclusion that "virtually all the more prominent Warwickshire gentry can be shown to have been of the affinity of at least one lord" (p. 515).

59. Bennett, *Community, Class and Careerism: Cheshire and Lancastire Society in the Age of Sir Gawain and the Green Knight* (Cambridge: Cambridge University Press, 1983), pp. 30–33, 67–89.

60. Not only the practice of lifetime indenture but other, more temporary, forms of indenture spread rapidly in the second half of the century. One measure of their progress is the bitter complaints in Commons against various dilutions of the system. Of particular concern was the practice of distributing liveries and other badges or signs by lords to those with whom they had agreed to make common cause in *querelles,* on a decidedly short-term basis. Petitions in Commons of 1384 and 1388 decry the depredations of such liveried retainers, saying that such *signi* encourage those who wear them, swollen with arrogance because of the power of their lords, to practice extortions upon the countryside (*West. Chron.,* p. 354). For a representative attempt to control short-term indenture by legislation, see *Statutes of the Realm,* vol. 1 (London: Basket, 1758), p. 335.

61. "Si avons ordenez et estroitement defenduz . . . que null Prelat nautre homme de Saint esglise ne bachiler ne esquier nautre de meyndre estat ne donne null manere de tiel liveree appelle liveree de compaignie et que nul Duc Cont Baron ou Banaret ne donne tiel liveree de compaignie a chivaler ne esquier sil ne soit retenuz ovesque luy a terme de vie pur pees et guerre par endenture sanz fraude ou male engyne ou que soit mesnal et familier demurant en son hostell ne a nul vallet appellez yoman archer nautre de meindre estat que esquier sil ne soit ensement familier demurant en son

hostell" (*Stat. Realm,* vol. 1, p. 396). Compare with *Stat. Realm,* vol. 2 (1816; rpt. Dawsons, 1963), pp. 74–75.

62. The intended stability of the arrangement may also be signaled by the introduction of "sanz . . . male engyne," which lightly echoes the feudal "per rectam fidem, sine ingan" (sine *malum ingenum* or false contrivance). See Ganshof, *Féodalité,* p. 103.

63. Only in respect to this distinction between gentle and nongentle household retainers do I differ from N. B. Lewis' comprehensive analysis of the 1390 statute in "The Organization of Indentured Retinues in Fourteenth-Century England," *Trans. Royal Hist. Soc.,* 4th ser., vol. 27 (1945), 29–39. Lewis tends to group the second and third categories as "resident household attendants" (p. 29), thus obscuring the significant position of the former group.

64. This sense of knights and esquires in "mesnal & familiar" capacities as fully *gentil* is borne out in the nearly contemporaneous statute by which Henry IV, newly come to the throne, sought further to limit the practice of retaining by indenture to himself and to the Prince of Wales. There we learn that the king may give his livery to knights and esquires who are resident in his household or retained for life, and that the prince may likewise give his livery to the gentlepersons of his household—here termed *meignalx gentilx* or *mesnals gentils.* See *Stat. Realm,* vol. 1, p. 443.

65. *West. Chron.,* pp. 82, 356.

66. McFarlane, "Bastard Feudalism," p. 169. On McFarlane's point see also Harriss, Introduction to *England in the Fifteenth Century,* with his conclusion that "the bastard feudal affinity represents an attempt . . . to contain the increasingly diversified armigerous class within the old traditions of lordship and chivalry" (pp. xxvi–xxvii).

67. Carpenter, "The Beauchamp Affinity," pp. 531–532. Scott L. Waugh would seem to agree with her assertion, but his emphasis on contractual retaining as a quest for a more "flexible" instrument of clientage would seem to suggest a considerable potential for modification of attitudes under the new system (see "Tenure to Contract," pp. 833–835).

68. Given-Wilson concludes that Richard engaged in little formal retaining before 1389, but pursued the practice avidly in the years 1389–1399; see *The Royal Household,* pp. 214–215, 256.

69. *Life-Records,* p. 303.

70. Lewis, "Organization of Indentured Retinues," p. 36.

71. "'King's esquire' also takes on a new meaning from 1377 . . . [when it is] applied to a large number of men who are not listed in the wardrobe account books, and who are clearly not of the household . . . Both Richard II and Henry IV spent a lot of money on these men, and obviously they set great store by them" (Given-Wilson, *The Royal Household,* p. 212).

72. *Life-Records of Chaucer,* ed. F. J. Furnivall, vol. 2 (London: Chaucer Society, 1876), p. 70.

73. Recall the pertinent anecdote of Froissart: Richard II received and admired his presentation volume and then removed it to his inner chamber or "chambre de retraite," presumably for solitary enjoyment (*Chroniques*, vol. 15, p. 167).

74. Langland, x.97–103.

75. N. H. Owen, "Thomas Wimbledon's Sermon," *MS*, 28 (1966), 181. This observation is of course a late medieval commonplace.

76. *Life-Records*, pp. 112, 144–146, 151.

77. Tout, *Chapters*, vol. 3, p. 457.

78. *Life-Records*, p. 514.

79. Ibid., pp. 46ff.

80. Although an accompanying exemption may suggest that the latter charge was a favor to Chaucer in the financial straits of his last years; see ibid., pp. 42–43, 62–64.

81. Ibid., p. 303.

82. Ibid., pp. 533–534.

2. *The King's Affinity*

1. "Class, Status, Party," in *From Max Weber*, p. 194.

2. *Memorials of London Life*, ed. Henry T. Riley (London: Longmans, Green, 1868), pp. 480–481.

3. Duby points out that communal oaths, designed to solidify relations within a class or closely related classes rather than relations of subordination between classes, were a recurring phenomenon throughout the middle ages (*The Three Orders*, pp. 139, 327–336). On the populist and antihierarchical attitude embodied in such oaths (as opposed to the descending attitude toward human relations), see Walter Ullmann, *The Individual and Society in the Middle Ages* (Baltimore: Johns Hopkins University Press, 1966), p. 56, and *Principles of Government and Politics in the Middle Ages* (New York: Barnes and Noble, 1961), pp. 217–230.

4. The metaphor, "series of concentric circles," is in fact the choice of two recent commentators on the subject. It is employed by Carpenter, "The Beauchamp Affinity," pp. 515–516, and by Given-Wilson, *The Royal Household*, p. 203.

5. Given-Wilson, *The Royal Household*, p. 203.

6. G. A. Holmes, *The Estates of the Higher Nobility in Fourteenth-Century England* (Cambridge: Cambridge University Press, 1957), p. 79.

7. Tout, *Chapters*, vol. 3, p. 457.

8. Hulbert, *Official Life*, p. 92.

9. S. Sanderlin, "Chaucer and Ricardian Politics," *The Chaucer Review*, 22 (1987–1988), 173.

10. Tout conveniently lists Richard's chamber knights, with conjectured terms of service and pertinent references, in *Chapters*, vol. 4, pp. 344–345.

11. See Bird, *Turbulent London,* esp. p. 29.

12. I am joining Anthony Goodman in his suggestion of the relatively greater intensity of commitment shared by the three "senior" Appellants and briefer, less intense commitment shared by the two "junior" Appellants. See *The Loyal Conspiracy: The Lords Appellant under Richard II* (London: Routledge and Kegan Paul, 1971), pp. 135–164.

13. On Northampton's collusive understanding with John of Gaunt, and on the limits of their reciprocal loyalty, see Usk's "Appeal," in R. W. Chambers and Marjorie Daunt, eds., *A Book of London English* (Oxford: Clarendon Press, 1931), p. 28.

14. Ibid., pp. 22–31. A fuller list is published in Bird, *Turbulent London,* pp. 134–135.

15. *Life-Records,* p. 168.

16. James Hulbert, "Chaucer and the Earl of Oxford," *MP,* 10 (1912–1913), 433.

17. *Life-Records,* p. 165.

18. Ibid., p. 361.

19. Ibid., p. 46.

20. Tout, *Chapters,* vol. 3, p. 331.

21. *Life-Records,* p. 360.

22. Ibid., p. 43.

23. Ibid., p. 95.

24. Ibid., p. 100.

25. In his *Testament of Love,* written in 1385–1387 in the hope of gaining preferment from the royal faction, Usk followed Chaucer's example in writing a prose treatise in English, borrowed a passage from his *House of Fame,* and praised him as the "noble philosophical poete in Englissh." See Chaucer, *Works,* ed. Skeat, bk. II, chap. 3, ll. 248–358; bk. III, chap. 4.

26. Tout, *Chapters,* vol. 4, pp. 344–345; G. L. Kittredge, "Chaucer and Some of His Friends," *MP,* 1 (1903–1904), 10.

27. On these respective activities, see *Life-Records,* pp. 24–25; *Chroniques,* vol. 8, pp. 383–386; *Life-Records,* pp. 490–493.

28. Kittredge, "Chaucer and Some of His Friends," pp. 13–18.

29. Edith Rickert, "Thou Vache," *MP,* 11 (1913–1914), 209–225.

30. *Oeuvres,* ed. Le Marquis de Saint-Hilaire and G. Raynaud, SATF, vol. 2, pp. 138–139.

31. K. B. McFarlane, *Lancastrian Kings and Lollard Knights* (Oxford: Clarendon Press, 1972), pp. 161, 185; William Dugdale, *The Baronage of England,* vol. 1 (London, 1675), p. 342.

32. May Newman Hallmundsson, "Chaucer's Circle: Henry Scogan and His Friends," *Medievalia et Humanistica,* n.s. 10 (1981), p. 130.

33. Hulbert, *Official Life,* p. 76.

34. Bird, *Turbulent London,* pp. 97–99.

35. Ibid., p. 97.

36. Ibid., p. 79.

37. *Life-Records,* p. 153.

38. Hulbert, *Official Life,* p. 88.

39. *CPR,* 1385–1389, p. 330. Evidently in greater favor than Chaucer, he was granted from the outset the right to appoint a permanent deputy.

40. *Stat. Realm,* vol. 2 (1816), p. 63.

41. Ibid., p. 77.

42. *Life-Records,* pp. 359–363. Crow puts Hugh Fastolf among the gentry, but see note 47, below.

43. Knighton, p. 237.

44. *West. Chron.,* p. 292.

45. Tout, *Chapters,* vol. 3, p. 432.

46. In this they might be compared with Mayor Nicholas Exton and others of the London aldermen who steadily supported royal policy until the emergence of the Appellants. Yet—according to an anecdote told by the Westminster Chronicler in which Devereux risked himself to restrain a rage of the king against the Archbishop of Canterbury in 1385—he and others might always have been a restraining influence in the household (*West. Chron.,* pp. 116, 210, and note). Cobham was to join the Appellants more wholeheartedly than Devereux; it would be he who joined Gloucester in dragging Robert Tresilian from sanctuary (*West. Chron.,* p. 332).

47. Fastolf is described as "burgess of Great Yarmouth" (*CPR,* 1381–1385, p. 108) and "citizen of London" (*CPR,* 1385–1389, p. 337).

48. *Turbulent London,* p. 94.

49. Carpenter, "The Beauchamp Affinity," p. 516.

50. *Life-Records,* pp. 276–293.

51. Ibid., pp. 95, 98, 99, 101, 107.

52. Bird, *Turbulent London,* p. 68.

53. Ibid., p. 98.

54. *Life-Records,* pp. 343–347.

55. Ernest P. Kuhl places Morel in the Brembre faction, but without supporting evidence. See "Some Friends of Chaucer," *PMLA,* 29 (1914), 270–276. See also *Letter-Book H,* p. 246; Bird, *Turbulent London,* pp. 29, 35; Usk's "Appeal," Chambers and Daunt, *A Book of London English,* p. 30.

56. *Life-Records,* pp. 54–55.

57. Gower did of course receive a collar in return for a presentation manuscript in 1393, but only with his celebration of Henry's accession in his 1399 *Chronica* may he be said decisively to have entered the Lancastrian camp. See John H. Fisher, *John Gower: Moral Philosopher and Friend of Chaucer* (New York: New York University Press, 1964), pp. 68, 109–115.

58. *Letter-Book H,* pp. 208, 245.

59. *CPR,* 1370–1374, p. 351; 1377–1381, p. 126; *Life-Records,* p. 99.

60. *Life-Records,* p. 60. This is the view of Fisher, *John Gower,* pp. 61, 338.

61. *Letter-Book H,* p. 290; *Life-Records,* p. 146.

62. Hulbert cites evidence that he was granted the royal manor of Beckele in 5 R II (Hulbert, *Official Life,* p. 74); see *CPR,* 1377–1383, p. 293.

63. Hulbert, *Official Life,* p. 92.

64. Haldeen Braddy, "Messire Oton de Graunson, Chaucer's Savoyard Friend," *SP,* 35 (1938), 522.

65. Braddy, "Graunson," p. 527.

66. A. Piaget, "Oton de Granson et ses poésies," *Romania,* 19 (1890), 251.

67. "Inventory of the Goods and Chattels Belonging to Thomas, Duke of Gloucester . . . ," *Archaeological Journal,* 54 (1897), 275–308. Some of the books may have belonged to his late wife Eleanor; see *A Collection of All the Wills . . . of Kings and Queens of England* (London: J. Nichols, 1780), pp. 177–183.

68. *CPR,* 1399–1401, p. 202.

69. *Life-Records,* pp. 436–437.

70. Ibid., pp. 61–62.

71. *West. Chron.,* p. 214.

72. Walsingham, p. 169.

73. Knighton, p. 244, 251.

74. *Baronage,* p. 239.

75. Hulbert, *Official Life,* p. 92.

76. *Life-Records,* p. 85.

77. Ibid., p. 271.

78. Ibid., p. 275.

79. Braddy, "Graunson," p. 522.

80. Goodman, *The Loyal Conspiracy,* p. 156.

81. When the accusations of a Carmelite friar and the machinations of Vere and others made a rupture seem inevitable (*West. Chron.,* pp. 68–80).

82. *John of Gaunt* (London: Constable, 1905), p. 136, 193.

83. May McKisack, *The Fourteenth Century, 1307–1399* (Oxford: Clarendon Press, 1959), p. 490. The same point is made even more forcibly by Anthony Tuck, *Richard II and the English Nobility* (London: Edward Arnold, 1974), p. 138.

84. Tuck, *Richard II and the English Nobility,* p. 126.

85. McKisack, *The Fourteenth Century,* pp. 487–489.

86. The following pages will suggest my substantial agreement with Sanderlin's analysis of Chaucer's circumspection in 1386–1389 ("Chaucer and Ricardian Politics," esp. pp. 171–175).

87. Ed. J. J. N. Palmer, "The Impeachment of Michael de la Pole in 1386," *Bull. Inst. Hist. Research,* 42 (1969), 97–101.

88. Ibid., p. 97.

89. *Life-Records,* pp. 348–363, 365–366. Given-Wilson notes that the number of king's knights and esquires returned to this Parliament was the

highest of the decade—possibly an aspect of an abortive Ricardian strategy (*The Royal Household,* p. 247).

90. *RP,* vol. 3, p. 221.

91. Ibid., p. 223.

92. *West. Chron.*, pp. 116–117.

93. *Life-Records,* pp. 268–270.

94. Crow reports, "There is no evidence that a general inquiry was made as a result of which Chaucer might have been removed from office nor that any of the controllers appointed for life were discharged as a result of the council's investigation." See *Life-Records,* p. 269.

95. Hulbert, *Official Life,* p. 88.

96. *RP,* vol. 3, p. 246.

97. Ibid., p. 247.

98. *Life-Records,* pp. 123, 338.

99. Ibid., p. 339.

100. This and the remaining observations made in this paragraph are based on *CPR,* 1385–1389, pp. 15, 41, 306, 363, 371, and passim.

101. *West. Chron.*, p. 456.

102. Ibid., p. 160.

103. *CPR,* 1385–1389, p. 214.

104. Since this April 19 pardon coincided almost exactly with the April 18 debate between the king and the Appellants over their recent action in removing Robert Tresilian from sanctuary in Saint Peter's, Westminster, Nevill's question may have been framed in order to reassert a traditional prerogative that the Appellants had overridden; if so, however, his gesture was oblique and nonconfrontational in nature. See *CPR,* 1385–1389, pp. 449, 454.

105. Rickert, "Thou Vache," pp. 10–11.

106. Walsingham, p. 156.

107. *CPR,* 1385–1389, p. 475.

108. McFarlane makes this point about the cases of Stury, Clanvowe, and Nevill in *Lancastrian Kings and Lollard Knights,* p. 171.

109. McFarlane, *Lancastrian Kings,* p. 180; *Chroniques,* vol. 15, p. 167.

110. *West. Chron.*, p. 480.

111. Rickert, "Thou Vache," p. 219; *RP,* vol. 3, p. 374.

112. Tout, *Chapters,* vol. 3, p. 457.

113. *Lavision-Christine,* ed. Mary Louis Towner (Washington: Catholic University, 1932), pp. 165–166. See also *Oeuvres poétiques de Christine de Pisan,* ed. Maurice Loy, vol. 1 (Paris: SATF, 1886), pp. 232–233.

114. Rossell Hope Robbins has cited convincing evidence that French was spoken in the English court. Other evidence, such as the decisions of Chaucer, Usk, and Gower to write in English and the existence of English wills for several chamber knights including Lewis Clifford and William Beauchamp, suggests that English was prevalent as well. In all probability,

linguistic choice was socially stratified throughout the 1370s and 1380s, the aristocracy preferring French and the gentry preferring English, with Montagu—the Ricardian chamber knight most closely connected with the aristocracy—to be considered within the former group. See Robbins, "Geoffroi Chaucier, Poète Français, Father of English Poetry," *Chaucer Review,* 13 (1978), 101. On the English wills of Lollard chamber knights, see McFarlane, *Lancastrian Kings,* pp. 209–210.

115. Virginia Bording Jellech, "*The Testament of Love* by Thomas Usk: A New Edition" (diss., Washington University, 1970), pp. 70–77.

116. See Jerome Mitchell, "Hoccleve's Supposed Friendship with Chaucer," *ELN,* 4 (1966–1967), 9–12.

117. Fisher, *John Gower,* pp. 116–117.

118. McFarlane, *Lancastrian Kings,* p. 25.

119. Skeat, "A Moral Balade," *Works,* pp. xli–xlii, 237.

120. Dugdale, pp. 238–240.

121. McFarlane, *Lancastrian Kings,* p. 162.

122. Ibid.; see also pp. 148–196, 230–232.

123. Rickert, "Thou Vache," pp. 4–5.

124. Hallmundsson, "Chaucer's Circle," pp. 129–139; G. L. Kittredge, "Henry Scogan," [Harvard] *Studies and Notes,* 1 (1892), 109–117.

125. *Minor Poems,* p. 140.

126. Whether Gower's career received impetus from possible connections to a knightly family or whether his own questionable real-estate deals were the foundation of his wealth, his was a position of economic autonomy suitable to his exercise of the role of independent commentator on contemporary events. See Fisher, *John Gower,* pp. 41–49.

127. On the familiar quality of Chaucer's address, see Alfred David, *The Strumpet Muse* (Bloomington: Indiana University Press, 1976), p. 122.

128. Both published as *The Works of Sir John Clanvowe,* ed. V. J. Scattergood (Cambridge: D. S. Brewer, 1975).

129. McFarlane shows that the copyist of the manuscript was probably Beauchamp's chaplain and clerk. See *Lancastrian Kings,* pp. 200–201; *The Works of Sir John Clanvowe,* pp. 21–22.

130. According to the "Vetus Catalogus," "Nobilis poeta fuit et versificavit librum elegiacum vocatum Phantasma Radulphi." See Israel Gollancz, *DNB,* vol. 19, p. 57.

131. *Chroniques,* vol. 15, p. 167; McFarlane, *Lancastrian Kings,* p. 185; V. J. Scattergood, "Literary Culture at the Court of Richard II," *English Court Culture in the Later Middle Ages* (London: Duckworth, 1983), p. 41.

132. Fisher, *John Gower,* pp. 249–250.

133. Hallmundsson, "Chaucer's Circle," pp. 129–139.

134. Strohm, "Chaucer's Fifteenth-Century Audience and the Narrowing of the 'Chaucer Tradition,'" *SAC,* 4 (1982), 15–16.

3. Audience

1. Middle English *tale* itself conveys a strong and etymologically based sense of oral narration. The bibliography on the oral delivery of literature before the invention of printing is too long for recitation here, but basic texts include: Ruth Crosby, "Oral Delivery in the Middle Ages," *Speculum,* 11 (1936), 88–110, and "Chaucer and the Custom of Oral Delivery," *Speculum,* 13 (1938), 413–432; Bertrand H. Bronson, "Chaucer's Art in Relation to His Audience," *Five Studies in Literature* (Berkeley: University of California Press, 1940), pp. 1–53; H. J. Chaytor, *From Script to Print* (1945; rpt. London: Sidgwick and Jackson, 1966), esp. pp. 1–21; Albert C. Baugh, "The Middle English Romance: Some Questions of Creation, Presentation, and Preservation," *Speculum,* 42 (1967), 1–31. To the extent that a private reading public was fostered by manuscript circulation in the course of the fourteenth and fifteenth centuries, these conclusions must of course be qualified. See Karl Brunner, "Middle English Metrical Romances and Their Audience," *Studies in Medieval Literature in Honor of Professor Albert Croll Baugh,* ed. MacEdward Leach (Philadelphia, 1961), pp. 219–227; M. T. Clanchy, *From Memory to Written Record* (Cambridge: Harvard University Press, 1979). Too recent for proper consideration here is Leonard Michael Koff's highly pertinent *Chaucer and the Art of Storytelling* (Berkeley: University of California Press, 1988).

2. See Renaud's "Livre de Mellibee et Prudence," in *Sources and Analogues,* pp. 572–573.

3. The rhetorical sense of audience I am describing here is less evident in rhetorical treatises like those of Geoffrey of Vinsauf and Matthew of Vendôme, with their focus on the internal amplification of literary works, than in medieval theories of preaching. On this general subject, see Charles Sears Baldwin, *Medieval Rhetoric and Poetic* (New York: Macmillan, 1928), pp. 1–51; G. R. Owst, *Preaching in Medieval England* (Cambridge: Cambridge University Press, 1926), pp. 331–354; Harry Caplan, "Classical Rhetoric and the Medieval Theory of Preaching," *Historical Studies of Rhetoric and Rhetoricians,* ed. Raymond F. Howes (Ithaca: Cornell University Press, 1961), pp. 86–87; and James J. Murphy, *Rhetoric in the Middle Ages* (Berkeley: University of California Press, 1974), pp. 269–355, esp. pp. 294–295. Of particular importance are the later medieval *artes praedicandi,* such as the fourteenth-century *De modo componendi sermones cum documentis* of Thomas Waleys, with its keen attention to matters of effective delivery and its advice that the preacher shape subject matter to the audience ("Necessarium tamen est ut discretionem habeat in loquendo, secundum diversitatem auditorium"). See *Artes Praedicandi,* ed. T.-M. Charland, *Publications de l'Institut d'études médiévales d'Ottawa,* 7 (1936), 339.

4. *Letters of Riper Years* (17, 3); quoted from *The Decameron,* ed. Mark Musa and Peter Bondanella (New York: Norton Critical Editions, 1977), p. 185.

5. Exemplified by H. Marshall Leicester Jr.'s discussion of the "self-constructing" voice embodied in the text of Chaucer's *General Prologue,* in "A General Prologue to the *Canterbury Tales,*" *PMLA,* 95 (1980), 213–234.

6. H. R. Jauss, "Literary History as a Challenge to Literary Theory," *Toward an Aesthetic of Reception,* trans. Timothy Bahti (Minneapolis: University of Minnesota Press, 1982), p. 19.

7. The same point can be made of those sociologists of art—including Arnold Hauser and others following in the nondogmatic Marxist tradition of Plekhanov—who have written illuminatingly on the importance of a socially defined group of readers in perpetuating an artistic style. In his *Philosophy of Art History* (New York: Meridian Books, 1963), Hauser argues that a style is confirmed when it finds "a point of attachment in the support of a socially defined group" (p. 230). This is a valuable theory in its capacity to explain the mixture of styles within the art of a given age or even within a given oeuvre (a result of different social and cultural currents within any society) and the phenomenon of stylistic change (a result of the rise of new classes or groups of interested persons). These formulations nevertheless omit the influence of an audience (or an author's sense of an audience) on the process of composition. Hauser's audience can be "attracted" by what it finds in a work and can "encourage" a stylistic tendency by means as indirect as approbation or as direct as patronage, but it remains in a consuming role, wholly reactive to what the artist has placed before it.

8. V. N. Voloshinov, *Marxism and the Philosophy of Language,* trans. Ladislav Matejka and I. R. Titunik (New York: Seminar Press, 1973), p. 86.

9. Jonathan Culler, *Structuralist Poetics* (Ithaca: Cornell University Press, 1975), pp. 131–132.

10. M. M. Bakhtin/P. M. Medvedev, *The Formal Method in Literary Scholarship,* ed. Albert J. Wehrle (Cambridge: Harvard University Press, 1985), p. 18.

11. Ibid., pp. 151–152.

12. Compare Stanley Fish's compatible argument that the writing of a text is governed by the same community-derived rules that govern interpretation: "Interpretive communities are made up of those who share interpretive strategies not for reading but for writing texts, for constituting their properties. In other words these strategies exist prior to the act of reading and therefore determine the shape of what is read rather than, as is usually assumed, the other way around." See *Is There a Text in This Class? The Authority of Interpretive Communities* (Cambridge: Harvard University Press, 1980), p. 14.

13. That such a group, consisting of gentle civil servants and a few Londoners, represents the heart of Chaucer's literary and social circle has previously been argued by Derek Pearsall, "The *Troilus* Frontispiece and Chaucer's Audience," *YES,* 7 (1977), 68–74; Paul Strohm, "Chaucer's Audience," *Literature and History,* 5 (1977), 26–41; and V. J. Scattergood,

"Literary Culture at the Court of Richard II," *English Court Culture in the Later Middle Ages,* pp. 29–43. See also P. R. Coss, "Aspects of Cultural Diffusion in Medieval England: The Early Romances, Local Society and Robin Hood," *Past and Present,* 108 (1985), 35–79. Evidence pertinent to the existence of such a circle is also presented in Michael J. Bennett, *Community, Class and Careerism* (Cambridge: Cambridge University Press, 1983), pp. 30–33, 67–89.

14. For Salter's warning not to overreact against "older accounts of Chaucer as court-poet, with patrons among the innermost circles of the English royal family," see "Chaucer and Internationalism," *SAC,* 2 (1980), 79. An argumentative context for the reassertion of Chaucer's connections with royalty is provided by Richard F. Green, *Poets and Princepleasers* (Toronto: University of Toronto Press, 1980). The argument for the continuing importance of Richard and his circle as the primary audience of Chaucer's poetry has been cogently restated by Donald R. Howard, *Chaucer: His Life, His Works, His World* (New York: Dutton, 1987). Howard's analysis reflects the influence of two arguments for the royal and occasional background of important works: Larry D. Benson, "The 'Love-Tydinges' in Chaucer's *House of Fame,*" *Chaucer in the Eighties,* ed. Julian Wasserman and Robert Blanch (Syracuse: Syracuse University Press, 1986), pp. 3–22, and "The Occasion of *The Parliament of Fowls,*" *The Wisdom of Poetry,* ed. Benson and Siegfried Wenzel (Kalamazoo, Mich.: Medieval Inst. Pubs., 1982), pp. 151–176. My argument is by no means intended as a refutation of these studies, which reassert an important element of Chaucer's situation of address to which I have given only brief attention. Chaucer's own activities in royal service provided him with ample incentive to address Richard and other magnates on selected occasions, and works like "Lack of Steadfastness" (almost certainly addressed to Richard, probably in support of the king's attempt to broaden his popular base by opposing livery and maintenance in 1388–1389) leave no doubt that he sometimes took advantage of these occasions. If his inscribed audiences are to be taken at all seriously as indicators of his intended audiences, one of his most ambitious poems—the *Legend of Good Women*—may be addressed almost exclusively to a socially elevated readership (see below, note 50).

Several considerations, however, argue that Chaucer's address to his monarchs was occasional and situational rather than constant. One is the fact that he seems rarely to have written for purposes of patronage; James Hulbert argued convincingly as long ago as 1912 that Chaucer's literary efforts can be connected with no marks of royal favor that decisively set him apart from his fellow, nonliterary esquires (*Official Life,* p. 79). Another is the suggestion of booklists and other evidence that Richard's court embraced two tiers of linguistic and literary preference, with Richard and highly placed associates like Simon Burley preferring literature in French and Chaucer and his associates preferring English. On Richard's reading preferences, see Edith

Rickert, "Richard II's Books," *The Library,* 4th ser., 13 (1933), 144–147; R. F. Green, "Richard II's Books Revisited," *The Library,* 31 (1976), 235–239; M. V. Clarke, "Forfeitures and Treason in 1388," *Fourteenth Century Studies* (Oxford: Clarendon Press, 1937), pp. 120–121; V. J. Scattergood, "Two Medieval Book Lists," *The Library,* 23 (1968), 236–239. Even Henry IV appears to have preferred literature written in languages other than English. Henry did, to be sure, address Parliament in English (*RP,* vol. 3, pp. 422–423), but the most concrete illustrations of his reading preferences are his invitation to Christine de Pisan to be his guest in England (see *Lavision-Christine,* ed. Mary Louis Towner [Washington: Catholic University, 1932], pp. 165–166) and his apparent interest in Latin works of disputation and theology (as described in William Dugdale, *Monasticon Anglicanum,* vol. 1 [London: Bohn, 1846], p. 41). Actually Henry V was the first English king who definitely owned English books. Notable among these volumes is the Campsall MS of *Troilus and Criseyde,* which bears his arms as Prince of Wales (see Robert Kilburn Root, *The Manuscripts of Chaucer's Troilus,* Chaucer Society, ser. 1, vol. 98 [1914], p. 5), and Edward Duke of York's Englishing of Gaston de Foix's *Livre de Chasse,* addressed to Henry as Prince of Wales (*The Master of Game,* ed. W. A. and F. Baillie-Grohman [London: Chatto and Windus, 1909]). On the other hand, we have good evidence that (excepting a few members of exceptionally elevated station) most knights and esquires of the royal household preferred literature in English. Consider, in this regard, works by Usk and Clanvowe as well as Chaucer, together with such relevant nonliterary evidence as the English wills of the Lollard chamber knights (McFarlane, *Lancastrian Kings,* pp. 209–210).

15. Supported by such details as the connection between the "ryche hil" and John of Gaunt's estate "Richemont," and between the "long castel" and "Lancaster." See F. N. Robinson, *The Works of Geoffrey Chaucer* (2nd ed.), note to lines 1318–19.

16. On the death of Blanche, see J. N. N. Palmer, "The Historical Context of the *Book of the Duchess:* A Revision," *The Chaucer Review,* 8 (1973–1974), 253–261. On Gaunt's remarriage see McKisack, p. 267. But if, as Howard Schless has argued, "this kyng" (1314) refers to Lancaster's claim on the throne of Castile, the date of the poem may be pushed to the end of 1371 or even to 1372. See "A Dating for the *Book of the Duchess:* Line 1314," *The Chaucer Review,* 19 (1984–1985), 273–275.

17. A mandate of 30 August 1372 provides for an annuity to Philippa Chaucer for services to the Duchess Constance (*Life-Records,* pp. 85–86).

18. The Black Knight is described as being "of the age of foure and twenty yer" (l. 455), when the Duke would actually have been 29 when Blanche died. Robinson (note to ll. 445ff.) offers a possible scribal explanation.

19. David, *The Strumpet Muse,* p. 11.

20. Lenaghan, "Chaucer's Circle of Gentlemen and Clerks," *The Chaucer Review,* 18 (1983–1984), 155–160.

21. The marriage had occurred by 1366; Philippa was in service with Constance by 1372 (*Life-Records,* pp. 67–68, 85–86).

22. *Chaucer's Dream Poetry: Sources and Analogues,* ed. and trans. B. A. Windeatt (Cambridge: D. S. Brewer, 1982), pp. 39–40.

23. *Life-Records of Chaucer,* part 4, ed. R. E. G. Kirk, Chaucer Society Publications, 2nd ser., no. 32 (London, 1900), pp. 162–165.

24. As noted in Chapter 2, Stury knew Froissart and possessed his own copy of the *Roman de la rose.*

25. Donaldson, "Criseyde and Her Narrator," *Speaking of Chaucer* (London: Athlone Press, 1970), pp. 65–83.

26. Brewer, "The Reconstruction of Chaucer," *SAC, Proceedings,* 1 (1984), 14. This point is usefully developed by David Lawton, *Chaucer's Narrators* (Cambridge: D. S. Brewer, 1985).

27. Ong, *PMLA,* 90 (1975), 9–21.

28. John H. Fisher, *John Gower: Moral Philosopher and Friend of Chaucer* (New York: New York University Press, 1964), pp. 225–235. A complementary view is that of R. F. Yeager, "'O Moral Gower': Chaucer's Dedication of Troilus and Criseyde," *The Chaucer Review,* 19 (1984–1985), 87–99. Yeager traces the meaning of "moral" to four elements of Gower's poetic reputation: "personal and social reformism; conscious (and conscientious) classicism; an advocate's stance; a thorough consistency in his approach to questions of evil and good" (p. 97).

29. Gower, *Works,* vol. 1; as cited and discussed in Fisher, *John Gower,* pp. 226–227.

30. Gower, *Works,* vols. 2 and 3.

31. This is a consensus view, but doubts have been entertained by such careful commentators as T. F. Tout, who points out that "if the one Ralph Strode did all these things he was a very remarkable man." See his "Literature and Learning in the English Civil Service in the Fourteenth Century," *Speculum,* 4 (1929), 388.

32. On the argument that this passage represents a late addition to Chaucer's poem, see Robinson, note to IV.953. Cf. B. A. Windeatt, ed., *Troilus and Criseyde* (London and New York: Longman, 1984), pp. 40–43.

33. Herbert B. Workman, *John Wycliff: A Study of the English Medieval Church,* vol. 2 (Oxford: Clarendon Press, 1926), pp. 127–128.

34. J. S. P. Tatlock's suggestion ("The Epilog of Chaucer's 'Troilus,'" *MP,* 18 [1920–1921], 656–657) that Strode would have been an "uncompromising critic" of Troilus' views on destiny is correct, but not in the sense that Tatlock intended. His view was that Chaucer's and Troilus' positions are similar and that Strode is invoked in order to mollify readers distressed by the paganism and determinism of the poem; my view is, rather, that Strode is proposed as a reader capable of "seeing through" the weakness of Troilus' position, as Chaucer intended him and other readers to do. In this regard I concur with Howard R. Patch's assertion that Troilus' soliloquy

shows him "giving way to his feelings rather than his intellect . . . in a situation on which the poem as a whole sheds ironic light." See "Troilus on Determinism," *Speculum,* 6 (1929), 235.

35. If Strode the lawyer is a separate person from Strode the theologian, we must be less sure of his reading of this dimension of the poem. Still he would seem to be *invited* to read the poem from the position of his philosophical namesake.

36. Chauncey Wood has offered an intriguing "Gowerian" reading of the whole of the *Troilus,* in *The Elements of Chaucer's* Troilus (Durham: Duke University Press, 1984), esp. pp. 168–169. My own inclination is to treat Gower and Strode less as ideal readers of the whole poem than as ideal respondents to the mood and outlook of the narrator at the particular moment they are invoked.

37. John Livingston Lowes, "The Date of Chaucer's *Troilus and Criseyde,*" *PMLA,* 23 (1908), 285–306.

38. B. A. Windeatt, "The Scribes as Chaucer's Early Critics," *SAC,* 1 (1979), 119–141.

39. A point made by Donaldson, *Speaking of Chaucer,* p. 98.

40. As Bertrand Bronson observes in "Chaucer's Art in Relation to His Audience," *Five Studies in Literature,* University of California Publications in English, 8 (1940), p. 53.

41. The period in which Chaucer worked on *Troilus* may be stated most broadly as late 1381 to late 1386. The former date represents the time when Richard's engagement to Anne, to culminate in marriage on 14 January 1382, would have been common knowledge (see Lowes, note 37 above). The latter date is set by Chaucer's removal to Kent and also by the reference to *Troilus* in Usk's *Testament,* which must have been complete before September-October 1387, when its author attained the preferment for which the *Testament* was written. I am not persuaded with Ramona Bressie that Usk had to have completed his poem during 1384–1385 ("The Date of Thomas Usk's *Testament of Love, MP,* 26 [1928–1929], 17–29). Nor am I convinced by John P. McCall and George Rudisill, Jr., that *Troilus* could not have been finished until after the Parliament of 1386 ("The Parliament of 1386 and Chaucer's Trojan Parliament," *JEGP,* 58 [1959], 276–288). My assumption is that *Troilus* was completed in late 1385 or early 1386 (a date consistent with the astrological reference discussed by R. K. Root and H. N. Russell, "A Planetary Date for Chaucer's *Troilus,*" *PMLA,* 39 [1924], 48–63), and that Usk's *Testament* was completed while he awaited preferment in 1386. Thus, tightening the termini slightly, I would argue that the period of composition of *Troilus* was roughly 1382–1385/86, and that late 1385 would be the most likely estimate of its completion.

42. Like Chaucer, Usk balanced secular aspirations and pious extremes; he met his death "cum magna contricione," reciting penitential psalms and other devotional pieces (*West. Chron.,* p. 314).

43. Derek Pearsall, *The Canterbury Tales* (London: George Allen and Unwin, 1985), p. 295.

44. Ibid., p. 294.

45. While Chaucer himself would naturally have been a member of the former group, his pilgrim-narrator seems to have been somewhat demoted; D. S. Brewer notes his "insecure" status in "Class Distinction in Chaucer," *Speculum,* 43 (1968), 303–304.

46. Mann, *Chaucer and Medieval Estates Satire* (Cambridge: Cambridge University Press, 1973).

47. According to Helen Cooper, "Other story-collections, such as legendaries or Aesopets or the *Monk's Tale,* concentrate on a single genre; potentially more varied collections, such as the *Gesta* or the *Decameron* or the *Confessio,* tend to reduce all their stories to the level of a 'tale.' Only the stories of the *Canterbury Tales* keep their individual structure and content as romance or fabliau or saint's life or tract, with different verse or prose forms to contain them." See *The Structure of the Canterbury Tales* (London: Duckworth, 1983), pp. 50 and 8–55 passim.

48. C. David Benson, *Chaucer's Drama of Style: Poetic Variety and Contrast in the Canterbury Tales* (Chapel Hill: University of North Carolina Press, 1986). Cooper has pointed to that moment in the *House of Fame* when the speeches upon entry to the palace reassume the guises of their original speakers as an example of the sense in which a speaker may, for Chaucer, be regarded as a projection of the thing said (*Structure,* p. 75).

49. *Decameron,* ed. Mario Marti, 2nd ed. (Milan: Rizzoli, 1967), pp. 49, 1066; ed. Musa and Bondanella, p. 3.

50. The audience fictionalized in the poem seems, as Alfred David has pointed out, to be "small and opinionated," wedded to "limited and established literary tastes," as distinguished from persons "like Scogan and Bukton, whose sense of comedy is clearly implied in the epistles Chaucer addressed to them" (*Strumpet Muse,* pp. 122–124). Although discussion of the poem's problems has tended to center on the difficulty of its charge, we should not overlook the difficulty of mobilizing the diverse and challenging poetry we have come to expect from Chaucer in address to so socially narrow (and, in the case of the God of Love, so obtuse) an audience. Seen in relation to its audience, the *Legend* seems shaped for outward compliance with demands for generic stability and explicit didacticism, even as it indulges in complicated and sometimes private tonal experiments that reflect awareness of the actual complexity of the poet's task. This point is effectively made by Lisa J. Kiser, *Telling Classical Tales* (Ithaca: Cornell University Press, 1983), esp. pp. 71–94. I agree fully with her observations about Chaucer's somewhat subversive response to his audience's restrictive demands. I would differ, however, with her occasional implication that his relation to his audience in this poem typifies his relations with his audience generally (e.g., p. 94), since I regard the situation of the *Legend* as somewhat atypical in

comparison with the more congenial audience situation implied by most of his poems.

51. A point emphasized by Dieter Mehl, "Chaucer's Audience," *Leeds Studies in English,* 10 (1978), esp. 66.

52. *Les Fabliaux: Etude d'histoire littéraire et de stylistique médiévale* (Copenhagen: E. Munksgaard, 1957), esp. pp. 20–28, 105–139.

53. Jean Rychner, "Les Fabliaux: Genre, Styles, Publics," *La Littérature narrative d'imagination* (Paris: Presses Universitaires, 1961), pp. 41–52.

54. Paul Strohm, "*Passioun, Lyf, Miracle, Legende:* Some Generic Terms in Middle English Hagiographical Narrative," *The Chaucer Review,* 10 (1974–1975), 69–70.

55. Renate Hass, "Chaucer's *Monk's Tale:* An Ingenious Criticism of Early Humanistic Conceptions of Tragedy," *Humanistica Lovaniensia,* 36 (1987), 44–70.

56. Strohm, "*Passioun,*" pp. 70–72, 161–164.

57. Lee Patterson, "The *Parson's Tale* and the Quitting of the *Canterbury Tales,*" *Traditio,* 34 (1978), 331–380.

58. Especially P. M. Kean, *Chaucer and the Making of English Poetry,* vol. 1 (London: Routledge and Kegan Paul, 1972), pp. 33–38; Alfred David, "Chaucer's Good Counsel to Scogan," *The Chaucer Review,* 3 (1968–1969), 265–274; R. T. Lenaghan, "Chaucer's *Envoy to Scogan:* The Uses of Literary Conventions," *The Chaucer Review,* 10 (1975–1976), 46–61.

59. Kean observes that "This is a complex example of a poem in which the poet, the friend addressed and a wider but congenial and known audience all participate" (*Chaucer and the Making of English Poetry,* p. 35).

60. Pace and David, *Minor Poems,* p. 145.

61. "Thou Vache," *MP,* 11 (1913–1914), 209–226.

62. "Chaucer's *Envoy to Scogan,*" p. 57.

63. Respective characterizations by Deschamps, Usk, and Lydgate. See Derek Brewer, *Chaucer: The Critical Heritage,* vol. 1 (London: Routledge and Kegan Paul, 1978), pp. 39–58; Caroline F. E. Spurgeon, *Five Hundred Years of Chaucer Criticism and Allusion,* vol. 1 (1925; rpt. New York: Russell and Russell, 1960), pp. 1–32.

64. See Paul Strohm, "Fourteenth- and Fifteenth-Century Writers as Readers of Chaucer," *Genres, Themes, and Images in English Literature: From the Fourteenth to the Fifteenth Century,* J. A. W. Bennett Memorial Lectures (Tübingen: Narr, 1988), pp. 90–104.

65. Virginia Bording Jellech, "*The Testament of Love* by Thomas Usk: A New Edition" (diss., Washington University, 1970), pp. 53–70.

66. Citations to *The Testament of Love* from *Works,* ed. Skeat.

67. Text from *Works,* ed. Skeat.

68. Pace and David, p. 73.

69. *The Works of Sir John Clanvowe,* ed. V. J. Scattergood (Cambridge: D. S. Brewer, 1975), pp. 14–18.

70. Ibid., pp. 18–22.

71. G. L. Kittredge, "Chaucer and Some of His Friends," *MP,* 1 (1903–1904), esp. 13–18.

72. *Works,* p. 13.

73. As described in F. J. E. Raby, *A History of Secular Latin Poetry in the Middle Ages,* vol. 2 (Oxford: Clarendon Press, 1934) pp. 282–308; H. Walther, *Das Streitgedicht in der lateinischen Literatur des Mittelalters* (Munich: Beck, 1920).

74. For discussion of further "Chaucerian" qualities of Clanvowe's other surviving work, "The Two Ways," see Strohm, "Fourteenth- and Fifteenth-Century writers as Readers of Chaucer."

4. *Selflessness and Selfishness*

1. I am borrowing the notion of "stance" from William J. Brandt, *The Shape of Medieval History* (1966; rpt. New York: Shocken Books, 1973). Brandt treats the stance as a public, aristocratic posture, though I will use the term somewhat more broadly.

2. See Chapter 1, note 4.

3. As shown by Jill Mann, *Chaucer and Medieval Estates Satire* (Cambridge: Cambridge University Press, 1973).

4. The argument that the Knight is a mercenary, fighting for gain, has been advanced by Terry Jones, *Chaucer's Knight* (London: Weidenfeld and Nicolson, 1980), a work that includes an extensive and jaundiced review of his campaigns. A preponderence of evidence, however, supports the traditional view of J. M. Manly ("A Knight ther was," *Trans. Amer. Phil. Assn.,* 38 [1907], 89–107) and of Albert S. Cook ("The Historical Background of Chaucer's Knight," *Trans. Conn. Acad.,* 20 [1916], 161–240), that the Knight's campaigns represent ideal conduct, unsullied by forays against fellow Christians. This conforms to the ideal of traditional knighthood endorsed by Gower in his *Mirour*—an ideal demanding that the knight reject the temptation to remain at home troubling the poor and litigating and engaging in trade (23725–60), and instead exert himself abroad in God's behalf, in such venues as "Espruce" and "Tartarie" (23893–963). A particularly apposite rejoinder to Jones is that of Maurice Keen, "Chaucer's Knight, The English Aristocracy and the Crusade," *English Court Culture in the Later Middle Ages* (London: Duckworth, 1983), pp. 45–61.

5. Among other elements of traditionalism in the Knight's behavior is his acceptance of responsibility for his own son. Georges Duby, *William Marshall* (1984; rpt. New York: Pantheon, 1987), pp. 65–66, points out that sons were rarely retained by their fathers. This observation, made of the thirteenth century, would seem to be even more true of the more mobile society of the late fourteenth century.

6. For a somewhat overstated but provocative argument that the pres-

ence of the Yeoman as retainer argues for the Knight's high social rank, see William B. McColly, "Chaucer's Yeoman and the Rank of his Knight," *The Chaucer Review,* 20 (1985-86), 14–27.

7. Mann, *Chaucer and Medieval Estates Satire,* p. 109.

8. Ibid., pp. 109–110.

9. "Dobest . . . bereth a bisshopes crosse; / Is hoked at that oon ende to holde men in good lif"—Langland, VIII.96–97.

10. On the decline of villeinage in the late fourteenth century see R. H. Hilton, *The Decline of Serfdom in Medieval England* (London: Macmillan, 1969), esp. pp. 32–43.

11. The Plowman is taken by Joseph Horrell as "a symbol of the rude, anonymous folk who might lead the beatific life" in "Chaucer's Symbolic Plowman," *Speculum,* 14 (1939), 82–92. But, as examples cited both by Horrell and by Mann, *Chaucer and Medieval Estates Satire,* pp. 67–74, would suggest, idealizations of plowmen and other *cultores* were rare before Langland and Chaucer. Elizabeth D. Kirk has recently argued in "Langland's Plowman and the Recreation of Fourteenth-Century Religious Metaphor," *Yearbook of Langland Studies,* 2 (1988), 1–21, that Langland's and Chaucer's idealizations represent an essentially new departure, the imaginative strength of which has persuaded modern readers that they were writing in an established tradition.

12. Harry Bailly seconds the Knight's interruption and confirms that the Monk was indeed on the brink of losing "audience" (VII.2801) from the company of pilgrims. That the Knight's and Harry Bailly's interruptions were welcomed by early readers is suggested by the early manuscript history of the *Tales,* including Jean of Angoulême's further cuts in the Monk's series of tragedies. See Paul Strohm, "Jean of Angoulême: A Fifteenth Century Reader of Chaucer," *Neuphilologische Mitteilungen,* 72 (1971), 69–76.

13. VI.962–967. This tradition is epitomized in Langland, 6, ll. 23–32.

14. In this behavior the Merchant exhibits a variant of the practice described by the merchant of the *Shipman's Tale,* who tells of putting the best face on affairs of business, while dealing privately with the misfortunes associated with trade (VII.230–238). See Gardiner Stillwell, "Chaucer's 'Sad' Merchant," *RES,* 20 (1944), 1–18.

15. Their ambitions are, in the light of the social history of the fourteenth century, misconceived. As indicated by materials collected by Sylvia Thrupp (*Merchant Class,* pp. 321–377), only three representatives of the Guildsmen's own trades ever became aldermen in the fourteenth and fifteenth centuries, and none earlier than the late fifteenth century. Also see Ernest P. Kuhl, "Chaucer's Burgesses," *Trans. Wisc. Academy,* 18:2 (1916), 652–675.

16. Thrupp points to the particular popularity of such parish guilds among citizens of middle rank (*Merchant Class,* p. 37), though some guilds and confraternities claimed more prominent members. The guild records assembled by Toulmin Smith include the interesting case of the relatively

exclusionary guild of St. Michael on the Hill, the members of which are to be of the same rank ("status") as that of the brothers and sisters who founded it, namely, of common and middle rank ("de statu communum et mediocrum vivorum"). See *English Gilds,* EETS, OS, 40 (1870), pp. 178–179.

17. For examples of mutual assistance see *English Gilds,* pp. 183–185; motives of personal advancement surface on pp. 94–95, 217.

18. On amity in guild regulations, see Carl Lindahl, *Ernest Games: Folkloric Patterns in the Canterbury Tales* (Bloomington: Indiana University Press, 1987), esp. pp. 80–82.

19. *Chaucer and Medieval Estates Satire,* p. 202.

20. This passage in fragment B of the *Romaunt* is unlikely to belong to the translation mentioned by the God of Love in the *Prologue* to the *Legend of Good Women* (F 329); see Alfred David's explanatory notes to the *Romaunt, The Riverside Chaucer,* pp. 1103–4. Aside from his own possible activities as translator, Chaucer repeatedly demonstrates intimate knowledge of Guillaume's text, as in VIII. 1–3.

21. See Ganshof, *Qu'est-ce que la Féodalité?,* pp. 98–99.

22. Ibid., pp. 105–106.

23. On the function of semantic domains within the metaphor, see Inge Crosman, *Metaphoric Narration,* North Carolina Studies in Romance Languages and Literatures (Chapel Hill, 1978), pp. 14–19.

24. Richards, *The Philosophy of Rhetoric* (London: Oxford University Press, 1936), p. 96.

25. For an argument that a term (and by implication any other social fact) may come to inhabit distinct social and literary planes, see P. R. Coss, "Literature and Social Terminology: The Vavasour in England," in *Social Relations and Ideas: Essays in Honour of R. H. Hilton,* ed. T. H. Aston et al. (Cambridge: Cambridge University Press, 1983), pp. 109–150.

26. The idea of vassalage as it is constituted within Guillaume's poetry is not wholly untouched by the social developments discussed in the opening chapter of this book. The God of Love, for example, professes himself often disappointed in vassalage: "'I have,' he seide, 'taken fele homages / Of oon and other, where I have ben / Disceyved often'" (2044–46), a disappointment that leads in this case to further elaboration of the ceremony, in which the lover offers his heart as "ostage" (2081). Yet his disappointment lies less in the institution itself than in the fallibility of its participants; this kind of treason is not peculiar to the thirteenth century, but is acknowledged as a possibility in the earliest chansons. Guillaume's poem uses vassalage in a way that suggests that good vassalage is still a possibility in the world.

27. As recently argued by Denis Walker, "*Contentio:* The Structural Paradigm of *The Parliament of Fowls,*" *SAC, Proceedings,* 1 (1984), 173–180.

28. Kate O. Peterson, *The Sources of the Parson's Tale* (1901; rpt. New York: AMS, 1973), p. 40.

29. Keen, "Brotherhood in Arms," *History,* 47 (1962), 1–17.

30. Peterson, *Sources,* p. 54; see the *Parson's Tale,* x.590–602.

31. The *Pardoner's Tale* is given a deliberately vague setting, in "Flaundres" (vi.463). Stephen Knight has pointed out that the treasure of "floryns" (vi.774) connects the action with fourteenth-century economic realities ("Rhetoric and Cash: The Socio-economic Progress of Chaucer's Pardoner," paper read at the 1984 NCS Congress), but such details are few.

32. Z. Dolly Hassan-Yusuff, "'Wynne Thy Cost': Commercial and Feudal Imagery in the *Friar's Tale,*" *Chaucer Newsletter,* 1:2 (1979), 15–18.

33. Richard F. Green has called my attention to the definition of *approver* in Black's law dictionary: "An accomplice in crime who accuses others of the same offense." John A. Alford cites the definition of *approver* in a thirteenth-century formulary: "one who serves as a witness against a former accomplice in crime, usually in exchange for a reduced penalty" (*Piers Plowman: A Glossary of Legal Diction* [Cambridge: D. S. Brewer, 1988], p. x).

34. The *MED*—as in the "duetee and honour" with which Arcite ends his life (i.3060).

35. The *MED.*

36. On lay confraternities see John V. Fleming, "The Summoner's Prologue: An Iconographic Adjustment," *The Chaucer Review,* 2 (1967–68), 101–107.

37. These interrelated aspects of the tale have been examined, respectively, by Albert H. Silverman, "Sex and Money in Chaucer's *Shipman's Tale,*" *PQ,* 32 (1953), 329–336; Lee W. Patterson, "Exchange and Alienation in the Shipman's Tale," (paper read the 1985 MLA meeting); V. J. Scattergood, "The Originality of the *Shipman's Tale,*" *The Chaucer Review,* 11 (1976–1977), 210–231; George R. Keiser, "Language and Meaning in the *Shipman's Tale,*" *The Chaucer Review,* 12 (1977–1978), 148–152; Keiser also takes note of the debasement of language, particularly the language of sworn oaths, in this tale.

38. See Scattergood, "The Originality," pp. 222–224.

39. David Wallace has observed in correspondence that "Troilus' commitments are religious oaths in the sense that *Paradiso* V defines them—they are binding in the afterlife. When he says to Pandarus 'it lith nat in my power,' he is, I think, following the medieval understanding of what making a religious oath implies: it means the voluntary renunciation of free will, the most precious power humans possess (*Par.* v.28–30). So, for Troilus, the change Pandarus seeks literally does not lie in his power, but in that of God (or, the gods)."

40. See Alan T. Gaylord, "The Promises in *The Franklin's Tale, ELH,* 31 (1964), esp. 341–350.

41. This is the view of Alfred David, who comments that "There *is* another way out of every contract involving a debt of honor. It may be voluntarily dissolved by the creditor" (*The Strumpet Muse,* p. 189).

42. Kathryn Jacobs contrasts the "self-interest and opportunism repre-

sented by the "contracts" of the tale, with the "affection and social responsibility" represented by a "beneficent cluster of social ties." The tale, in her view, proposes an ideal society, based on the superiority of the "law of love" to the "law of interest." See "The Marriage Contract of the *Franklin's Tale:* The Remaking of Society," *The Chaucer Review,* 20 (1985–1986), 132–143.

43. G. H. Gerould, "The Social Status of Chaucer's Franklin," *PMLA,* 41 (1926), 262–279; George Lyman Kittredge, *Chaucer and His Poetry* (1915; rpt. Cambridge: Harvard University Press, 1970), pp. 209–210.

44. The notion of the Franklin as a character beguiled by his own social aspirations has been put forward with the most conviction by R. M. Lumiansky, *Of Soundry Folk* (Austin: University of Texas Press, 1955), pp. 180–193.

45. Henrik Specht, *Chaucer's Franklin in the Canterbury Tales* (Copenhagen: Akademisk Forlag, 1981).

46. Nigel Saul, "The Social Status of Chaucer's Franklin: A Reconsideration," *Medium Aevum,* 52 (1983), 10–26.

47. "His tale," according to Alfred David, "reflects the values of the emerging class to which he belongs." See "Sentimental Comedy in the *Franklin's Tale,*" *Annuale Medievale,* 6 (1965), 21.

48. Middleton, "Chaucer's 'New Men' and the Good of Literature," *Literature and Society,* ed. Edward Said (Baltimore: Johns Hopkins University Press, 1980), 16.

49. The latter work reproduces "Gentilesse" in full and paraphrases passages both from that poem and from relevant sections of the *Wife of Bath's Tale.* See Chaucer, *Works,* ed. Skeat, pp. 237–244.

50. I borrow the word from Alfred David, (note 47, above), who connects it with the rise of sentimental comedy, written for a predominantly bourgeois audience at the turn of the eighteenth century. Chaucer also uses the term, and relevantly, in reference to the expression of strong feeling; see *Troilus and Criseyde,* II.13; III.43, 1797; *LGW,* F, 69.

5. Time and the Social Implications of Narrative Form

1. *Civ. Dei,* XI.6.

2. Gordon Leff has discussed the different, but ultimately related, senses in which fourteenth-century philosophers widened the gap between God's eternal present and human choices in time. See "The Fourteenth Century and the Decline of Scholasticism," *Past and Present,* 9 (1956), esp. 36–37.

3. Similarly temporal are those forms of narrative which depart from *ordo naturalis* in favor of *ordo artificialis,* or nonsequential action, but which nevertheless present their episodes in ways that permit the audience to engage in temporal or chronological reconstruction. See Geoffrey of Vinsauf, *Poetria nova,* II.167, in Edmond Faral, *Les Arts poétiques du XIIe et du XIIIe siècle* (Paris: Champion, 1924), p. 202.

4. Ricoeur, *Time and Narrative,* vol. 1 (Chicago: University of Chicago Press, 1984), p. 81.

5. As in Hayden White's description of the Annals of St. Gall as "a representation of temporality." See "The Value of Narrativity in the Representation of Reality," *Critical Inquiry,* 7 (1980), 5–27.

6. White, "The Value of Narrativity," pp. 26–27; Ricoeur, *Time and Narrative,* p. 67.

7. *Time and Narrative,* p. 81.

8. A development described by Sherry L. Reames, "The Cecilia Legend as Chaucer Inherited It and Retold It," *Speculum,* 55 (1980), 38–57. See also Reames, *The Legenda Aurea: A Reexamination of Its Paradoxical History* (Madison: University of Wisconsin Press, 1985).

9. LeGoff, "Merchant's Time and Church's Time in the Middle Ages," *Time, Work, and Culture in the Middle Ages* (Chicago: University of Chicago Press, 1980), p. 33.

10. Bakhtin, "Forms of Time and Chronotope in the Novel," in *The Dialogic Imagination,* ed. Michael Holquist (Austin: University of Texas Press, 1981), pp. 151–155. Formal receptivity to the miraculous within both saints' lives and romances may be a factor in their generic interpenetration in the later middle ages. See Ojars Kratins, "The Middle English *Amis and Amiloun:* Chivalric Romance or Secular Hagiography," *PMLA,* 81 (1966), 347–354.

11. As, for example, John Livingston Lowes' discussion of the way Chaucer "casts off trammels" in his movement from the "conventional frames" of the vision poems to the richer "narrative fabric" of *Troilus* and the *Tales.* See *Geoffrey Chaucer and the Development of His Genius* (Boston: Houghton Mifflin, 1934), pp. 168–169, 191–192.

12. These poems embrace a pattern noted by John Norton-Smith for the *Legend of Good Women,* in which "the general narration leads up by *ordo naturalis* to a passage of rhetorically elegant, pathetic utterance, thus showing an overall formulation similar to that of the narrative-amatory complaints such as *Mars, Anelida,* and *Pity.*" *Geoffrey Chaucer* (London: Routledge and Kegan Paul, 1974), p. 73.

13. Until the very end of the fourteenth century, astronomical time virtually *was* time, providing the most authoritative model of regularity in succession. Chaucer's pilgrims calculate sublunary or terrestrial time by rough-and-ready approximations of celestial time based on the length of shadows cast by the sun (as in II. 1–14). The mechanical clocks of the fourteenth century were designed in the first instance to provide information about the motions of the planets, and regular division of the hours of day and night developed only later. See Jean Gimpel, *The Medieval Machine: The Industrial Revolution of the Middle Ages* (London: Penguin, 1976), pp. 147–170.

14. Paul Strohm, "Guillaume as Narrator and Lover in the *Roman de la Rose,*" *Romanic Review,* 59 (1968), 3–9.

15. Gardiner Stillwell observed that "Chaucer does not go so far as to

say that Venus becomes Mercury's mistress, but Mercury . . . receives Venus heartily as his friend full dear (l. 147), and she accepts his hospitality. And whatever goes on in Mercury's mansion, Mars does not know of the proceedings, so that when in his complaint he supposes Venus to be on the point of death and woe, we have unmistakable dramatic irony" ("Chaucer's *Complaint of Mars*," *PQ*, 35 [1956], 73). His point has been extended—and possibly a bit overextended—by Edgar S. Laird, "Astrology and Irony in Chaucer's *Complaint of Mars*," *The Chaucer Review*, 6 (1971–1972), 229–231, and by Melvin Storm, "The Mythological Tradition in Chaucer's *Complaint of Mars*," *PQ*, 57 (1978), 329.

16. Boccaccio, "A Fiametta."

17. One reader's response to Statius' *Thebaid/Roman de Thèbes* is that of Criseyde in book II of *Troilus*. When her hearing of "the geste / Of the siege of Thebes" (83–84) is interrupted by Pandarus' arrival, she is able to describe her location in the poem in terms of its succession of episodes (102–105).

18. Edgar Finley Shannon, *Chaucer and the Roman Poets* (Cambridge: Harvard University Press, 1929), pp. 15–44.

19. Wolfgang Clemen observes that these stanzas are "full of promises that are not kept and statements that are not true." *Chaucer's Early Poetry* (New York: Barnes and Noble, 1963), p. 199.

20. Vincent J. DiMarco, in *The Riverside Chaucer*, p. 991.

21. Clemen, *Chaucer's Early Poetry*, pp. 203–204.

22. Aage Brusendorff argues that the stanza is a scribal addition (*The Chaucer Tradition* [Oxford: Clarendon Press, 1925], p. 260). Norton-Smith argues tellingly that this stanza obscures the pattern of the poem, in which—as in the "Complaint of Mars"—a brief story introduces a complaint ("Chaucer's Anelida and Arcite," *Medieval Studies for J. A. W. Bennett* [Oxford: Clarendon Press, 1981], pp. 81–99).

23. The fact that two manuscripts reverse the order of "storie" and "compleynte" might be taken as evidence that comparison, rather than any particular ordering of parts, was Chaucer's main motive here; yet the fact that four manuscripts copy the complaint alone might simply suggest the fifteenth-century preference for that form. See *The Riverside Chaucer*, pp. 1144–46.

24. Monica E. McAlpine has discussed *Troilus* as a mixture of elements of Boethian comedy and Boethian tragedy, in *The Genre of Troilus and Criseyde* (Ithaca: Cornell University Press, 1978). The full generic complexity of the poem—including its numerous generic embeddings—has not, to my knowledge, been reviewed.

25. As explained by Joseph A. Longo, "The Double Time Scheme in Book II of Chaucer's *Troilus and Criseyde*," *MLQ*, 22 (1961), 37–40.

26. This treatment of narrative time has been insightfully discussed by Gerry Brenner, who finds the first two books characterized by "sequential narration," the third by "unified" time, the fourth by "strained unity," and

the fifth by the "complete dismissal of time." He finds in this disruption of narrative time—together with other structural inversions, ironic foreshadowings, and multiple points of view—a "metaphor of cacaphony and disorder." I can certainly agree with this analysis, so long as due attention is given to the senses in which the ruination of temporal narration prepares the audience for an enhanced reassertion of an extratemporal view. See Brenner's "Narrative Structure in Chaucer's *Troilus and Criseyde,*" *Annual Medievale,* 6 (1965), 5–18.

27. On the narrator's multiple vision, see E. Talbot Donaldson, "The Ending of 'Troilus,'" *Speaking of Chaucer* (New York: Norton, 1972), pp. 84–101.

28. LeGoff, *Time, Work, and Culture,* pp. 29–42.

29. See Chenu, *Nature, Man, and Society,* on the natural state, with its assertion of "the autonomy of the forms of nature, of the methods of the mind, and of the laws of society" and with its emphasis on "an administration based on functions rather than on feudal oaths" (pp. 196–197). Chenu's observations are based on John of Salisbury, but are equally true of Marsilius of Padua, with his emphasis on the ultimate authority of the whole body of citizens; see *Defensor pacis,* vol. 2, ed. Alan Gewirth (New York: Columbia University Press, 1956), I.xii.5 and xix.2.

30. On theocratic kingship see Ullmann, *Principles of Government and Politics in the Middle Ages,* pp. 117–149. The forceful analogy of the rule of the universe by a single being ("mundus ab uno gubernetur") influenced Aquinas and others ("De Gubernatione Rerum in Communi," *Summa Theologica,* Qu. 103, art. 3, in *Aquinas: Selected Political Writings* [Oxford: Blackwell, 1948], p. 106), and was reinforced by those tenets of Aristotle's *Politics* that had become available in Latin translation in the early thirteenth century.

31. On the practical use of the mechanical clock, publicly displayed and striking equal hours, see Gimpel, *The Medieval Machine,* pp. 168–170, as well as LeGoff, "Labor Time in the 'Crisis' of the Fourteenth Century: From Medieval Time to Modern Time," *Time, Work, and Culture,* pp. 43–52.

32. LeGoff argues that the regulatory practices of confession arose in the thirteenth century as an aspect of the church's attempt to organize and evaluate activities occurring in secular time. Yet he observes that the two realms of time again diverged in the late fourteenth and fifteenth centuries, with men and women of the later middle ages gaining mastery of secular time, and with church time "relegated to the sphere of unpredictable decisions of an omnipotent God" ("Merchant's Time and Church's Time," pp. 37–42).

33. Thrupp, *Merchant Class,* pp. 234–287.

34. Eberle, "Commercial Language and the Commercial Outlook in the *General Prologue,*" *The Chaucer Review,* 18 (1983–1984), 161–174.

35. See V. J. Scattergood, "Literary Culture at the Court of Richard II," *English Court Culture,* which includes a partial listing of devotional and

service books bestowed in wills enrolled in the Court of Husting during Richard's reign (esp. pp. 42–43).

36. LeGoff, *Marchands et banquiers du moyen âge,* 4th ed. (Paris: Presses Universitaires, 1969), pp. 85–91.

37. Armando Sapori, *The Italian Merchant in the Middle Ages* (New York: Norton, 1970), pp. 21–28.

38. "Merchant's Time and Church's Time," p. 37. See Georges Poulet, *Studies in Human Time* (Baltimore: Johns Hopkins University Press, 1956), pp. 3–7.

39. The disapprobation embodied in Chaucer's presentation of Venus' segment of the garden is suggested by its dependence on Boccaccio's "second Venus," "the one who causes all kinds of lust to be desired." Chaucer transfers to the activities of Nature those productive aspects in which Venus "can and should be seen to represent all worthy and legitimate desires—such as the desire to have a wife in order to have children." *Teseida,* 7.55–60 and glosses; see *Chaucer's Boccaccio,* ed. and trans. N. R. Havely (London: D. S. Brewer, 1980), pp. 129–133.

40. See Paul A. Olson, "*The Parlement of Foules:* Aristotle's *Politics* and the Foundations of Human Society," *SAC,* 2 (1980), 63.

41. Several such efforts are cited by F. N. Robinson, *Works*, n. to l. 323.

42. *The Parlement of Foulys,* Nelson's Medieval and Renaissance Library (London: Nelson, 1960), p. 35.

43. Robinson, *Works,* n. to l. 323.

44. Bédier, *Les Fabliaux* (Paris: E. Champion, 1893), p. 384.

45. As Brewer points out, the French analogues to this poem concerned themselves mainly with debates among a noble council or retinue (and, one might add, with forms of judgment delivered by a presiding figure), but Chaucer adds an overlay of terminology appropriate to the deliberations of a national parliament (*The Parlement,* pp. 37–38). As I have already implied, Chaucer is also the first of the poets employing this debate form to associate particular views on love with socially based groups or factions. On debates and judgments analogous to Chaucer's poem, see *Chaucer's Dream Poetry: Sources and Analogues,* ed. and trans. B. A. Windeatt (London: D. S. Brewer, 1982), pp. 84–124.

46. I am in general agreement with Paul Olson's reading of the *Parliament* as a "civic" poem that recognizes the essential "interdependency of corporate groups" ("*The Parlement,*" pp. 53–69).

47. Chaucer's hint that the royal tercel may receive the ultimate reward would seem both appropriate and prudent, in view of evidence connecting the *Parliament* with actual marriage negotiations conducted on behalf of Richard II. See Larry D. Benson, *The Wisdom of Poetry: Essays . . . in Honor of Morton W. Bloomfield* (Kalamazoo, Mich.: Medieval Institute Publications, 1982), pp. 123–144.

48. As discussed in Chapter 3, one such debate concerns the assignment of a narrative about *gentillesse* to the not quite *gentil* Franklin.

49. Paul Strohm, "Some Generic Distinctions in the *Canterbury Tales*," *MP*, 68 (1970–1971), 322–323.

50. Among recent studies that argue for Chaucer's intentional evocation of the idea of romance, and of the *Knight's Tale* as a romance, see Cooper, *The Structure of the Canterbury Tales*, pp. 91–93. The contrary position is represented by Robert M. Jordan, "Chaucerian Romance?" *Yale French Studies*, 51 (1974), 223–234.

51. See Robert S. Haller, "The *Knight's Tale* and the Epic Tradition," *The Chaucer Review*, 1 (1966–1967), 67–84.

52. "Merchant's Time and Church's Time," pp. 33–34; see also Chenu, *Nature, Man, and Society*, pp. 162–201.

53. J. G. A. Pocock, *The Machiavellian Moment* (Princeton: Princeton University Press, 1975), pp. 8–9.

54. In the terminology of Bakhtin, the tale represents a fusion of chronotopes: one temporal/historical and one extratemporal/vertical. See "Forms of Time and Chronotope," esp. pp. 155–158, in which Bakhtin discusses the mixed form of Dante's and Langland's vision poems.

55. Muscatine, *Chaucer and the French Tradition* (Berkeley: University of California Press, 1957), pp. 175–190.

56. Derek Pearsall observes that all Boccaccio's "attention to the why and the how is passed over by Chaucer, in favour of sudden and unexplained impulse, and the operations of chance or destiny on mysteriously momentous days" (*The Canterbury Tales*, p. 130).

57. Walter Clyde Curry, *Chaucer and the Mediaeval Sciences*, 2nd ed. (New York: Barnes and Noble, 1960), pp. 119–163; Chauncey Wood, *Chaucer and the Country of the Stars* (Princeton: Princeton University Press, 1970), pp. 62–76.

58. As pointed out by Joseph Westlund, "The *Knight's Tale* as an Impetus for Pilgrimage," *PQ*, 43 (1964), 526–537.

59. On the broad relations of celestial to terrestrial bodies, and the ways in which these relations were called into question in the thirteenth and fourteenth centuries, see Edward Grant, "Medieval and Renaissance Scholastic Conceptions of the Influence of the Celestial Region on the Terrestrial," *Journal of Medieval and Renaissance Studies*, 17 (1987), 1–23.

60. See, for example, P. M. Kean, *Chaucer and the Making of English Poetry*, vol. 2 (London: Routledge and Kegan Paul, 1972), pp. 94–96.

61. A slight temporal reversion occurs at line 3657, when the action switches from the Monday evening preparations to Absolon at Oseney earlier that day; despite this narrative rearrangement, however, Chaucer's clear temporal indications permit the audience to retain a firm sense of "natural" sequence.

62. Bakhtin aptly describes Petronius' *Satyricon* as "a completely real-life

narrative, one whose component parts are all necessary" ("Forms of Time and Chronotope," p. 222).

63. The "Aristotelian" plotting of the *Miller's Tale* is discussed by E. M. W. Tillyard, *Poetry Direct and Oblique* (London: Chatto and Windus, 1948), pp. 85–92.

64. In this regard, R. Howard Bloch's argument for the specifically literary and nonreferential qualities of the fabliaux (*The Scandal of the Fabliaux* [Chicago: University of Chicago Press, 1986]) must be preferred to Charles Muscatine's appreciation of the fabliaux as a "rich source of factual data" (*The Old French Fabliaux* [New Haven: Yale University Press, 1986], p. 153).

65. J. A. W. Bennett, *Chaucer at Oxford and Cambridge* (Toronto: University of Toronto Press, 1974), pp. 28, 35–40.

66. Most suggestively by Earle K. Birney, "The Inhibited and the Uninhibited: Ironic Structure in the *Miller's Tale,*" *Neophilologus,* 44 (1960), 333–338, and by Paul E. Beichner, "Characterization in *The Miller's Tale,*" *Chaucer Criticism, The Canterbury Tales,* ed. Schoeck and Taylor (Notre Dame: University of Notre Dame Press, 1960), pp. 117–129. Less faithful to the spirit of the tale is Paul Olson's departure from norms established within the narrative in order to analyze the justice of the tale according to avarice, pride, and lechery, in "Poetic Justice in the *Miller's Tale,*" *MLQ,* 24 (1963), 227–236.

67. Donaldson shows how Absolon's idealizing aspirations are undermined by the world of the tale and the awareness of its contemporary audience, in "Idiom of Popular Poetry in the Miller's Tale," *Speaking of Chaucer,* pp. 13–28.

68. Tirelessly demonstrated by Robertson, Kaske, Bolton, Rowland, and Olson; full references are to be found in Macklin Smith, "'Or I wol Caste a Ston,'" *SAC,* 8 (1986), 3–30.

69. Ibid., p. 30.

70. "Thus the gown, the university-interest, asserts itself," says Bennett. I would differ, however with Bennett's conclusion that strife is subsumed in the laughter of "every wight," believing as I do that some elements of strife remain unsubsumed. See his *Chaucer at Oxford and Cambridge,* p. 56.

71. On the debt of the *Teseida*—and hence the *Knight's Tale*—to the cantare, see David Wallace, *Chaucer and the Early Writings of Boccaccio* (London: D. S. Brewer, 1985), pp. 75–93. On the atemporality of epic and geste, see LeGoff, "Merchant's Time and Church's Time," p. 33.

72. Carl Lindahl is undoubtedly correct in connecting Chaucer's comic tales with the broad popular tradition which he designates as that of the *Schwank,* which also embraces the fabliau—and, for that matter, the varieties of *fablel, conte,* and *dit.* See *Ernest Games: Folkloric Patterns in the Canterbury Tales* (Bloomington: Indiana University Press, 1987), pp. 124–127.

73. As observed by J. A. Burrow, *Medieval Writers and Their Work* (Oxford: Oxford University Press, 1982), pp. 79–80.

74. Derek Pearsall, "Middle English Romance and Its Audiences," in *Historical and Editorial Studies in Medieval and Early Modern English, for Johan Gerritsen,* ed. Mary-Jo Arn and Hanneke Wirtjes, with Hans Jansen (Groningen: Wolters-Noordhoff, 1985), pp. 37–47.

75. On the power of Chaucer's assignments—which, though drawn from literary convention, persuade us that they represent social reality—see Burrow, *Medieval Writers,* p. 78.

76. As argued by C. David Benson in his critique of the "roadside drama" argument, *Chaucer's Drama of Style: Poetic Variety and Contrast in the Canterbury Tales* (Chapel Hill: University of North Carolina Press, 1986), pp. 72–75.

77. On Richard's atavistic aspirations, see Ullmann, *Principles of Government and Politics in the Middle Ages,* pp. 181–185.

78. Terry Eagleton, *Criticism and Ideology* (London: NLB, 1976), pp. 177–181.

79. Such an analysis would follow the approach outlined by Raymond Williams in "Hegemony," *Marxism and Literature* (London: Oxford University Press, 1977), pp. 108–114. Whether the two ideological ensembles under discussion are regarded as aspects of a single hegemonic formation under pressure (according to Eagleton) or as aspects of hegemony and counterhegemony (according to Williams) seems to me finally a matter of emphasis, and perhaps not so crucial a difference as the combative opening chapter of Eagleton's *Criticism and Ideology* would imply.

80. A point paralleled in Lee Patterson's review of Stephen Knight's *Geoffrey Chaucer,* in *SAC,* 9 (1987), 224–225.

81. The generic and stylistic mix of the *Canterbury Tales* has been effectively asserted in the opening chapters of Cooper's *The Structure of the Canterbury Tales* as well as in Benson's *Chaucer's Drama of Style*—though neither proposes a social explanation for Chaucer's attraction to literary diversity.

6. A Mixed Commonwealth of Style

1. On the reconciliation of the medieval idea of the artificial state and the Aristotelian idea of the natural state, see Otto Gierke, *Political Theories of the Middle Age,* trans. F. W. Maitland (1900; rpt. Boston: Beacon Press, 1958), esp. pp. 88–89. More generally, see J. W. Gough, *The Social Contract,* 2nd ed. (Oxford: Clarendon Press, 1957), pp. 36–48.

2. On Harry Bailly's evolution from tyrannical misgovernance to good Christian rule, see David R. Pichaske and Laura Sweetland, "Chaucer on the Medieval Monarchy: Harry Bailly in the *Canterbury Tales,*" *The Chaucer Review,* 11 (1976–1977), 179–200.

3. Ioannis Saresberiensis, *Episcopi Carnotensis Policratici,* ed. Clemens C. J. Webb, 2 vols. (Oxford: Clarendon Press, 1909), VI.25.

4. *De ecclesiastica potestate: Un Trattato inedito di Egidio Colonna,* ed.

Giuseppe Boffito (Florence: B. Seeber, 1908), II.13. See also *Giles of Rome on Ecclesiastical Power,* trans. R. W. Dyson (Woodbridge, Suffolk: Boydell Press, 1986).

5. Ibid., II.6. See also the similar views of Nicholas of Cusa, cited in Gierke, pp. 23–24.

6. *Politica* (based on the translation of William of Moerbeke), *Aristoteles Latinus,* ed. P. Michaud-Quantin (Bruges-Paris: Desclee de Brouwer, 1961).

7. On the early dissemination of Aristotle, see Jean Dunbabin, "The Reception and Interpretation of Aristotle's *Politics,*" in *The Cambridge History of Later Medieval Philosophy,* ed. Kretzmann et al. (Cambridge: Cambridge University Press, 1982), pp. 723–737.

8. Ibid., pp. 725–728.

9. *De regimine principum,* ed. Joseph Mathis, 2nd ed. (Rome: Marietti, 1971).

10. "De potestate regia et papali," in Jean Leclercq, *Jean de Paris et l'ecclésiologie du XIIIe siècle* (Paris: J. Vrin, 1942). See also *On Royal and Papal Power,* ed. Arthur P. Monahan (New York: Columbia University Press, 1974).

11. *Defensor pacis,* ed. Richard Scholz (Hanover: Hahnsche Buchhandlung, 1932). See also *The Defender of the Peace,* vol. 2, ed. and trans. Alan Gewirth (New York: Columbia University Press, 1956).

12. "Of Dominion," *Wyclif: Select English Writings,* ed. Herbert E. Winn (London: Oxford University Press, 1919), pp. 62–63. Consider also Wyclif's view that the state is a natural body, with the clergy and the communality as its members, and with God-given power to resist its enemies. See R. Buddensied, ed., *John Wiclif's Polemical Works in Latin,* vol. 1 (London: Wyclif Society, 1883), p. xlii; translated in *The Tracts and Treatises of John de Wycliffe,* ed. Robert Vaughan (London, 1845), pp. 295–297.

13. "A Petition to King and Parliament," *Select English Writings,* pp. 64–65. On the context of this document, see Herbert B. Workman, *John Wyclif,* vol. 2 (Oxford: Clarendon Press, 1926), pp. 250–251.

14. Text from S. Harrison Thomson, "Walter Burley on Aristotle's *Politics,*" *Mélanges Auguste Pelzer* (Louvain: Bibliothèque de l'université, 1947), 557–578.

15. *Li Livres du Gouvernement des Rois,* ed. Samuel Paul Molenaer (New York: Macmillan, 1899).

16. Such ideas were in turn reinforced by vernacular popularizations. The primacy of a natural state guided by natural law was, for example, affirmed in the Middle English *Dialogus inter Militem et Clericum,* based on a work by William of Ockham, which argues that "rightful & unrightful in temporalte schal be demed by lawes, that men haueth made of temporalte." See the edition of Aaron Jenkins Perry, EETS, OS, 167 (London, 1925), p. 12.

17. Leclercq describes Jean's work as "une série de traités juxtaposés" (p. 39).

18. Fredric Jameson develops the concept of the narrative "ideologeme," in which an ideological construct is opened not only to conceptual summary but to narrative treatment. See *The Political Unconscious* (Ithaca: Cornell University Press, 1981), pp. 87–88.

19. Turner, *Dramas, Fields, and Metaphors: Symbolic Action in Human Society* (Ithaca: Cornell University Press, 1974), pp. 23–59.

20. I do not of course mean that Chaucer or his audience would have mistaken the imaginary conciliations that occur along the road to Canterbury as direct representations of their own social experience. Turner's social dramas are as likely to end in irreparable schism as in reintegration, and Chaucer's conciliatory strategies would inevitably have seemed utopian to persons confronted on every hand with evidences of schism, up to and including the Avignon papacy, the "Great Schism" itself! But to say that Chaucer's representations of conciliation are imaginary, and therefore false, is not necessarily to brand them as cynically deformative or malign. As Clifford Geertz points out, ideologies have a constructive role to play in addressing the social dislocations ensuing from the development of differentiated polities. The fact that ideologies are not truthful does not necessarily make them willfully obfuscatory or intellectually depraved; ideologies (and, by extension, ideologically conditioned works) can also be viewed more affirmatively as "maps of problematic social reality," as hypothetical solutions to otherwise intractable situations. See Geertz, "Ideology as a Cultural System," *The Interpretation of Cultures,* esp. pp. 218–220.

21. This general view of the social ordering of the Canterbury pilgrims is developed by Stephen Knight, *Geoffrey Chaucer* (Oxford: Basil Blackwell, 1986), p. 73.

22. David, *The Strumpet Muse,* p. 92.

23. On the importance of the artisan element, see Rodney Hilton, *Bond Men Made Free: Medieval Peasant Movements and the English Rising of 1381* (New York: Viking, 1973), pp. 176–185.

24. Lee Patterson argues for a shift from political to privatistic meaning in "'No man his reson herde': Peasant Consciousness, Chaucer's Miller, and the Structure of the *Canterbury Tales,*" *South Atlantic Quarterly,* 86 (1987), 457–495.

25. I am indebted for this observation to David Wallace, whose keen awareness of the limits of Chaucer's conciliatory strategies has considerably enriched my own understanding of the subject. A recent, partial presentation of his views is "Chaucer's Body Politic: Social and Narrative Self-Regulation," read at Rochester University, April 1988.

26. Especially by R. M. Lumiansky, *Of Sondry Folk: The Dramatic Principle in the Canterbury Tales* (Austin: University of Texas Press, 1955), pp. 184–185.

27. This aspect of the tale is extensively discussed in a new book by H. Marshall Leicester, Jr. (University of California Press, forthcoming).

28. Patterson, "'No man his reson herde,'" pp. 487–488.

29. Delany, "Politics and the Paralysis of Poetic Imagination in *The Physician's Tale, SAC,* 3 (1981), 47–60.

30. J. Burke Severs, "The Clerk's Tale," *Sources and Analogues,* pp. 288–289.

31. Despite the notoriety of the Wyclifite and Lollard movement, most members of the ecclesiastical hierarchy in late fourteenth-century England were resolutely conservative in their social opinions. For a suggestive portrait of Archbishop Courtenay—with his reliance on authority, firm moderation, and deference to papal authority—see K. B. McFarlane, *John Wycliffe and the Beginnings of English Nonconformity* (London: English Universities Press, 1952), esp. pp. 71–74, 105–116.

32. Wallace's splendid and definitive study, "'Whan she translated was': A Chaucerian Critique of the Petrarchan Academy," is to be published in *Social Action and Literary Practice in the Later Middle Ages,* ed. Lee Patterson, (University of California Press, forthcoming).

33. See the pertinent discussion of Griselda's benign rulership in David Aers, *Chaucer* (Atlantic Highlands, N.J.: Humanities Press International, 1986), pp. 34–35.

34. *Sources and Analogues,* pp. 330–331.

35. On the responses of Petrarch's friends to his rendering of Boccaccio's story, see Anne Middleton, "The Clerk and His Tale: Some Literary Contexts," *SAC,* 2 (1980), 121–150.

36. As observed by Charles A. Owen, Jr., "The *Tale of Melibee,*" *The Chaucer Review,* 7 (1972–1973), 267–280.

37. On the date of Albertanus' original version, see Albertano of Brescia, *Liber consolationis et consilii,* ed. Thor Sundby, Chaucer Society, ser. 2, vol. 8 (London, 1873), pp. v–xxi.

38. Paul A. Olson, *The* Canterbury Tales *and the Good Society* (Princeton: Princeton University Press, 1986), p. 120.

39. Interpretations supportive of Olson's position, though not nearly so pointed in application, are provided by Gardiner Stillwell, "The Political Meaning of Chaucer's *Tale of Melibee,*" *Speculum,* 19 (1944), 433–444, and Richard Firth Green, *Poets and Princepleasers* (Toronto: University of Toronto Press, 1980), p. 164.

40. Benson, *Chaucer's Drama of Style,* p. 64.

41. Cooper, *The Structure of the Canterbury Tales,* p. 53.

42. Spearing, "Al This Mene I Be Love," *SAC, Proceedings,* 2 (1986), 169–177. The arguments to which he responds are those of Bruce Kent Cowgill, "The *Parlement of Foules* and the Body Politic," *JEGP,* 74 (1975), 315–335 (who concludes that the poem contrasts the "ordered state wisely governed" with the "chaos of a state whose leadership is selfish and irresponsible"), and Paul A. Olson, *"The Parlement of Foules:* Aristotle's *Politics* and the Foundations of Human Society," *SAC,* 2 (1980), 53–69 (who finds in the poem an illustration of civic charity operating under the laws of nature).

43. On Jameson's notion of history as absent cause, see *The Political Unconscious,* p. 35.

44. Such polyvocality, whether expressed through voice or perspective, is taken for granted in what Derek Pearsall characterizes as the "Muscatine-Donaldson" tradition of commentary. See Pearsall, ed., *The Nun's Priest's Tale,* The Chaucer Variorum, II, pt. 9 (Norman: University of Oklahoma Press, 1984), pp. 67–81.

45. On the relation of style to different "states of men" as exemplified by John of Garland, see James J. Murphy, *Rhetoric in the Middle Ages* (Berkeley: University of California Press, 1974), pp. 178–179. These presuppositions are examined in Erich Auerbach, *Literary Language and Its Public in Late Latin Antiquity and in the Middle Ages* (New York: Pantheon Books, 1965).

46. *Problems of Dostoevsky's Poetics* (Minnesota: University of Minnesota Press, 1984), p. 30. Bakhtin would restrict total polyvocality, in which "every thought" is represented as "the position of a personality" (p. 9) to the capitalist era (pp. 20–21), and he may be correct in this most rigorous application of his term. But, even while recognizing that many passages of the *Canterbury Tales* bear meanings that cannot be attributed to their imaginary speakers, I would nevertheless argue for the general applicability of his concept to works by Chaucer, Langland, and other pre-nineteenth-century authors.

47. Especially in the influential formulation of G. L. Kittredge, who believed the *Franklin's Tale* to propose a solution with which "the whole debate has been brought to a satisfactory conclusion." "Chaucer's Discussion of Marriage," *MP* (1911–1912), 467.

48. See Cooper, pp. 54–55; Larry Sklute, *Virtue of Necessity: Inconclusiveness and Narrative Form in Chaucer's Poetry* (Columbus: Ohio State University Press, 1984), pp. 3–12; Jesse M. Gellrich, *The Idea of the Book in the Middle Ages* (Ithaca: Cornell University Press, 1985), pp. 213–214.

49. For example, those critics listed in the previous note, together with David A. Lawton, *Chaucer's Narrators* (Cambridge: D. S. Brewer, 1985), and Paul Strohm, "Form and Social Statement in *Confessio Amantis* and the *Canterbury Tales,*" *SAC,* 1 (1979), 17–40.

50. Bakhtin, *Dostoevsky's Poetics,* p. 27.

51. These observations are developed at greater length in Strohm, "Form and Social Statement," pp. 26–30.

52. Renate Haas, "Chaucer's *Monk's Tale:* An Ingenious Criticism of Early Humanist Conceptions of Tragedy," *Humanistica Lovaniensia,* 36 (1987), 44–70.

53. Especially Lisa J. Kiser, *Telling Classical Tales: Chaucer and the* Legend of Good Women (Ithaca: Cornell University Press, 1983).

54. H. C. Goddard, "Chaucer's Legend of Good Women," part 2, *JEGP,* 8 (1909), 47–111. The entire subject of Chaucer's boredom with his task is surveyed by Robert Worth Frank, Jr., *Chaucer and the Legend of Good Women* (Cambridge: Harvard University Press, 1972), pp. 189–210.

55. Cooper, p. 55.

56. Bakhtin, *Dostoevsky's Poetics,* p. 40.

57. Ibid., p. 27.

58. As in Claude Lévi-Strauss, "The Structural Study of Myth," *Structural Anthropology* (New York: Anchor Books, 1967), esp. pp. 217–227.

59. Etienne Balibar and Pierre Macherey, "On Literature as an Ideological Form," in *Untying the Text: A Post-Structuralist Reader,* ed. Robert Young (London: Routledge and Kegan Paul, n.d.).

60. "The Plowman's Tale," in *Works,* ed. Skeat, ll. 41–42.

61. Patterson, "'No man his reson herde.'"

62. The Miller would, for example, be considered a prosperous "yoman" in the terms of the 1363 statute; an "artificer" in the 1379 poll tax; a "man of craft" in the Norwich guild ordinance.

63. I accept some aspects of Patterson's persuasive description of the exclusion of the peasantry from the *Canterbury Tales* ("'No man his reson herde'"). My disagreement involves the emphasis to be given to this exclusion in a total evaluation of Chaucer's poetry. Patterson associates himself with the general position of the ideological critics, that the text is constituted in the struggle between a dominant ideology to which it offers ostensible expression and a dominated and repressed ideology contained within it and perceptible in telltale incidentals (Macherey, "On Literature as an Ideological Form"; Eagleton, *Criticism and Ideology,* p. 93). He thus finds that noble/feudal and bourgeois/urban ideologies are "together part of the hegemonic ideology that dominates late medieval English society; and both are to be set against the largely inarticulate but nonetheless insistent pressure of rural commodity production." My own tendency is rather to locate the principal conflict in Chaucer's poetry where he seems to mean to put it—between contending hierarchical and antihierarchical ideologies—rather than between a fusion of these elements on the one hand and a repressed ensemble representing a partially formed peasant consciousness on the other.

64. Most notably, James Dean, "Dismantling the Canterbury Book," *PMLA,* 100 (1985), 746–759.

65. Donaldson, "Idiom of Popular Poetry in the Miller's Tale," *Speaking of Chaucer* (1970; rpt. New York: Norton, 1972), pp. 13–29.

66. On *fable* as a narrative with invented plot, see Paul Strohm, "Some Generic Distinctions in the *Canterbury Tales,*" *MP,* 68 (1971–1972), 321–328.

67. "Forms of Time and of the Chronotope in the Novel," *The Dialogic Imagination,* ed. Michael Holquist (Austin: University of Texas Press, 1981), p. 157.

68. Patterson observes that the *Parson's Tale* "cancels out . . . that which precedes." "The *Parson's Tale* and the Quitting of the *Canterbury Tales,*" *Traditio,* 34 (1978), 379.

69. On the orthodox proscription of swearing, see G. R. Owst, *Literature*

and Pulpit in Medieval England (Cambridge: Cambridge University Press, 1933), pp. 414–425.

70. With respect to Chaucer's source, see Kate Oelzner Peterson, *The Sources of the Parson's Tale* (1901; rpt. New York: AMS Press, 1973), n. to pp. 34–35.

71. Giles, *De. eccl. pot.*

72. Compare Peterson, p. 40.

73. *Dostoevsky's Poetics*, p. 293.

74. For a discussion of the activities of the Ellesmere and Hengwrt scribes, with accompanying bibliography, see Derek Pearsall, *The Canterbury Tales* (London: Unwin Critical Library, 1985), pp. 1–23. An interesting account of the "bookish" pretensions of the Ellesmere manuscript has been given by Alan T. Gaylord (unpublished paper, 1982 NCS Congress).

75. Baldwin, *The Unity of the "Canterbury Tales," Anglistica*, 5 (Copenhagen, 1955).

76. Robertson's argument that the "litel tretys" of the Retraction is the whole of the *Tales* occurs in *A Preface to Chaucer* (Princeton: Princeton University Press, 1962), p. 369. For a corrective, see John W. Clark, "'This Litel Tretys' Again," *The Chaucer Review*, 6 (1971–1972), 152–156.

77. Pearsall observes that the text should ideally be presented to modern readers "partly as a bound book (with first and last fragments fixed) and partly as a set of fragments in folders, with the incomplete information as to their nature and placement fully displayed" (*The Canterbury Tales*, p. 23).

78. For arguments that some manuscript glosses may ultimately be authorial, see Daniel S. Silvia, "Glosses to the *Canterbury Tales* from St. Jerome's *Epistola Adversus Jovinianum*," *SP*, 62 (1965), 28–39; Robert E. Lewis, "Glosses to the *Man of Law's Tale* from Pope Innocent III's *De Miseria Humane Conditionis*," *SP*, 64 (1967), 1–16. On the scribal origin of the glosses as an enhancement of the prestige of Chaucer's compilation, see A. I. Doyle and M. B. Parkes, "The Production of Copies of the *Canterbury Tales* and the *Confessio Amantis* in the Early Fifteenth Century," *Medieval Scribes, Manuscripts and Libraries: Essays Presented to N. R. Ker*, ed. Parkes and A. G. Watson (London: Scolar Press, 1978), pp. 190–191.

79. Though manuscript circulation of individual tales and fragments prior to Chaucer's death remains a possibility. An argument for the circulation of individual tales in his lifetime, based on independent textual traditions as inferred from textual variants in fifteenth-century manuscripts, is advanced by Charles A. Owen, Jr., "The *Canterbury Tales:* Early Manuscripts and Relative Popularity," *JEGP*, 54 (1955), 104–110.

80. Paul Olson's *The* Canterbury Tales *and the Good Society* also argues for the social significance of Chaucer's literary text. Readers of both studies will note, however, my essential point of difference with Olson's conviction that Chaucer's reconstruction of society depends on a reassertion of hierarchy and a discouragement of pervasively "epicurean" tendencies.

Index